Legislating Morality

Legislating Morality

Pluralism and Religious Identity in Lawmaking

LUCINDA PEACH

OXFORD
UNIVERSITY PRESS

2002

OXFORD
UNIVERSITY PRESS

Oxford   New York
Athens   Auckland   Bangkok   Bogotá   Buenos Aires   Cape Town
Chennai   Dar es Salaam   Delhi   Florence   Hong Kong   Istanbul   Karachi
Kolkata   Kuala Lumpur   Madrid   Melbourne   Mexico City   Mumbai   Nairobi
Paris   São Paulo   Shanghai   Singapore   Taipei   Tokyo   Toronto   Warsaw

and associated companies in
Berlin   Ibadan

Copyright © 2002 by Lucinda Peach

Published by Oxford University Press, Inc.
198 Madison Avenue, New York, New York 10016

Oxford is a registered trademark of Oxford University Press

Library of Congress Cataloging-in-Publication Data
Peach, Lucinda J.
Legislating morality : pluralism and religious identity in lawmaking / Lucinda Peach.
    p.   cm.
ISBN 0-19-514371-X
1. Legislation—United States—Moral and ethical aspects.   2. Religion and law—United States
3. Law and ethics.   I. Title.
KF4930 .P43   2002
340'.112—dc21   2001133042

9 8 7 6 5 4 3 2 1

Printed in the United States of America
on acid-free paper

For His Holiness, the fourteenth Dalai Lama of Tibet, who is unsurpassable in facilitating human understanding of religious pluralism and the necessity of acknowledging and respecting the differences as well as the similarities among the world's religious and cultural traditions in the pursuit of global peace.

Acknowledgments

This book has had a long gestation period, which began with my dissertation several years ago, and has included numerous revisions amid a myriad of other projects and life changes. The book is a kind of hybrid, reflecting my earlier training in law, as well as my doctoral work in religion, philosophical ethics, and feminist theory. Both the underlying research and the approaches to religious lawmaking that I recommend reveal that hybridization of training: the work not only examines the Supreme Court's jurisprudence on the issue and recommends a legal solution but also analyzes prominent philosophical perspectives and recommends a theoretical solution to the issues raised by religious lawmaking.

In keeping with this multiplicity of influences, I would like to acknowledge the many streams of assistance that I received during this long gestation period. First, the largest debt of gratitude goes to my mentors and friends at Indiana University, where I did my doctoral work. Primacy of place goes to my dissertation director and main graduate advisor, Richard B. Miller, who not only maintained patience and good humor through reading several drafts of each chapter during the dissertation writing stage but also had the stamina to read and make many helpful comments on a revised draft of the entire work.

Next in the list of indebtedness are the other members of my dissertation committee: Karen Hanson of the Department of Philosophy, who introduced me to the American Pragmatist philosophers and piqued my interest in George Herbert Mead; David Smith of the Department of Religious Studies, who not only acted as a mentor and instructor but also employed me as a research assistant at the Poynter Center for Ethics and American Institutions at Indiana University (where he is the director); and Dan Conkle, a professor in the School of Law, who was generous enough to be on my committee despite his own burdensome professional commitments and personal convictions that differed in some significant ways from my own.

In addition, my classmate and then significant other Jason David BeDuhn provided me with immeasurable advice and encouragement throughout the process of research and writing; despite having few other scholarly interests in common with me (being a scholar of the Manichean religion), he shared my interest in Mead. Other friends and fellow students who lent support and solidarity in the process of graduate study include Sarah Pike, Leslie Bloom, Pauline Schlosser, and Teresa Treat.

More recently, I received the astute advice of Vincent Fruchart. I am indebted to Herb Ferris, who provided companionship and sustenance during a critical phase of the revising process while I was working in Vermont over the past two summers, to Bear Hollyday, Ted Emerson, Suzanne Jones, and Greg Elder, who provided me with the opportunity to do that revising work in Vermont; and to Bear's yellow Labrador retriever, Hopi, who was an ever enthusiastic companion on my jogs and walks in the woods during breaks between revising sessions.

My American University colleagues Ellen Feder, David Rodier, Amy Oliver, and Jeffrey Reiman have been generously supportive throughout the publication process. I would also like to thank my colleagues at the University of Baltimore, where I did my first two years of postdoctoral teaching, for supporting my research and seeing the merit in the thesis underlying this book, especially Jeffrey Sawyer, Catherine Albrecht, Donald Mulcahey, Fred Guy, Tim Sellers, and Walter Schwidetzsky.

To those who assisted me during those "formative years" of legal training, before the idea behind this book was even conceived, I would like to acknowledge David A. Menken, who encouraged me to attend law school in the first place; Susan J. Stabile, my best friend and compatriot throughout law school at New York University and in law practice at Cleary, Gottlieb, Steen & Hamilton both during and following law school; and Burt Neuborne, who inspired me with his lectures on constitutional law to pursue the idea that the notion of "legal justice" is not an oxymoron. And, finally, to Michael Perry, whose work I address here and who I first encountered as the articles editor for an essay he published in the *New York University Law Review* during my tenure on that journal. Despite, or perhaps because of, my disagreement with Perry about the place of religion in politics, his has been perhaps the most significant influence on this book.

Contents

Legislating Morality

Introduction

Imagine the following scenarios:

A. A state senator in a politically liberal state is contemplating how to vote on an upcoming bill regarding the abortion rights of minors. The bill would require the written consent of at least one parent before a doctor could legally perform an abortion requested by the minor. Many of the senator's constituents think the parental consent requirement is too restrictive, at least in the absence of some alternative procedure that would enable the minor to obtain the mandated authorization, and that a less burdensome parental notification requirement like several surrounding states have passed would be preferable. Despite the views of these constituents, the senator is reluctant to vote against the bill. Abortion is morally wrong according to his religious beliefs, and he is thus inclined to restrict the right to abortion whenever possible.

B. A governor in a politically conservative state has just been presented with a piece of legislation for his approval and signature. The bill, which passed by a substantial margin in both houses of the legislature, would require women seeking abortions to wait at least forty-eight hours after an initial visit to a doctor or other abortion service provider before being allowed to undergo the procedure. The governor is reluctant to sign the bill into law because she is convinced that this requirement will make access to abortion unduly burdensome for some women, especially indigent rural women who have to travel hundreds of miles from home to obtain access to abortion services. Although she is personally opposed to abortion on the basis of her religious belief that all life is sacred and should be preserved whenever possible, she also recognizes that the Supreme

Court has read the Constitution to prohibit abortion restrictions that create an undue burden on the woman's right to choose. The governor believes that a forty-eight-hour waiting period may present an undue burden on women who cannot afford the expense, delays, and other inconveniences that the waiting period would involve.

C. A federal appellate judge has just finished hearing a case involving the constitutionality of new legislation that would ban all abortions at overseas military facilities that are not necessary to save the life of the mother. The judge is aware that the sponsor of the bill is a long-time opponent of abortion who has consistently argued that abortion is contrary to God's will for how human beings should live their lives. The judge also knows that without access to military facilities American enlisted women seeking abortions may be forced to leave the service if they are not able to secure a rarely granted leave of absence to return to the United States or face the specter of an illegal abortion, especially in countries where abortion is prohibited by law. Although the judge holds personal religious beliefs that are consistent with a prochoice position on abortion, he doubts that his personal disagreement with the religious motivations underlying the law is a sufficient basis for striking it down as unconstitutional.

Although hypothetical, each of these scenarios illustrates the kinds of real-life conflicts that may arise—indeed, have arisen—between religious beliefs and lawmaking. How should the lawmakers in these scenarios make their decisions? Should they rely on their personal religious convictions or those of interested parties to these cases? Or should they view religious considerations as inappropriate or even unconstitutional grounds for decision?

These hypothetical cases suggest some of the difficulties involved in the determination of what role, if any, lawmakers' religious convictions should play in their public decisions, especially with regard to abortion regulations. Other examples in which religious convictions have actually played (or may potentially play) a role in public policy making include the legality of euthanasia and physician-assisted suicide, the validity of cloning and manipulation of genetic material (especially that of humans), capital punishment, the ordination of women as priests, the right of religious landlords to discriminate against tenant applicants on the basis of their sexual orientation, moments of silence and sex-education programs in public schools, the use of fetal tissue in scientific research, the legalization of marijuana, the regulation of prostitution and surrogacy contracts, the disposition of human embryos used for in vitro fertilization and other scientific research, and the right of religious groups to discriminate against others on the basis of their race, gender, or sexual orientation.

The legitimacy of such instances of "religious lawmaking" has been debated since the founding of our nation. The issue is especially relevant today, given the range of political and moral issues that religious views have had an influence in resolving. Notably, many of these issues have gender-specific dimensions, either because they directly concern women and female bodies or because they bear on the equal rights and status of women in society.

On one side of the debate over the proper role of religion in lawmaking are those who oppose religious influences on lawmaking as an infringement on the constitutional guarantees of separation of Church and State and the free exercise of religion by all citizens in a religiously pluralistic society. On the other side of the dilemma are those who contend that excluding religious beliefs, principles, and values as grounds on which lawmakers may rely in making political decisions is unduly restrictive and fails to respect the moral identity and constitutional rights of religious lawmakers and communities to the free exercise of their religion.

In part, the dilemma of religious lawmaking results from a lack of clarity in the Constitution itself, which does not provide a simple or straightforward resolution to the dilemma that religious lawmaking presents. Rather, the First Amendment religion clauses extend protection to both the free exercise rights of lawmakers to rely on their religious convictions, as well as the Establishment Clause rights of nonbelievers to the separation of Church and State.

Neither the Supreme Court nor scholars who have considered the matter have developed a resolution that accords adequate recognition and respect for the values at stake on both sides of the debate. In particular, the Supreme Court's decisions in this area lack adequate protections for the rights protected by the First Amendment religion clauses because they fail to consider how religiously influenced laws often infringe on interests protected by the Establishment Clause (Establishment Concerns). Although these infringements may not constitute full-scale violations of constitutional rights, they frequently do involve constitutional interests that contribute to violations of constitutional rights that are fundamental to equal citizenship (Citizenship Rights).

The Court's decisions in the area of abortion laws in particular have disregarded the ways that religious lawmaking may violate Citizenship Rights protected by the Fourteenth Amendment's substantive due process and equal protection clauses. They ignore how religiously motivated abortion restrictions may deprive women of the liberty and autonomy to make fundamental decisions regarding their own lives to the same extent to which men are legally enabled.

The Court's failure to provide a satisfactory resolution of the constitutional issues involved in religious lawmaking has contributed to the proliferation of conflicting scholarly proposals. The prevailing scholarly debate has been mired in opposition between liberal and communitarian political theorists and their incompatible emphases on the place of religion in relation to moral identity and pluralism.

Liberals have tended to address the issue principally as one involving moral pluralism in a religiously and culturally diverse society. Their theories have focused on the need to protect the free exercise of religion for all citizens, especially religious minorities, by the prohibition of most religious influences on the political and lawmaking processes. Communitarians, in contrast, have largely fixed on the centrality that religion may have to moral identity and the positive role of religion in the formation of a strong moral community. They have conceptualized moral identity as inextricably linked to the values and ideas of the moral agent's community and tradition, including his or her religious community and tradition. Their position has emphasized the difficulties of separating religion from other aspects of moral identity and the unfairness in making religious (but not other personal) bases for decision making illegitimate in the lawmaking arena.

Despite their significant conceptual differences, liberal and communitarian approaches to religious lawmaking share certain practical problems. One, as already mentioned, is the tendency to privilege one aspect of the dilemma, either pluralism or moral identity, while undervaluing the other. Liberal approaches to religious lawmaking tend to undervalue the importance of religion to moral identity, whereas communitarian views tend to underestimate the significance of religious pluralism as well as the potential of religious lawmaking to harm the constitutional rights and interests of certain groups of citizens, especially women and religious minorities. Whereas liberal approaches too easily assume that religion can be severed from legal decision making, communitarians too quickly assume that religion is inextricable from moral personhood, regardless of the particular social roles that a moral agent occupies. Communitarian theorists (and also some liberals) fail to recognize that lawmakers have special moral and legal obligations as a consequence of their roles as public officials, which may require them to modify the grounds of their public decision making.

Liberal and communitarian theorists also share a blindness to the significance of gender and power inequalities in the formulation of a satisfactory resolution to religious lawmaking. Although much attention has been given to the potential problems that religious lawmaking may create for religious minorities in a pluralistic society such as the United States, scant consideration has been accorded to the ways that religiously influenced laws have adversely affected the status of women. However, as Elizabeth Frazer and Nicola Lacey argue, any "explanatory political theory which simply fails to advert to gender will be deeply flawed, for it will fail to account for an important aspect of the very social relations it seeks to analyze" (1993: 37).

Although the most blatant forms of gender inequality have been eliminated from law and from many religious traditions as well, more subtle forms of exclusion, marginalization, and subordination of women are still operative in both institutions, as the following chapters illustrate. These injustices are magnified in religious lawmaking because the coercive power of the State is brought to bear to enforce gender ideology often proclaimed to be divinely ordained or sanctioned, if not mandated, by God.

These problems with religious lawmaking are evident in recent American experiences with abortion regulation. In fact, Michael Perry suggests that "the debate about what public policy regarding abortion should be—looms large . . . as a subtext, of the debate about the proper role of religion in politics" (1997: 70). Abortion lawmaking has been the site of public struggle among and within religious groups and secular interests over the legality and morality of abortion in the United States for decades. These debates have been so acrimonious that Ronald Dworkin suggests that they represent "America's new version of the terrible seventeenth-century European civil wars of religion" (1993: 4).

In addition to being the site of struggle between a variety of religious and secular views of abortion, abortion lawmaking reflects inequalities of social and political power and authority between lawmakers and other citizens, inequalities based not only on social roles and religious differences but also on gender hierarchies. Abortion regulation, therefore, is not simply a question of the human rights of the fetus, as some antichoice theorists would argue. Rather, because it is centrally involved with the rights and social status of women in society, it is a gender issue as well. Because most traditional religious views of abortion ignore the oppressiveness inherent in coercing women to continue unwanted pregnancies, laws incorporating such religious views are likely to lack respect for women as moral agents. They may also restrict women's ability to exercise their own freedom of conscience (whether religiously informed or not) in determining whether to carry a pregnancy to term.

If the law imposes severe restrictions on a woman's ability to obtain an abortion, it denies her the ability to determine for herself whether an abortion would be the most moral choice for her to make. As Teresa Phelps observes, "Clearly restrictive abortion laws that take decision making out of the hands of women and place it under the power of the government tell a story about women and society that portrays women as less capable of moral reflection than the state. These laws do not encourage women to be autonomous and moral, but instead tell them they cannot be so trusted" (1992: 568). Such laws may thus hamper women's self-confidence in being able to think and act in the world (Karst 1989: 119), as well as their ability to define their own moral identities independently of State power (see Karst 1993: 196). Thus, by focusing on abortion regulation in this investigation, we can better examine the gendered implications of religious lawmaking.

Some advocates of a larger role for religion in the public sphere have argued that religion has a valid place in political discourse and public policy making, including lawmaking, because it is constitutive of the moral identity of many Americans. Proponents of this view tend to overlook or ignore the problems presented by the allowance of personal religious beliefs to provide the basis for public laws. Laws that are based on or influenced by religious considerations carry the potential for alienating and coercing citizens who do not subscribe to the religious beliefs that underlie them and thus risk fostering political divisiveness among citizens of different religious (or nonreligious) affiliations. The distinctively coercive character of public law makes religious lawmaking morally problematic in a religiously pluralistic society in ways that religious influences on more general public discussion and debate are not and makes it necessary and appropriate to evaluate religious lawmaking apart from other religious influence on public life.

The coercive character of laws establishes the possibility that religious rationales will provide the basis for restricting individual freedoms, in violation of constitutional protections to substantive due process and equal protection of the laws. This problem is not remedied by the theoretical freedom that members of all religious persuasions have to participate in establishing public law and policy because, realistically, the opportunities for members of less politically and socially powerful religious groups to influence lawmaking are more limited than for members of majoritarian religious faiths. Lawmakers still overwhelmingly are members of mainstream Christian religions and do not reflect the diversity of religious traditions that are found in the larger society. The breadth and depth of religious pluralism in America is evident in the radical diversity of and frequent conflicts among views on the morality and legality of abortion included among the public statements of American religious groups (see Melton 1989).

My aim in this book is to advance the discussion relating to the place of religion in political life beyond its current impasse between liberal and communitarian proposals by bringing fresh perspectives to the discussion, particularly those of feminism and American pragmatism. Rather than choosing sides and promoting either the liberal or the communitarian vision of the appropriate place of religion in lawmaking, in this study I approach the dilemma by starting with the concrete particulars of lived experience rather than abstract theory. In focusing specifically on lawmaking, this study addresses one limited aspect of the larger issue of religious influence on public life or on civil society more generally.

I do not dispute the claims made in recent years by a number of scholars, including Perry, Greenawalt, and Stephen Carter, that religion has a valid and valuable role to play in public moral discourse. As Carter explains in *The Culture of Disbelief* (1993), religion provides an important role as an independent voice or counterbalance to the secular society. Carter's claim that "democracy is best served when the religions are able to act as independent moral voices interposed between the citizen and the state" has considerable value (16). Public discussion and debate that includes religious discourse can enrich the breadth and depth of moral consideration on many social issues.

Religious convictions presented in public discourse may succeed in persuading even nonbelievers of their merit, or they may be shown to be less persuasive to their original proponents. Thus, the influence of religion on civil society, broadly defined, can be a salutary one that increases the diversity of moral considerations in the public sphere and helps to shape public policies that benefit all citizens. But religious influences on lawmaking are of a different character because of the coercion inherent in law.

In the following chapters, I explore a variety of resolutions to the dilemma of religious lawmaking proposed by liberal and communitarian theorists, especially those recommended by legal theorists Kent Greenawalt and Michael Perry. To demonstrate the problems with religious lawmaking, especially in relation to gender inequality, in chapter 1 I describe how religion has actually influenced the process of lawmaking, using the case of abortion regulation to illustrate these elements. I provide an overview of some of the many ways that religion historically has influenced abortion regulations enacted by legislatures, courts, and other lawmakers, especially since the Supreme Court's landmark *Roe v. Wade* decision in 1973.

In the first chapter, I also define what constitutes religious lawmaking, describe why it is problematic in a religiously pluralistic society, and establish the framework for understanding why religious lawmaking presents such a seemingly intractable dilemma in contemporary American society. I explore not only the ways that religious influence on lawmaking risks alienating and coercing citizens, especially women, but also why the moral identity of religious lawmakers precludes the option of simply prohibiting such influences.

Chapter 2 begins with a fuller description of the citizenship rights that may be involved in religious lawmaking. I analyze problems with the Supreme Court's interpretations of religious lawmaking when these constitutional provisions are at issue, focusing especially on deficiencies in the Supreme Court's interpretations of religious lawmaking in abortion cases.

Chapter 3 examines the other side of the dilemma of religious lawmaking, the central role that religion may have in the life of political leaders. Rather than assuming that either liberal or communitarian conceptions of the relationship of religion to moral identity is accurate, I examine how several prominent American political leaders have articulated the place of religion in their political and lawmaking activities and the influence of their religious convictions in their public policy making on abortion. An examination of how former New York governor Mario Cuomo, Judge John Noonan, Congressman Henry Hyde, Senator Mark Hatfield, former president Ronald Reagan, and former presidential candidate the Reverend Jesse Jackson have understood the role of religion in their own public policy-making activities, particularly on abortion, illuminates some of the inaccuracies of both liberal and communitarian theories of moral identity, which consider only theoretical conceptions of persons, and also lays an empirical groundwork for considering alternative approaches.

In chapters 4 and 5, I assess the prevalent approaches to resolving the dilemma of religious lawmaking in liberal and communitarian thought. Chapter 4 focuses on the liberal proposals offered by law professor Kent Greenawalt and shows where his views diverge from more traditional liberal approaches, such as those of John Rawls and Robert Audi. Despite some divergences, I conclude that Greenawalt's proposals do not escape the major limitations of liberal approaches that address religious lawmaking.

Chapter 5 follows a similar format in describing communitarian theories, here focusing on the proposals of law professor Michael Perry. Although Perry's views regarding religious lawmaking diverge in certain respects from those of more traditional communitarian theorists (as I show by comparing his views with those of communitarian political theorist Michael Sandel), I conclude that Perry's approach shares certain deficiencies with other communitarian proposals. At the end of chapter 5, I detail the prerequisites for an adequate approach to religious lawmaking, one that neither unduly limits the ability of public officials to rely on their religious convictions in their lawmaking nor sacrifices respect for religious pluralism and/or gender differences.

In chapter 6, I offer the first of two alternative strategies that I claim better protect the constitutional rights and interests of all relevant parties than either the Supreme Court's jurisprudence or the liberal or communitarian approaches. The twentieth-century American Pragmatist philosopher George Herbert

Mead's theory of the social self provides the foundation for this strategy. In particular, Mead's ideas about the socially constructed character of the self and the special requirements of role-based morality provide a model for understanding that lawmakers, as public officials, are both practically able and morally obligated to take the attitudes of all of their constituents into account in their public policy making. In a culturally and religiously diverse society, I argue, this requires lawmakers to support their policy decisions with publicly accessible rationales.

However, given the practical limitations of theoretical solutions that I discuss, in chapter 7 I propose a practical legal framework for the resolution of the constitutional problems posed by religious lawmaking. The *legal assessment* model I propose is based on an expanded test for Establishment Clause violations. It invalidates religiously influenced laws in a limited range of circumstances when Establishment Concerns are present and when infringements on Citizenship Rights cannot be fully justified by a secular rationale and/or by a compelling State interest.

This framework modifies current Supreme Court standards for the assessment of the constitutionality of religious lawmaking. It provides that religious lawmaking be subjected to heightened standards of scrutiny to ensure that Citizenship Rights are not violated. Applying the proposed legal model, first in the abortion context and then in relation to two significantly different moral issues—the regulation of homosexual conduct and environmental protection—I demonstrate its efficacy for resolving dilemmas of religious lawmaking in a wide range of cases. The alternative approaches to religious lawmaking that I propose in chapters 6 and 7 better protect both the values of gender equality and religious pluralism on the one side and the religious identity and individual constitutional rights of lawmakers on the other than prevalent approaches have done.

In the conclusion, I offer some reflections on the particular advantages of these proposed ethical and legal frameworks for the resolution of problems of religious lawmaking that impact disproportionately on women and members of politically subordinate religious groups. With this overview in hand, let us now explore in more detail the problems that religious lawmaking poses to the rights and interests of citizens in a religiously pluralistic society, especially those of women and religious minorities.

ONE

The Dilemma of Religious Lawmaking

Religious influences on the political process may result in laws that are both constitutionally and morally problematic. As I discuss in this and the following chapters, these problems are especially disadvantaging to the Citizenship Rights and interests of women and religious minorities. However, what makes religious lawmaking a dilemma is that it does not simply involve the constitutional rights and interests of citizens who may be negatively impacted or disadvantaged by its effects. If it did, the solution to the problem would be simple: prohibit religious influences on the lawmaking process.

Because the moral identity and free exercise rights of religious lawmakers are also at stake, it is inappropriate to simply expect (or demand) that they not draw on their religious convictions in making public policy decisions, especially those concerning difficult moral issues such as abortion. As we will see, it is the combination of these two frequently conflicting sets of rights and interests of lawmakers on one side and the rights and interests of citizens obligated to obey the results of those lawmakers' political decision making on the other that makes religious lawmaking such a difficult dilemma to resolve.

In this chapter, I first discuss what I mean by the term *religious lawmaking*, describing the kinds of activities that religious lawmaking encompasses and what persons qualify as religious lawmakers. Second, I describe a number of factors that make religious lawmaking constitutionally problematic in a morally and religiously pluralistic society. I show how these problems result, in part, from the special characteristics of religion and the religious pluralism

11

of American society. In particular, I describe how these problems frequently have a gendered impact that results in particularly putting the citizenship rights and interests of women at a disadvantage. I use the case of abortion regulation to illustrate these problems, providing an overview of the range of religious influences on abortion regulation. This discussion sets the stage for the discussion of the specific constitutional problems with religious lawmaking in the next chapter.

What Is Religious Lawmaking? Defining the Terms for Discussion

In this section, I define the terms relevant to the discussion of the dilemma of religious lawmaking and then discuss three prevalent styles or types of religious influences on lawmaking.

Terminology Relevant for the Analysis of Religious Lawmaking

Before proceeding to look in more depth at the problems presented by religious lawmaking in the context of the religiously pluralistic United States, let us consider more precisely what *religious lawmaking* involves. I use this term generally to refer to the process of enacting, validating, interpreting, applying, or enforcing legally binding regulations (those backed by the coercive power of the State) on the basis of religious considerations.

Religion and *religious* are extremely difficult terms to define accurately. Although religion has been interpreted in numerous ways by the courts and by scholars studying the relationship of religion and politics, most Americans use the term to mean "a personal affirmation of faith in God and an identification with a religious denomination" (Kosmin and Lachman 1993: 1). Traditional definitions are typically based on western monotheistic religions and, thus, do not encompass the full range of religious experience and expression found in the contemporary United States. In view of the difficulties of attempting to formulate a definition of religion adequate to encompass the diversity of religious phenomenon present in the United States, I use a more pragmatic definition here.

Based on Ludwig Wittgenstein's idea of family resemblances, there is no single feature or set of characteristics that defines all religions. There are, however, substantial areas of overlap among different religions. Because the problem of religious lawmaking as it has arisen in the United States virtually always involves institutionalized religions, I use the terms *religion* and *religious* to refer primarily to those religions that have established institutional bases in the United States: Christianity and Judaism and, to a far lesser extent, Islam, Buddhism, and Hinduism. These terms should consequently be interpreted as including those organizations and institutions that have traditionally been recognized as religious by their adherents as well as by outsiders.

The family resemblances among different institutional religions generally involve some or most of the following characteristics: a faith in teachings or doctrines that profess access to a universal truth, reality, or morality; concern with some kind of liberation or salvation that extends beyond this world; and acceptance of certain premises that are based on faith, revelation, or spiritual authority and cannot be fully supported or understood on the basis of secular reasons.

In addition, many religious beliefs are dependent on personal experiences that cannot be assessed on interpersonal grounds (see Greenawalt 1990: 1031). In general, a significant criterion for distinguishing what is religious from what is secular is that the former is not publicly accessible, empirically verifiable or falsifiable, or universally accepted (or potentially so) by members of society at large (cf. Solum 1993: 741). I refer to persons who are religious in this sense as *believers*, *adherents*, *members*, and *practitioners* and use nonbelievers to refer to those who do not ascribe to the religious convictions that have influenced a particular law. Nonbelievers may or may not be religious.

As already mentioned, the term *lawmaking* refers broadly to the procedures by which the several types of public policy enactments and regulations are made legally binding and enforceable on citizens through the coercive power of the State. *Lawmaking* thus encompasses not only the formal enactments of a legislature but also official executive rules and orders, policy enactments by other government officials, and judicial decisions. This definition of lawmaking enables a more complete assessment of the many different ways that religion affects the promulgation and enforcement of laws than would be allowed by restricting the term to refer only to legislation.

Lawmakers are government and public officials whose roles involve, in whole or in part, the passage or enactment of laws. The category includes, most obviously, legislators, as well as executive-branch officials such as presidents, governors, mayors, city and town council members, and also members of the judiciary. Ordinary citizens are encompassed by the term *lawmaker* only when they enact specific public policies, such as through voting on public referenda. However, because most of the cases that address religious lawmaking on abortion involve state and federal statutes, much of the discussion here involves legislators and judges as opposed to other types of lawmakers. As I later discuss in greater detail, lawmakers' roles generally distinguish them from other citizens in several respects, especially in terms of their responsibilities as public representatives and their greater power and authority to use the law to coercively bind other citizens.

Thus, religious lawmaking designates the process of enacting, administering, executing, or enforcing laws on the basis of, in reliance on, or as a result of religion or religious beliefs. To focus specifically on the decisions of lawmakers for whom religion is a significant defining aspect of their identity, I have excluded other kinds of religious influences on government, such as attempts by religious institutions to directly lobby for or against certain laws or public policies, from this inquiry. The determination of whether lawmaking is religious is an objective one. That is, there must be evidence that religious considerations play a significant part in the enactment of a law, one that results in discernible effects or consequences, for it to be considered to be *religiously* based or influenced.

To warrant the designation of *religious lawmaking*, religious influences must be evident either in the content or the effect of a law. The contribution of religion may be evident on the face of a particular law, such as by language that makes explicit references to religion, religious institutions, or distinctively religious themes. The presence of an explicitly theological rationale may also be inferred from the absence of an adequate secular rationale or purpose for the law or in the consequences of the law for particular groups of religious believers and nonbelievers. Religious influence may also be evident if the language of a law is directly traceable to the teachings or pronouncements of a particular religion (*Wallace v. Jaffree*, 472 U.S. 38, 56 [1985]).

Religious rationales may also be reflected in the statements of lawmakers themselves, either in connection with the enactment of a particular law or relating to the subject matter of the law on some other occasion. Such statements are often included in the legislative history or background that underlies the passage of a law, such as in testimony in support of or opposition to a law made at legislative hearings.

Religious lawmaking may conflict with the fundamental rights of citizenship protected by the U.S. Constitution (Citizenship Rights). The principle of equal citizenship mandates that all citizens have an equal right to participate in society, regardless of their race, gender, or religion (see generally Karst 1993, 1989). In addition to the constitutional guarantee of equal protection, Citizenship Rights include those constitutional rights that are most centrally impacted by religious lawmaking. In connection with our case study of religious lawmaking on abortion, the main Citizenship Rights that may be impacted are those granted by the First Amendment religion clauses, which guarantee the free exercise of religion and prohibit government from establishing religion, and the principle of substantive due process protected by the Fifth and Fourteenth Amendments. Religious lawmaking on other matters (e.g., the property rights case I consider in chapter 7) may more centrally implicate other fundamental constitutional rights, in which case the term *Citizenship Rights* refers to them.

Religious lawmaking may raise *Establishment Concerns*, or problems of alienation, exclusion, coercion, and political divisiveness, which the Supreme Court has identified as relevant to its decision making under the Establishment Clause. As I argue, the presence of Establishment Concerns in a particular case is an important consideration in analyzing the validity of religious lawmaking, even though they may not be sufficient, by themselves, to establish that Citizenship Rights have been violated.

As I explain further in the following chapter, religiously grounded laws are more likely to raise Establishment Concerns and, consequently, to infringe on Citizenship Rights in a religiously pluralistic society such as the United States than are laws based on other kinds of considerations. Religious pluralism, in combination with disparities in political power among members of different religions, makes it more likely that lawmaking influenced by religion will result in the unjustified coercion of religious minorities, in violation of constitutional protections. Historical examples include the banning of certain Mormon and Seventh Day Adventist religious practices, failure to protect Native American religious practices against infringement, jailing of conscientious objectors (prior to the passage of the *Exemptions Act*), required prayer in public fora, posting of the Ten Commandments in public school classrooms, and the teaching of creation science in public schools.

Three Styles of Religious Lawmaking

From the range of possible types of influence that religion may have on lawmaking, three general types or categories are especially pertinent to the investigation here. The first type, *Authority*, involves reliance on a religious authority (e.g., the "word of God," scripture, one's spiritual leader, overarching religious orientation) to provide the basis for decisions. This first type of religious influence provides the lawmaker's motivation for making a particular decision. Motivation will usually be evident on the face of a law, even if no specific scriptural authority or religious language is explicitly used. A law prohibiting the sale or consumption of pork because of biblical prohibitions against eating swine is an example of this first type of influence.

In the second category, *Justification* or *Rationale*, the religious influence in a sense follows after the decision and provides legitimating reasons for it. It would include, for example, a legislator's justification for voting against the death penalty on the basis that killing others is prohibited by the Ten Commandments. This kind of influence may or may not be evident in the expressed content of a law. A bill sanctioning the death penalty for certain heinous crimes might be justified by a legislator's interpretation of biblical teachings on retribution, for example, but may not be evident anywhere in the text of the bill.

In the third category of religious influence, *Guidance*, the lawmaker relies on his or her religious convictions to provide a source of guidance or moral principles and norms to assist in making a legal decision. The religious influence in this third category thus precedes the law's enactment. It may, but does not necessarily, provide the actual content of the lawmaker's decision. An example here would be a lawmaker's decision to vote against imposing criminal penalties on drug-addicted pregnant women based on the understanding that such penalties would be inconsistent with the Christian principle of neighborly love (*agape*).

To further illustrate the differences among these three types of influence, let us return to the hypothetical cases mentioned at the beginning of the introduction. The decisions of a sponsor of a bill that bans abortions at overseas military facilities based on the strictly prolife teachings of his church reflect the Authority, or Motivation, type of influence. The judge who upholds the constitutionality of the bill based on his interpretation that abortion is prohibited by the Ten Commandments exemplifies the second type of influence, that of

Justification, or Rationale. If the judge instead strikes down the law's constitutionality because of the hardship this would impose on American military women stationed overseas and its inconsistency with *agape*, this would illustrate the third, Guidance, or Resource, style of religious influence. There is obviously a degree of overlap between the three types and room for different degrees of intensity of religious conviction within each of these three categories. Nonetheless, as later discussion clarifies, the three types of religious influence are problematic to different degrees, with the first two, in general, more likely to create Establishment Concerns or infringements on Citizenship Rights than the third.

What Makes Religious Lawmaking Problematic?

There are at least four components embedded in the question of what makes religious lawmaking problematic. The first component has to do with the character of law. The second concerns the character of religion. The third component is an effect or consequence of the interaction of law and religion in a morally and religiously pluralistic polity. The fourth is related—it concerns interaction of law and religion in a gender-based society. I consider each of these components in turn.

The Character of Law

What distinguishes religious influences on law from such influences on public discussion and debate more generally? Although there is no bright line distinction between the realms of social life designated as public, political, governmental, legal, civic, social, and private, the potential for officially sanctioned coercion provides a key distinction between government and lawmaking on the one side and the realms of civil society and private associations on the other. Although the presence of religious rationales in public discussion and debate (e.g., lawmaking) may alienate and exclude some nonbelievers and/or foster political divisiveness, these dangers are far less pernicious there than in the context of lawmaking. In public discussion and debate, religious arguments are subject to contestation and rejection in ways they are not when they form the basis for legal regulations backed by the enforcement apparatus of the State. Because of the coercive character of the law itself, religious influences on lawmaking carry special risks of being coercive that are not evident in the context of religious influences on other aspects of public life.

Certainly, nonreligious laws can also be coercive and disrespectful of individuals' personal convictions. To some extent, coercion is built into the very concept of law because it is designed to regulate society on principles that are authoritative, regardless of the agreement or acceptance of everyone subject to obeying them. However, as Martin Luther King, Jr., taught, it is axiomatic to justice that laws in a democratic society must permit some form of participation by those subject to obeying them. When laws are based on inaccessible religious premises that cannot be openly discussed and debated on terms available to nonbelievers in the way that laws based on secular rationales can, their coerciveness is enhanced. Such laws also may fail to gain widespread support or obedience, which may exacerbate problems of enforcement, because the effectiveness of law ultimately is dependent on citizens' willingness to accept it (see Woodard 1984: 797; Alexander 1993: 776).

Nonetheless, this problem alone does not warrant singling out religion as an especially problematic basis for lawmaking. After all, the lawmaking process is fraught with all sorts of ideological and value-laden influences, from political action committees and special interest lobbies to the advice and suggestions of a lawmaker's spouse or partner, friends, or associates to the political pressures on some lawmakers to satisfy the desires of those constituents who can assure reelection. Rather, I suggest that it is also necessary to examine the other two components of the question, the character of religion and the character of the United States as a morally and religiously pluralistic society. Together, these factors create a significant danger that religious lawmaking will abridge Citizenship Rights and interests and provide a convincing justification for according special scrutiny to religious lawmaking.

The Character of Religion

As noted in the introduction, although it is difficult to generalize about religion, given the incredible diversity of forms of religious belief and expression that can be found in the United States, nevertheless, it is possible to make a few generalizations about characteristics common to institutional religions that make religious lawmaking problematic, especially in the context of a religiously pluralistic polity. As an umbrella heading, I use *public inaccessibility* to describe one set of such problems with using religious beliefs in lawmaking. These encompass the tendency of religious beliefs, which are inaccessible to the general public understanding, to also be exclusionary, alienating, coercive, and politically divisive (i.e., to raise Establishment Concerns). The other set of problems stems from the basis of many religious beliefs in sexist and patriarchal traditions that are disadvantaging to the needs and interests of women.

Public Inaccessibility of Religious Beliefs

A number of characteristics of institutional religious beliefs contribute to their not being accessible to nonbelievers. Traditional religions are concerned with the deepest questions and issues of human existence—issues about the ultimate meaningfulness of life; the purpose of creation, life, and death; the possibility of a better existence elsewhere than that afforded in this world; and questions about how to live rightly—in relation to fellow human beings, to the rest of the natural world, and especially to God or some ultimate reality. Many traditional religions claim to hold "the" truth about such matters of ultimate concern as the meaning of the universe, the nature of God, and the way to salvation.

For many religious adherents, the tenets of faith are authoritative: they are understood to be God's word or revelation, to be faithfully and rigidly adhered to, regardless of the consequences for others, even nonbelievers. Some religious adherents, for example, are more concerned about the spiritual consequences of their beliefs and actions than the temporal, this-worldly ones (Conkle 1988: 1164). Adherence to the teachings of their faith may take precedence over a commitment to democratic values, including a respect for religious pluralism or the constitutional rights of others. This orientation is evident in the convictions of many religious fundamentalists who believe in the inerrancy of scriptural revelation. An extreme form of religious faith is represented in the beliefs of religious adherents willing to die in defense of their faith or their spiritual leader (e.g., Jim Jones's cult in Jonestown, Guyana; the Branch Davidians in Waco, Texas; and more recently, Om Shin Rikyo in Japan and the Heaven's Gate doomsday cult in Rancho Santa Fe, California).

In addition to the authoritative and unquestionable character of many religious beliefs, a second problem is the absence of reference points by which outsiders can assess the validity of those beliefs. Even Stephen Carter, a proponent of greater religious influence in public life, admits that those outside a particular religious tradition "have no standpoint from which to judge what counts as a 'superior' or 'inferior' position or, indeed, whether the words have any meaning within the faith community" (1993: 40; see 215). The foundation of many religious beliefs in faith rather than reason or fact means that they may lack any basis likely to persuade nonbelievers of their validity. Although some nonreligious beliefs also lack publicly accessible reasons to support them, religious beliefs more frequently are based on faith, revelation, and emotion (or what Abner Greene refers to as "an extra-human source of value" [1993: 1614]) than on reason, empirically demonstrable facts, or some other basis rooted in shareable human experience.

These characteristics of many traditional religious beliefs contribute to their lack of public accessibility, that is, their reliance on premises that are either not publicly intelligible and/or are not widely shared by nonmembers. Kent Greenawalt uses the term *public accessibility* to refer to reasons that "would be acknowledged by any competent and level-headed observer" and are "commonly accepted as valid" (1988: 57, 59). Publicly accessible premises can be understood without reference to any religious metaphysic; they do not require access to faith or some sort of special knowledge, experience, or belief to be accepted.

This is not to say that there is necessarily a qualitative difference between religious and nonreligious beliefs. Certainly, some religious beliefs are publicly accessible (e.g., the belief that murder is wrong) and some secular reasons are not (e.g., the postulates of quantum physics). Even if, as a matter of epistemology, religious beliefs ultimately are not any less publicly accessible than secular beliefs (see, e.g., Alexander 1993), as a symbolic matter religious beliefs are more likely to be perceived to be inaccessible by nonbelievers and disbelievers than are secular ones. In addition, religious reasons are often associated in the public's perception with the institutional authority of the traditions from which they originate. For example, when a Catholic bishop gives congressional testimony about health care, the Catholic Church's broader worldview (including its stance on issues such as abortion and birth control) is likely to be evoked, even if not explicitly expressed. Thus, religious beliefs may symbolize the spiritual authority and coercive potential of religious institutions being brought to bear on the resolution of a secular problem. Such perceptions themselves present pragmatic reasons for according special consideration to religious beliefs (see Greenawalt 1988: 205–6).

These problems are enhanced by the tendency of some religions to encourage or demand adherence to rigid, dogmatic beliefs. Religious claims to have primary, if not exclusive, access to the truth are often linked to intolerance for those who do not share or accept it. Traditional religions, especially historically, have been intolerant of dissenters, as Justice Oliver Wendell Holmes's dissenting opinion in the Supreme Court case of *Abrams v. U.S.* (250 U.S. 616, 630 [1919]) argues. Even today, a number of traditional religious groups claim to have the exclusive path to salvation, from which all nonadherents are damned (see Wald 1992: 340; Liebman 1988: 40).

Deeply held religious beliefs thus have the potential to lend themselves to zealousness, intolerance, and even persecution of those with different views or practices (see Marshall 1993: 862), as history has amply demonstrated. Part of the tendency of religious beliefs to be intolerant of divergent views may relate to the emphasis of many religions on subjects of ultimate concern. This emphasis tends to make religious beliefs more significant, more important, and more compelling to believers and, thus, more trenchantly held and less willingly relinquished than nonreligious beliefs.

These characteristics of many religious beliefs make them more likely than nonreligious beliefs to be the subjects of coercion, conflict, and political divisiveness. The risk that such beliefs will violate the constitutional rights of others are enhanced when they are incorporated into public laws backed by the threat of coercive sanctions. The potential of religious lawmaking to coerce nonbelievers by compelling them, under penalty of punishment, to abide by the dictates of laws that are rooted in religious beliefs that conflict with their own personal convictions raises an additional concern. Such laws are unfair in a democracy based on notions of citizen participation in government.

James Madison recognized this danger of religious influences on politics in stating that even in its "coolest state," religion "may become a motive to oppression as well as a restraint from injustice" (quoted in Meyers 1981: 60). He was especially cognizant that the danger of oppression was heightened when an "unjust and interested majority" representing mainstream religion has the power to "outnumber and oppress the rest," especially members of nondominant religious groups (quoted in Meyers 1981: 63; see also Sinopoli 1992: 96).

A more subtle aspect of legal coercion results from the government endorsement of the particular religious tradition or traditions from which religiously influenced laws are derived, whether actual or perceived. As Justice Blackmun's concurrence in the Supreme Court case of *Lee v. Weisman* (505 U.S. 557 [1992]) suggests, because "religious faith puts its trust in an ultimate divine authority above all human deliberation . . . when the government appropriates religious truth, it 'transforms rational debate into theological decree'" (112 S. Ct. 2666). This may reinforce the confidence of the believers in the accepted group that they have the truth, making them less willing to compromise with or even tolerate those of other faiths (see Wald 1992: 340, citing Liebman 1988: 40). Reciprocally, it sends a message to nonbelievers that they do not have the truth and that their beliefs are not valued or respected. Such messages make nonbelievers become political as well as religious outsiders. In these respects, religious lawmaking may be alienating, exclusionary, and politically divisive, as well as coercive, especially to nonbelievers.

Gender Bias in Traditional Religions

A second way that religion contributes to making religious lawmaking problematic is through gender bias and sex discrimination against women. All of the major world religions traditionally have taught that women are physically and emotionally, if not spiritually, inferior to men. These religions have limited women's control over their sexuality, reproduction, marital choices, ownership of property, and access to material, spiritual, political, and social resources and have otherwise constrained their freedom of movement and decision making. In addition, women have been devalued within religious teachings, viewed as the origin of sin, sexual temptresses, untrustworthy, unintelligent, irresponsible, and, in general, inferior to men. Traditional religions have also vested males with the power to determine who and when women married, if and under what conditions they were allowed to divorce, and their rights, if any, to their children.

Traditional religions have not viewed women as moral agents on a par with men in making responsible ethical choices. Hierarchical gender relations that subordinate women to men have been legitimated in religious teachings variously as the result of God's will, the workings of karma, or the result of natural law. These characteristics of traditional religions make their influence on law likely to perpetuate the oppression and secondary status of women in society. This result is both morally and constitutionally problematic.

The following brief survey describes how women are viewed in a number of prominent religious traditions represented in the United States, including both majority and minority religious institutions. This survey is not comprehensive, but it does illustrate the kinds of gender bias still pervasive in dominant religious institutions active in the United States. It vividly demonstrates the problems of basing laws on religious beliefs in a democracy constitutionally committed to gender equality. This discussion has special relevance to abortion lawmaking, but it is also pertinent to religious lawmaking on other, less evidently gendered issues as well.

Roman Catholicism.   The traditional status of women in the Catholic Church has been subordinate and secondary to that of men. Church patriarchs such as Tertullian, Chrystostom, and Augustine viewed women primarily as passive reproductive vessels or "fetal containers" for active male seed and attributed original sin to be the fault of woman (Eve's eating of the forbidden fruit in the Garden of Eden).

Throughout Christian history, women have been prohibited from positions of spiritual and administrative leadership in the Church and denied participation in the formulation and interpretation of scripture and theology (see Ruether 1983; Ranke-Heinemann 1990). The Catholic Church still bars women from ordination as priests and deacons and, thus, precludes them from performing many sacramental functions. Despite efforts by Catholic women in recent decades for fuller participation in the Church, the hierarchy has thus far refused to change its policy on women's ordination, thereby continuing to prohibit women from participation in the leadership and policy-setting functions of ecclesiastical life. This has meant that Catholic women's voices continue to be silenced, and their views about moral issues such as abortion are not reflected in official Church teachings.

Within the larger Catholic Church, women have been limited to distinctly secondary roles, generally those of wives and mothers. The Church has counseled women that their primary responsibility is to the home and family and has discouraged them from outside occupations. Pope John Paul II's Apostolic Letter in 1988 states that "women must not appropriate to themselves male characteristics contrary to their feminine originality. . . . Parenthood, although it belongs to both—is realized more fully in the woman. Motherhood involves a special communion with the mystery of life . . . which profoundly marks the woman's personality" (Rhode 1991: 1747). The American Catholic bishops have concurred with this view (see Cook, Jelen, and Wilcox 1992: 96).[1] As I discuss in chapter 3, such views of women as mothers are also evident in the views of some Catholic lawmakers.

Consistent with their perspective about women's special roles as mothers and foundations of the family, the American Catholic bishops have characterized the vast majority of abortions as "for convenience" and as selfishly motivated, demonstrating their lack of understanding of the actual social status and circumstances of many women's lives (see Segers 1992: 42–43). Church officials have also characterized women who seek abortions as killers. In addition, those adhering to the Church's official teachings on abortion seldom consider the coerciveness of forcing women to carry unwanted pregnancies to term, nor the burden and hardships such coerciveness often entails.

Protestant Christianity.   In contrast to Orthodox Roman Catholicism, Protestant Christianity reflects a broad spectrum of different views of women. Although Protestantism shares the Catholic heritage of sexist and patriarchal views about women, many mainstream denominations have incorporated contemporary social norms that promote equality for women. Many have opened their churches to women ministers and priests and have made efforts to eliminate gender bias in all aspects of ecclesiastical life, including liturgy, hymns, administration, and leadership. The statements of some denominations explicitly take women into consideration in determining the legitimacy of abortion.

Other Protestant churches continue to reflect more traditional sexist and patriarchal attitudes that promote rigid notions of gendered social roles and accord women primary roles as wives and mothers. This is especially true of many fundamentalist and evangelical churches. In these churches, such views are often accompanied by an insistence on the subservient role of women and the dominant role of men (see Tamney, Johnson, and Burton 1994: 42; Cook, Jelen, and Wilcox 1992: 98). Traditional family values promoted by many conservative Protestant groups such as the Promise Keepers include the beliefs that the father is the natural leader and head of the household, the woman's place is in the home, the wife and children are obligated to obey the male head of household, and children are subject to physical punishment as a legitimate response for their disobedience (see Blanchard 1994: 44; Kosmin and Lachman 1993: 273).

In the view of one prolife leader, "Abortion also permits the woman to adopt the same sexual pattern as the male, although it is a pattern alien to her nature. Blessed by God with a much longer view of society and the world, the woman is normally the stabilizing force in the male-female relationship, insisting that the man subordinate his sexual passions to the need to provide for the family over the long run" (Jones 1983: 240, quoted in Ginsburg 1989: 216). In this view, abortion alleviates the consequences of unrestrained sexuality, from which unmarried women should have refrained to begin with (Melton 1989: 86). Requiring teenagers or unwed women to continue unwanted pregnancies is considered to be an appropriate response to the woman's sin of having been sexually active outside of marriage (the male's role is not accorded any corresponding punishment). Traditional moral values are enforced, even coerced, for the person's own good, regardless of the personal hardships or difficulties that may result (see Tamney, Johnson, and Burton 1994: 42).

Judaism.   Traditional Jewish teachings do consider the status and rights of women in many areas, such as by granting women conjugal rights and an important role in running the household, including domestic religious ceremonies. Rachel Biale even speculates that wives were exempted from the obligation of procreation to which males are subject to spare them from being required to put their lives at stake in the processes of pregnancy and childbirth (1989: 28). However, because women are viewed primarily as wives and mothers in traditional Judaism, they were expected to have children. This remains the perspective of Orthodox Judaism today and is still an underlying assumption in some other Jewish organizations.

In addition, like most other religious traditions, Judaism has developed out of a very sexist and patriarchal culture. Even today, women have a secondary role in many synagogues and can only become rabbis in the Reformed and Conservative movements. Jewish law, *Halakhah*, continues to constrain women from study of the Torah, synagogue rituals, and communal leadership, by exempting them from these duties based on the understanding that a woman's primary role is as wife and mother. In Orthodox Judaism, this has excluded women from being counted as part of the *minyan* (quorum required for acts of public worship), from reading the Torah at prayer services, and from being seated in the same area of the synagogue as men (see Wright 1994: 113). *Halakhah* also prohibits women from initiating divorce and enables husbands to override a wife's refusal to grant a divorce (see Baker 1993: 55–57; Biale 1984). Reform of the *Halakhah*, which is a male-derived and dominated body of law, has remained virtually closed to women (see Davis 1992: 320; Umansky 1985; Biale 1984: 3).

The insensitivity of Jewish spiritual leaders to pregnant women is reflected in the response of Immanuel Jakobovits, formerly the Chief Rabbi of the United Kingdom, to arguments that restrictive abortion laws force women into having illegal abortions or unwanted children. He states that "There is, inevitably, some element of cruelty in most laws. For a person who has spent the last cent before the tax bill arrives, the income tax laws are unquestionably 'cruel,' and to a man passionately in love with a married woman, the adultery laws must appear 'barbaric'" (Jakobovits 1979: 124–25). Such opinions do not reflect a genuine understanding of or respect for the extreme hardship that restrictive abortion statutes impose on women who have unwanted pregnancies.

Islam.   The general status of women in Islam is secondary to that of men, although the Prophet Muhammad improved women's status significantly from what it had been in the pre-Islamic Arab countries. The holy book of Islam, the Qur'an, states that men are a degree above women (Surah 2:228) and that "men are in charge of women, because Allah hath made the one of them to excel the other, and because they spend of their property (for the support of women)" (Surah 4:34, quoted from Pickthall 1977: 83). Men have the right to marry up to four wives if they can provide for them all, but women have the right to only one husband. Husbands (but not wives) are granted an almost absolute right to obtain a divorce (see Pickthall 1977; see generally Smith 1984), whereas women must petition the courts to obtain a divorce (see Badawi 1994: 102, 106). In addition, the Qur'an accords women's legal testimony only half the value given to men's.

It is difficult to generalize about the status of women in American Islam because most of the Muslims in this country, with the exception of the Nation of Islam and the American Muslim Mission (the Black Muslims), immigrated from other cultures in recent generations (see generally Haddad and Smith 1994; Muhammad 1984). These cultures differ significantly in the status and roles accorded to women, such as whether women are allowed to work outside the home, take active roles in the Muslim centers and community life, and interact with members of the non-Muslim community (see generally Haddad and Smith 1994). In addition, the social practices of Islam have been influenced by American culture as well and are, thus, apt to differ from either Islam as practiced in its cultures of origin or from that set forth in the Qur'an (see, e.g., Haddad and Smith 1994; Haddad and Lummis 1987; Haddad 1991).

In some Islamic cultures, women are expected to wear veils and stay in the domestic sphere, are limited to social roles as wives and mothers, and are expected generally to take a subservient role to males, even in western countries.

In traditional Islamic practices, the mosques are strictly segregated, with women seated behind the men or in a separate area from the main hall (see Badawi 1994: 109). More conservative schools declare women legally incompetent to contract a marriage without the permission of a legal guardian and allow women to be coerced into marriage without their consent by their father or grandfather.

Although prohibited by U.S. law, polygamy (the practice of taking multiple wives) is practiced in some Islamic cultures, whereas polyandry (taking multiple husbands) is not. The Sharafi'i school allows the husband the unconditional right to choose whether or not to use contraception, regardless of the wife's consent because the wife has no automatic right to children (Rahman 1984: 114–15). The doctrine of "blocking the way to sin" that was once the basis for the ban on contraceptives in Muslim Pakistan has also been applied to prevent the public education of women, on the theory that once women were allowed beyond the protection of their homes, their chastity would be threatened (Rahman 1984: 117).

Buddhism.   It is impossible to generalize about the status of women in American Buddhism because there are so many different schools and lineages represented in this country. As with Islam, many forms of Buddhism arrived in America with immigrants, whose cultures reflect significant variations in authoritative scriptures, teachings, and practices. In addition, unlike Islam, many Buddhist groups in America today were designed primarily for Euro-Americans and, thus, have a distinctively American character.

However, as seen with the other world religions examined here, traditional Buddhism is also rooted in sexist and patriarchal values. Buddhist *sutras* (scriptures) describe the Buddha's agreement to admit women to the *Sangha* (monastic community) only after repeated entreaties and even then with the proclamation that the admission of women would shorten the existence of Buddhism in this world by 500 years! Many Buddhist scriptures and teachings portray women as sexual temptresses intent on seducing unsuspecting males from their spiritual paths (see Gross 1992; Lang 1986; Paul 1981).

Women generally have a secondary status in Buddhist culture, usually valued by religious leaders primarily for their provision of alms (donations of food, etc.) to maintain the primarily male monastic communities. Where female monastic orders do exist, such as in Taiwan and Korea, they are given far less financial and social support than the male orders.

Views on abortion in Buddhism, like those of the other religions described here, differ widely among different cultures and aspects of the tradition. In general, however, they tend to be prolife and to leave the moral agency of pregnant women out of consideration (see, e.g., Buddhist Churches of America Social Issues Committee 1984; Gibson and Stott 1993; Gross 1992).

This brief overview of traditional beliefs in a number of prominent religious traditions reveals their gender-biased character. The following section describes the problems that result when these biases are given the coercive sanction of State authority in religious lawmaking.

Interaction of Law and Religion in a
Gender-Biased Society

The preceding survey illustrates that none of the major world religions has recognized women as full and equal participants in social and political life. The sexist and patriarchal aspects of many religious traditions make it easier to devalue the importance of women as moral agents whose own lives must be considered in the abortion decision and, thus, to justify the conclusion that the fetus is of equal worth to the pregnant woman, regardless of the state of its development. As Siegel argues, "These *are* the assumptions which make it 'reasonable' to force women to become mothers. Absent these deep-rooted assumptions about women, it is impossible to explain why this society insists that restrictions on abortion are intended to protect the unborn, and yet has never even considered taking action that would alleviate the burdens forced motherhood imposes on women" (1992: 379).

In early judicial decision making, religious rationales were expressly used to validate laws that discriminated against women,[2] including the denial of women's right to vote until 1920 on the ground that the "divine intention" was to make women's place in the home bearing and raising children (Tribe 1988: 410). Religion also has obstructed women's rights in spheres of American law relating to property ownership (*Helms v. Franciscus*, 2 Bland. 544, 20 Am. Dec. 402, 407 [Md. Ch. 1830]; see Weigand 1980: 584), employment (*Bradwell v. Illinois*, 83 U.S. [16 Wall] 130, 141 [1873]), marital rights (*Ritter v. Ritter*, 13 Pa. 396, 398 [1858]; see Weigand 1980: 585), and violence against women (see *Poor v. Poor*, 8 N.H. 307, 312 [1836]; *Joyner v. Joyner*, 59 N.C. 322 [1862]; McDonald 1989: 265), as well as sexuality and reproduction, sex discrimination, and abortion. Religious influences contributed to the derailment of the Equal Rights Amendment, which would have outlawed discrimination against women.

The history of restrictive abortion laws illustrates that they were premised on the very views we have just seen as central to several world religions, views of women as child rearers and as "destined solely for the home and the rearing of the family" (see Siegel 1992: 356, citing *Mississippi University for Women v. Hogan*, 458 U.S. 718 at 726 n. 11 [1982]). Unfortunately, religious influences on lawmaking that result in adverse consequences for women are not a relic of history. Despite the formal legal equality of women in most spheres of American society, vestiges of such traditional religious beliefs continue to influence religious lawmakers' attitudes about women's proper roles and appropriate status, as the discussion in chapter 2 shows. Because women have been excluded from participation in the formulation of religious beliefs and practices in most traditional and institutional religions, it is likely that laws based on beliefs and values rooted in religious traditions will fail to incorporate women's self-determined interests. As Karst points out: "If your culture regards male power as a 'family value' ordained by God, you will see nothing amiss in using the power of the state to impose that value on women, even those who disagree" (1993: 180; see Siegel 1992: 362).[3]

Legitimating the influence of religious beliefs in lawmaking means legitimating such still extant patriarchal and oppressive attitudes toward women with the imprimatur of State sanction. Consequently, an important factor to consider in evaluating the validity of religious lawmaking is whether religiously influenced laws will perpetuate traditional views of women, views that conflict with women's formal legal equality and citizenship rights. Thus, in addition to the general problems with religious lawmaking already discussed, the gender bias in traditional religions presents an additional, gender-specific problem that is generally overlooked.

Interaction of Law and Religion in a Morally and Religiously Pluralistic Society

As much as problems with religious lawmaking discussed in the previous sections present persuasive reasons for limiting its practice, these problems are compounded in the context of the moral and religious pluralism of the United States. One of the most salient features of the cultural and religious landscape in this nation is its radically pluralistic character. It is one of the most religiously diverse nations in the world. At last count, there were more than 1,500 different religious bodies and sects in the United States (Woodward 1993: 80).

Although the large majority (86 percent) profess membership in one of the hundreds of Christian denominations that exist in America and 62 percent of these are Protestants, recent surveys indicate that the country has become less Protestant and more pluralistic and secular in recent decades (see Gallup and Castelli 1989: 23–24). There are substantial and growing numbers of citizens who are Jewish, Muslim, Buddhist, Hindu, and Native American, in addition to smaller numbers of Baha'i, Taoist, New Age, Ekankar, Rastafarian, Sikh, Wiccan, Shintoist, Deity, and other unclassified believers (Kosmin and Lachman 1993: 2, 17; see Conkle 1993: 3–4; Gaustad 1982; Hudson 1987; Adler 1986; Eller 1993).

Of course, not all Americans are religious, at least in any traditional sense of being actively involved or committed members of religious groups. A study conducted in the late 1980s indicated that secularists comprise approximately 11 percent of the population, presently the fastest growing community (or potential community) of moral conviction in America (Williamsburg Charter Foundation 1988).

Not only do Americans follow a wide variety of different religious traditions, but the tenets of these different religions are incredibly diverse. The result is a lack of any moral agreement or religious consensus with respect to any major social issues, including the justifiability of war and/or pacifism; euthanasia; experimentation with animals; environmental protection; sexual ethics; economic, racial, and gender justice; school prayer; and the rights of homosexuals.

There are also significant differences within religious groups. Even among Christian Protestants, for example, the so-called mainline denominations often disagree with the views of the evangelical ones. Similarly, there are marked divergences among American Catholics between traditionalists, who are generally critical of the reforms instituted with Vatican II, and modernists, who generally embrace these reforms. Similar divergences are evident among Orthodox, Conservative, and Reform Jews (see Wald 1989: 107–8).

Despite these realities of contemporary social life in America, consideration of religious pluralism and the importance of respect for religious differences are absent from most proposals to expand the role of religion in government, especially those made by members of the dominant religious traditions. Rather than affirming this religious diversity, conservative political leaders, including former president Ronald Reagan (see Lear and Reagan 1984), Randall Terry (see *Church and State* Editorial Staff 1993: 19), Paul Weyrich (Kosmin and Lachman 1993: 198), and the Reverend Jerry Falwell (see Johnston 1986: 135; see generally Marty 1987: 3), in recent years have promoted the claim that "America is a Christian nation." These echo earlier sentiments articulated even in Supreme Court decisions (e.g., *United States v. MacIntosh*, 283 U.S. 605, 625 [1931]; *Church of the Holy Trinity v. United States*, 143 U.S. 457, 472 [1892]; see Conkle 1993: 5; Wenz 1992: 85; Berman 1986: 779). Such assertions about the Christian identity of this country and the need to return the nation to its "Christian roots" (Neuhaus 1984; Carter 1993; Gaffney 1990; 99–101; Coleman 1982: 184–98; see Moen 1989; Pierard 1986: 100; Johnston 1986: 136) overlook America's non-Christian beginnings in Native American religions and its uninterrupted history of religious diversity.

The reality of religious pluralism in America makes laws based on or influenced by religious convictions (which are likely to be those of a majoritarian church) inevitably in tension if not outright conflict with the views of at least some nonbelievers and disbelievers. Permitting religious views to influence lawmaking in a context of religious pluralism enhances the effect of government giving official sanction to certain religious convictions at the expense of others. At a minimum, nonrepresented groups are bound to feel resentful. In extreme situations, they may be angered enough to rebel (see Conkle 1988: 1168; Zimmerman 1986: 1106).

Because the legitimacy of law is ultimately based on its public acceptability and because laws based on religion are unlikely to gain widespread public acceptance, religious lawmaking risks political divisiveness. Indeed, the potential for political divisiveness exists any time government agencies choose to give priority to one religion over another, whether in the distribution of benefits or favoritism in the establishment of public policy. In *Lemon v. Kurtzman* (403 U.S. 602 [1973]), the Court noted that the history of many countries "attests to the hazards of religious intrusion into the political arena" (622–23). Political strife resulting from government involvement in religious conflicts also can be illustrated by recent examples from around the world, including those in India, Pakistan, Bosnia, Israel, Northern Ireland, Lebanon, Sri Lanka, and the Philippines.

These problems are exacerbated in the United States, where the vast majority of lawmakers belong to traditional Christian faiths, but many of their constituents do not. More than 75 percent of the Senate and almost two-thirds of the House have been Protestant for decades: almost three-fourths affirm the divinity of Jesus, and just short of one-half regard Jesus as their personal savior (Pierard 1986: 72; Fowler 1985: 126). Yet at least 14 percent of the U.S. population is non-Christian. Further, moderate Protestants, especially Lutherans and Black Protestants, are underrepresented in Congress, whereas Episcopalians, liberal Protestants, and Jews are substantially overrepresented, and Orthodox Christians, Mormons, and Methodists are somewhat overrepresented (Duke and Johnson 1992: 325–26; see Fowler and Hertzke 1995: 112, 120, 122).

The disproportionate representation of certain dominant Christian faiths in government indicates that religious lawmaking is likely to infringe on the Free Exercise and other Citizenship Rights and interests of citizens from other religious groups, particularly those from minority religious traditions who are more likely to be lacking in political power. Indeed, the historical legal treatment of Mormon and Native American religious beliefs illustrates this problem (see *Lyng v. Northwest Indian Cemetery Protective Association*, 485 U.S. 439 [1988]; *Employment Division v. Smith*, 494 U.S. 872 [1990]).

The discussion thus far has shown the problems presented by religious lawmaking. I have focused on the public inaccessibility of many religious beliefs; the risks of exclusion, alienation, coercion, and political divisiveness that use of such beliefs in lawmaking entails; the gender bias present throughout the prominent religious traditions prevalent in the United States today; the history of such biased beliefs being incorporated into law; and the way that these problems are enhanced within a context of religious pluralism. In the following section, I provide an illustrative example of these problems in abortion regulation.

An Illustration of the Problems with Religious Lawmaking: The Case of Abortion Regulation

In this section, I discuss the prevalence of religious influences on abortion lawmaking. Focusing on this issue enables us to see not only the general problems with religious lawmaking but also how this activity has had particularly disadvantageous consequences for the citizenship rights and interests of women. This clarifies the inadequacies in the Supreme Court's approach to religious lawmaking covered in the following chapter and also sets the stage for the theoretical analysis of the dilemma, which follows in chapters 4 and 5.

The legal regulation of abortion has been closely identified with religious morality, especially since the Supreme Court's decision in the landmark case of *Roe v. Wade* (410 U.S. 113) in 1973, which established a woman's constitutional right to choose whether or not to terminate a first- or second-trimester pregnancy. This identification has been largely the result of efforts of the Roman Catholic Church to outlaw abortion (see Blanchard 1994: 33; Byrnes 1991: 54; Kelley 1991: 154–56).

Immediately following the Court's decision in *Roe*, several religiously affiliated groups, many of them associated with the Roman Catholic Church, mobilized their ranks in a highly developed, well-organized, and generously funded campaign to reverse its effect through legislation and a constitutional amendment (see Petchesky 1990: 241–42; Tribe 1990: 143–47). The "Pastoral Plan for Pro-Life Activities," issued in 1975 by the National Conference of Catholic Bishops, specified that a "comprehensive pro-life legislative program" must include "passage of a constitutional amendment providing protection for the unborn child to the maximum degree possible" and "passage of federal and state laws and adoption of administrative policies that will restrict the practice of abortion as much as possible" (*McRae v. Califano*, 491 F. Supp. 630, 704 [E.D.N.Y. 1980]; see Byrnes 1991: 58–59).

The plan also called for a "pro-life action group" to be formed in each congressional district for the purpose of organizing people to persuade elected representatives to pass a human life amendment and to restrict abortion legally, as well as to monitor the prolife position of elected representatives and work for the election of prolife candidates. Each January, on the anniversary of *Roe v. Wade*, the Catholic clergy has organized an annual March for Life rally in Washington, D.C., which includes visits to legislators' offices to lobby them on prolife issues (see Segers 1990a: 219). Although none has succeeded to date, many different amendments to the Constitution have been proposed since 1973 to reverse the effect of *Roe* (see Bopp 1993; Byrnes and Segers 1992: 7; Bopp and Coleson 1989; Moen 1989; Bopp 1984: 434; Destro 1975). Several religious prolife groups have participated in those hearings (Miller 1983: 282).

Among the many religiously influenced restrictions on abortion that Congress has enacted since *Roe v. Wade*, one of the most striking and controversial has been the Hyde Amendment, first proposed by Representative Henry Hyde, a Catholic Republican whom I discuss in greater detail in chapter 3. First enacted in 1976, the initial version of the Hyde Amendment prohibited the use of Medicaid funds for abortions "except where the life of the mother would be endangered if the fetus were carried to term."[4] Some form of the amendment has been enacted every subsequent year as a rider to an appropriations bill, generally permitting exceptions only if the woman's life is endangered or the pregnancy is the result of rape or incest. Because Medicaid is provided only to those living in poverty, the effect of the Hyde Amendment has been to enhance distinctions among categories of women by denying indigent women the ability to exercise their constitutional right to choose to have an abortion.

The legislative history of the congressional debates on the Hyde Amendment clearly portrays the role that religion played in passage of the law (see *McRae v. Califano*, 491 F. Supp. at 742–844). A research study of votes by members of the House of Representatives on the original Hyde Amendment revealed that religion was the second most significant factor influencing voting behavior, following party affiliation (Tatalovich 1993: 112). Several members of Congress, during the hearings on the Hyde Amendment, made explicit reference to religion and religious themes in expressing their opposition to abortion (see *McRae v. Califano*, 756–835). Many prolife congresspersons used explicit references to God in their arguments. Prochoice members of Congress also used religious references to argue to a contrary conclusion. Members of

Congress on both sides of the issue also referred to their own religious convictions in their testimony. More frequently, however, they made reference to the religious beliefs of constituents and generalized others rather than themselves. For instance, Representative Hyde argued that he was not attempting to impose "somebody's religious beliefs on other people" (*McRae v. Califano*, 832).

The tendency of religious lawmakers to discount or denigrate women's experience is also evident in the congressional debates on the Hyde Amendment. Consideration of women was almost completely absent from their testimony (see also Tribe 1990: 136), as it was from the arguments of religious lawyers promoting prolife legislation (see, e.g., Bopp and Coleson 1989; Cox 1990, who discusses Bopp and Coleson's proposals for a Human Life Amendment and a reversal of *Roe v. Wade*). As noted earlier, one version of the Hyde Amendment was passed that denied funding even for abortions necessary to save the life of the mother (see Tribe 1990: 155). The lack of consideration of pregnant women in Senator Helms's declaration that support for public funding for abortion reflected a judgment that "it is cheaper to the State to kill the unborn children of the poor man than it is to let them be born" (*McRae v. Califano*, 745) is conspicuous.

When women were mentioned at the hearings by religious legislators, it was generally in negative terms, reflecting their opinions that women are untrustworthy, irresponsible, and even dangerous. Representative Hyde argued more than once that "when the mother, who should be the natural protector of her unborn child becomes its deadly adversary, then it is the duty of this legislature to intervene on behalf of defenseless human life" (*McRae v. Califano*, 773, see also 753). Senator Bartlett reasoned that "to defer to the moral judgment of the mother who does not want the child and a doctor paid by the government forces the fetus to have its life taken, and ignores the moral question of the unborn child" (491 F. Supp. 748).

Representative Rudd argued that women should choose not to become pregnant, and "she should not ask the taxpayer to pay for her failure to exercise that choice" (*McRae v. Califano*, 775). Representative Bauman asserted that "the death of one unborn child was as important as the life of the mother who does not want the child" (*McRae v. Califano*, 825). Congressman Oberstar objected to the Supreme Court's focus on the mother in *Roe v. Wade*, criticizing it for ignoring the "vital issue" of the "rights of the unborn" (*McRae v. Califano*, 757). Similarly, Senator Bartlett argued that it was wrong to discuss abortion in terms of the mother and not the unborn child because the unborn were the "true minority" (491 F. Supp. 749).

In addition to the impact of religion within the congressional debates on the Hyde Amendment, religious groups lobbied hard from the outside both in favor and against the proposed amendment. Pursuant to the Pastoral Plan, the Catholic hierarchy encouraged its parishioners to support the amendment and to lobby their legislators in favor of it. Evidence suggests that these efforts were partially responsible for the amendment's passage (see Hofman 1986: 39–40; Petchesky 1990: 253 n. 25).

The constitutionality of the Hyde Amendment was struck down under the Free Exercise Clause by the district court in *McRae v. Califano* (491 F. Supp. 630 [E.D.N.Y. 1980]), but the lower court's decision was reversed by the Supreme Court in *Harris v. McRae* (448 U.S. 297 [1980]), a case that is discussed in more detail later. In addition to the Hyde Amendment, Congress has enacted a number of other religiously influenced restrictions on abortion in the years following *Roe v. Wade*. Conservative Christian congresspersons were instrumental in enabling prolife groups to influence Congress in the passage of much of this legislation (see Moen 1989: 56–58).

The *Adolescent Family Life Act (AFLA)*, enacted in 1981, includes a restriction on abortion rights, which indicates that religious influences factored into its enactment. Originally sponsored by conservative prolife Senators Jeremiah Denton and Orrin Hatch, *AFLA* provides that grants may be made only to programs or projects that do not provide abortions or abortion counseling or referral "or subcontract with anyone who does," except where a pregnant adolescent and her parents request such referral (*U.S. Code*, vol. 42, secs. 300z–10).

The influence of religion is not apparent in the language of the statute but instead in its effects. *AFLA* enables religious organizations to receive grants and requires that grant applicants specify how they will "involve religious and charitable organizations" in their provision of services. A number of grants funded pursuant to the Act have been given to organizations affiliated with religious institutions (see *Bowen v. Kendrick*, 487 U.S. 589, 597 [1988]), raising potential Establishment Clause concerns about excessive entanglements between Church and State. In particular, the Act as written "makes it possible for religiously affiliated grantees to teach adolescents on issues that can be considered 'fundamental elements of religious doctrine'" and "the teaching of 'religion qua religion'" (599), thereby involving government in financially supporting and endorsing religious influences on the adolescents served pursuant to the Act. As if in anticipation of future challenge, the report accompanying the 1981 bill states the Senate committee's view that "provisions for the involvement of religious organizations do not violate the constitutional separation between church and state."

Religious influences have sometimes had an inhibiting effect on legislation. The now defeated effort to pass a *Freedom of Choice Act*, for instance, which would have given the ruling in *Roe v. Wade* a federal statutory basis, met resistance from religious prolife forces (see, e.g., Alvare 1992: 66, 68). The inhibiting influence of religion is also evident in connection with the bill preceding the *Religious Freedom Restoration Act (RFRA)*, which some religious prolife political groups opposed on the ground that it would give women a basis to demand abortions by claiming that restrictions violated their free exercise rights (see Idelson 1993: 760; Masci 1993: 676; Chopko 1993; Bopp 1993; Biskupic 1991: 913).

Religious lawmaking has pervaded abortion regulation at the state level as well as the federal one. In *Webster v. Reproductive Health Services* (492 U.S. 490 [1989]), the Supreme Court upheld a Missouri abortion statute against a challenge to its constitutionality based on the Establishment Clause. The preamble to the Missouri abortion law at issue in *Webster* contained "findings" of the legislature that "the life of each human being begins at conception" and "unborn children have protectable interests in life, health, and well-being" (501).

Further, the Act provides that "all Missouri laws be interpreted to provide unborn children with the same rights enjoyed by other persons, subject to the Federal Constitution and this Court's precedents" (501, 504–5, n. 4). It includes a number of restrictions on abortion, including a prohibition on the use of public facilities and employees for abortions or abortion counseling (where not required to save the mother's life) and informed consent requirements. In particular, the Court upheld the constitutionality of the Missouri law, finding the preamble's language facially unobjectionable, because it "does not by its terms regulate abortion" and merely expresses Missouri's legitimate "value judgment favoring childbirth over abortion" (506).

The *Webster* decision resulted in a flurry of religiously motivated and influenced lobbying of state legislatures to adopt increasingly restrictive laws (see Byrnes 1991: 139; Byrnes and Segers 1992; Segers 1992: 33–34; Smolin 1989). For instance, 41 of the 46 Mormons in the Idaho legislature voted in favor of an extremely restrictive law designed by the national Right-to-Life organization to test the limits of the constitutionality of restrictive abortion laws after *Webster* (see Witt and Montcrief 1993: 124). Since *Webster*, Catholic bishops also have reasserted pressure on prochoice Catholic candidates and officeholders, publicly and vehemently attacking the prochoice positions of 1984 vice-presidential nominee Geraldine Ferraro and New York governor Mario Cuomo (see Byrnes 1991: 119–20, 140; Tribe 1990: 165–66).

The success of this activity to date has been significantly furthered by the Supreme Court's 1992 decision in *Planned Parenthood v. Casey* (505 U.S. 833 [1992]). *Casey* replaced the trimester framework of *Roe v. Wade* with an assessment of whether statutory restrictions constitute an "undue burden" on a pregnant woman's right to choose an abortion. The passage of the Pennsylvania abortion statute at issue in *Casey* was itself strongly influenced by the Pennsylvania Catholic Conference (see O'Hara 1992: 96, 99; see Rubin 1982: 105).

Religious lawmaking is evident in the executive as well as legislative arenas of government. Presidents Ronald Reagan, George H. W. Bush, and George W. Bush were elected with overwhelming support from conservative Christian groups, in part because of their publicly stated prolife views on abortion. The Catholic hierarchy has also been at the forefront of these efforts (see Byrnes 1991; Petchesky 1990). As described more fully in the following chapter, former President Reagan attempted to influence public policy on abortion by using explicitly religious terms to support his prolife views. While in office, Reagan rewarded his prolife supporters by influencing the passage of several restrictive abortion policies at the federal level.

The preceding discussion illustrates that religion has influenced abortion regulation in a variety of ways and in all branches of government, both at the state and federal levels. In chapter 2, I explain how this religious legislation raises constitutional concerns and examine the inadequacies of the Supreme Court's response to religious influences in the abortion cases that it has reviewed.

Why Religious Lawmaking Presents a Dilemma

As mentioned at the beginning of this chapter, if religious lawmaking is problematic in the ways just described, why not simply prohibit it? As I discuss in chapter 4, this is the approach that traditional liberal theorists have taken to protect free exercise and other Citizenship Rights in a religiously diverse society. This liberal solution, as we will see, is flawed for at least two reasons. The first is that it ignores the significance of religion to the moral identity of many citizens, including lawmakers. The second is that it overlooks the protections afforded to the religious beliefs of all citizens, including religious lawmakers, by the First Amendment Free Exercise Clause.

The Significance of Religion to Moral Identity

Religion is fundamental to the *moral identity* of many citizens. By moral identity, I mean the basic assumptions underlying an individual's moral and ethical decisions. Such considerations encompass both formal and informal frameworks of moral norms and values embodied in religious and ethical codes, creeds, principles, and guidelines. Constituents of moral identity may be derived from several different levels of social organization, ranging from the so-called private sphere of family and personal relationships to the public sphere of government, including laws and public educational institutions. It also includes the groups, organizations, and institutions of civil society that mediate between the public and private spheres of social life. The latter category for many, but not all, people includes religious organizations and institutions. Thus, on this definition, the category of religious identity may overlap significantly with that of moral identity but is not synonymous with it.

Given this centrality, a demand that religious adherents set aside or bracket their religious convictions in the spheres of lawmaking may infringe on and even violate their sense of identity. Daniel Conkle suggests that "religious beliefs, by their very nature, form a central part of a person's belief structure, his inner self. They define a person's very being—his sense of who he is, why he exists, and how he should relate to the world around him" (1988: 1165). Similarly, Carter suggests that "what is most special about religious life is the melding of the individual and the faith community in which, for the devout, much of reality is defined" (1993: 35).

From these perspectives, religious teaching is a way of looking at the world that cannot simply be set aside because it is constitutive of the believer's very identity (see Garvey 1993: 972). For Conkle, for example, "a person's religious beliefs cannot meaningfully be separated from the person himself; they are who he is. The essential identity of a person and his religious beliefs means that these beliefs often will be grounded on intense convictions. . . . For a person to challenge his own religious beliefs in any fundamental way is for him to challenge his sense of self, a sense of self that may depend on faith and that may give rise to eternal consequences" (1988: 1165).

According to these views, religion is so intertwined with a person's moral identity that it cannot be separated out. As Carter speculates: "It is not easy to imagine a religious self coping with the question of what life is through a relentlessly secular analysis" (1993: 241). This means that the choices a person makes, whether they be personal or political, inevitably will be influenced by the person's religious convictions (Benson and Williams 1982: 187, see 191; Curran 1982: 16).

Given this view of the relationship of religion to personal and moral identity (which is the dominant view of the communitarian theorists I discuss in chapter 5), asking a person to bracket their religious views in their public decision making, as do the proposals of some liberal theorists I consider in chapter 4, unfairly requires that person "to destroy a vital aspect of the self—in order to gain the right to participate in the dialogue alongside other citizens" (Carter 1993: 229). For example, Conkle argues that "religious believers can be torn apart in their efforts to maintain a private religiosity alongside a public secularity, and it is hard to believe that this kind of religious schizophrenia can be maintained indefinitely" (1993: 31). Although these views may overstate the actual significance of religion to moral identity, they emphasize that religion may be an indispensable element of the moral identity of persons, including lawmakers.

From another perspective, however, religion is never the exclusive determinant of the moral identity of persons, even for the most devout, regardless of how important it may be. For example, Robert Wuthnow describes modern religious identity as more of a voluntary or "achieved" characteristic than an ascribed or inevitable one, less a central feature in defining identity than it was in an earlier era (see Wuthnow 1993: 190; Wuthnow 1993: 190; see Wald 1989: 108–9). This is consistent with studies that indicate that the profession of faith frequently is more fervent than the level of actual religious activity and that only a minority of Americans take their religion seriously (Gallup and Castelli 1989: 3, 19; see Woodward 1993: 80). For example, one study found that the proportion of Americans who felt religion was "very important" in their lives fell from 75 percent in 1952 to about 55 percent in the late 1970s and 1980s. This study also found that church attendance has steadily declined since the 1950s (Gallup and Castelli 1989: 3). These statistics suggest that religion is not as inextricably related to personal and moral identity as communitarian views contend.

In addition, it is not uncommon for persons raised in one religious tradition to convert later to another religion or to become nonbelievers. As Steven Smith argues, "Even for self-conscious religious believers . . . the contention that religion is central to personal identity should be understood as an *aspirational* statement" rather than one of uncontroverted fact (1991: 221). These views support a conception of religion as a potentially significant aspect of moral identity but by no means the primary determinant or even a fixed and inalterable aspect, especially one that would or should preclude consideration of moral views other than and different from one's own.

Nevertheless, because many citizens consider religion to be fundamental, if not integral, to their moral identity, it seems unfair, if not unjust, to demand that they put aside their religious beliefs when acting in roles that include political decision making. As citizens, lawmakers are also entitled to the free exercise of their religion under the First Amendment. Despite their special roles as public officials, lawmakers are similar to most other citizens in viewing themselves as religious persons. In fact, lawmakers may be even more religious as a body than citizens generally. According to Benson and Williams's study, 95 percent of the members of Congress profess a belief in God, and 90 percent belong to a church or synagogue (1982: 24).[5]

Religious Lawmakers as Citizens

The free exercise rights of lawmakers may be infringed on by a prohibition on religious lawmaking, just as those of their constituents may be infringed on by the presence of such lawmaking (although, as I argue later, some constraints on lawmakers are permissible to protect the Citizenship Rights of other citizens). Further, if religion is as inextricably linked to moral identity as some views described here have suggested, the effort to require that lawmakers keep their religious beliefs separate from their political decision making may be futile. This is especially likely to be the case when the beliefs involve issues of ultimate concern, as with abortion, euthanasia, capital punishment, the use of reproductive technologies, cloning, genetic research, and so on.

Summary and Conclusions

In this chapter, I have described a number of respects in which religious influences on lawmaking are potentially problematic in a religiously pluralistic and gender-stratified society. To summarize the discussion thus far, religious lawmaking in the United States is contentious for a number of reasons, including the publicly inaccessible character of religion; the consequent tendency of religiously based laws to alienate, exclude, coerce, or be politically divisive for nonbelievers; the gender bias of the religious traditions prominent in the United States; and the magnification of that bias when incorporated into the binding laws of a morally and religiously pluralistic society. Such problems are starkly evident in the religious influences on abortion laws. Together, they make religious lawmaking potentially problematic in a constitutional democracy committed to religious liberty and gender justice.

However, because the moral identity and free exercise rights of religious lawmakers are also at stake, simply prohibiting religious influences on public lawmaking is not a viable solution. As chapter 3 further illuminates, religion plays an important, perhaps constitutive, role in the moral identity of many lawmakers. A blanket prohibition on religious lawmaking would fail to respect this role or the lawmakers' constitutionally protected free exercise rights. These complicating factors call for a more sophisticated analysis of the competing interests at stake and preclude a simple solution to religious lawmaking.

In the following chapter, I suggest that the U.S. Constitution is an important component in both the analysis of religious lawmaking and in the fashioning of an adequate response to the dilemma. As I discuss, religious lawmaking potentially violates a number of important constitutional rights and interests of citizens. However, because the Constitution also protects the rights of religious lawmakers, it does not give us a clear method for addressing the dilemma. In addition, because the Supreme Court has failed to satisfactorily address either the gender and pluralism side or the moral identity side of the dilemma in the cases it has decided that involve religious lawmaking, it also is necessary to go beyond a straightforward or simplistic approach to the constitutional issues involved in the course of fashioning a resolution for the dilemma.

TWO

The Constitutional Dimensions of Religious Lawmaking

In this chapter, I focus on the problems that religious lawmaking poses for constitutional rights and interests, both those of citizens subject to the results of such lawmaking as well as those of the lawmakers themselves. In part, I have chosen to focus on the constitutional problems with religious lawmaking because scholars in the past have emphasized the moral dimensions of the dilemma and undervalued the significance of the constitutional implications. But in addition, focusing on the constitutional rights and interests at stake in religious lawmaking will establish a foundation for developing a practical, legal solution to the dilemma. This chapter begins with a brief overview of religious lawmaking in the specific context of abortion regulation. In the second section, I describe the problems with religious lawmaking.

After describing how religious lawmaking raises a number of specific constitutional problems, including Establishment Concerns and potential infringements on Citizenship Rights. I illustrate how religious lawmaking interferes with these constitutional rights and interests in the context of abortion regulation. This focus highlights the gender dimensions of the issue. In the second part of the chapter, I show how the Supreme Court has failed to resolve the constitutional problems raised by religious lawmaking. I again use Supreme Court decisions on abortion regulation to illustrate overlooked gender inequalities involved in religious lawmaking.

Chapter 3 illustrates the inadequacies in the Court's approach to the other side of the dilemma of religious lawmaking, illustrating its inattention to the religious identity of lawmakers. Together, these first three chapters provide the foundation for considering the theoretical approaches to religious lawmaking discussed in chapters 4–6.

Constitutional Problems Raised by Religious Lawmaking

Before discussing the specific constitutional provisions that are relevant to religious lawmaking, it is important to discuss the basic relevance of the U.S. Constitution to religious lawmaking, especially in view of the skeptical reception some have given to the notion that religious influences on law implicate constitutional law. A typical argument is that religious influences on laws constitute an issue of religion and politics not addressed by the Constitution. The argument claims that the only relevant provision of the document, the First Amendment's Establishment Clause, is restricted in scope to matters of the institutional separation of Church and State.

For example, in *Private Consciences and Public Reasons*, Kent Greenawalt argues that the First Amendment's guarantee of religious liberty constrains government promotion of religious truth but does not resolve the appropriateness of individual government or public officials making decisions on the basis of their religious convictions (Greenawalt 1988: 18–19; see also 58–60). Michael Perry has also argues that the Constitution does not speak directly to religious lawmaking, especially the religion clauses of the First Amendment (1993: 706, 723).[1] The following discussion demonstrates how misplaced such views are.

The Relevance of the U.S. Constitution to Religious Lawmaking

In significant contrast to the stance that the Constitution is of little relevance to the issue of religious lawmaking, my position here is that the Constitution is of critical and central relevance. In particular, the religion clauses of the First Amendment and the Citizenship Rights to due process and equal protection guaranteed in the Fifth and Fourteenth Amendments are of central importance to religious lawmaking.

The Relevance of the First Amendment Religion Clauses to Religious Lawmaking

The so-called religion clauses of the First Amendment explicitly address the proper relationship of religion and government by specifying that "Congress shall make no law respecting an establishment of religion, or prohibiting the free exercise thereof" (U.S. Constitution, amend. 1). The Framers of the First Amendment evidently thought religion warranted special treatment by expressly using the term *religion*, not *conscience* or some more inclusive term in the language used in the final version of the Amendment. They also accorded a special status to religious freedom by mentioning it first among the several rights enumerated in the First Amendment, among them rights to free speech, free press, and free association.

In addition, the Constitution, with the Bill of Rights protecting basic civil liberties, provides a minimal framework for regulating the basic structure of government in a pluralistic polity. As the supreme law of the land, the tenets of the Constitution must be adhered to whenever applicable. Although the meanings of constitutional rights are not completely fixed and stable but shift over time in accordance with changes in context and interpretation, there nonetheless has been a remarkable degree of constancy and stability in the interpretation of rights guaranteed by the Constitution. The Constitution is, thus, of direct relevance in addressing the dilemma of religious lawmaking.

Although the term *religion* appears only once in the First Amendment, it qualifies two different clauses, one relating to the establishment of religion; the other to free exercise. The meaning of these clauses is ill-defined, however, in part because the Supreme Court appears to have defined religion differently for the Free Exercise Clause than for the Establishment Clause (see Alexander 1993: 792–94; Wenz 1992: 78–160; Richards 1986).

In a general sense, the Establishment Clause relates more directly to the concerns that religious lawmaking raises for religious pluralism, whereas the Free Exercise clause relates more directly to religious identity. However, the Free Exercise Clause also relates to religious pluralism in the sense that it is directed toward securing religious liberty for all citizens, regardless of their religious faith (or lack thereof). The Establishment Clause also concerns moral and religious identity in the sense of protecting the rights of those religious believers who would be excluded, alienated, or otherwise disadvantaged by religious influences on government.

Religious lawmaking presents two general types of problems for which constitutional analysis is appropriate: one, it may raise concerns that the Establishment Clause was designed to address, and two, it may abridge other Citizenship Rights protected by the Constitution, including those protected by the religion clauses. I take up each of these considerations in turn, beginning with Establishment Clause issues.

Interpreting the Establishment Clause for Purposes of Religious Lawmaking

There are two somewhat distinct occasions when the Establishment Clause is relevant to religious lawmaking. The first is when the core principle of the Establishment Clause has been deemed to be violated, as determined by interpretations of the Supreme Court. The second is when religious lawmaking infringes on what I call here *Establishment Concerns*, that is, the problems of alienation, exclusion, coercion, and political divisiveness that underlie the principles of the separation of Church and State presented in the Establishment

Clause. The latter may or may not rise to the level of a full-fledged violation of the Establishment Clause (in accordance with the Supreme Court's interpretations). Before addressing both of these aspects, I briefly examine how the Establishment Clause has been and should be interpreted in relation to religious lawmaking.

Rival Interpretations of the Establishment Clause.   A good deal of controversy has circulated around the issue of how the Establishment Clause should be interpreted because there is little historical evidence that illuminates what interpretation the Founders intended the Establishment Clause to have (see Levy 1985: 47, 52, 58). Both scholars and the Supreme Court have offered contrasting and sometimes contradictory perspectives on the extent to which the Establishment Clause prohibits religious lawmaking.

The Supreme Court originally stated that the purpose of the Establishment Clause was "to erect a wall of separation between Church and State" (see *Everson v. Board of Education*, 330 U.S. 1, 15–16 [1947]; *McDaniel v. Paty*, 435 U.S. 618, 637 [1978; Brennan, J., concurring]). The purpose of the wall has been viewed in numerous ways. For some, it is primarily to protect the free exercise rights of citizens. For political conservatives such as the Reverend Pat Robertson and Supreme Court Justice William Rehnquist, it was meant to prohibit only the official establishment of a church by the federal government and government preferences among religious sects or denominations (see Kosmin and Lachman 1993: 194; *Wallace v. Jaffree*, 472 U.S. 38, 106 [1985; Rehnquist, J., dissenting]; Berman 1986: 785).

For others, the point of Church-State separation is to maintain the secular character of government (see Sullivan 1992; Swomley 1987: 17; Wood 1991; Merel 1978: 813; see Smith 1991: 181; Fowler 1985: 236). For still others, it is to prevent the corruption of religion with worldly concerns (Carter 1993: 105, 107, 115–16). These different perspectives have resulted in a variety of conflicting proposals about the extent to which the Establishment Clause applies to religious lawmaking.[2]

Beyond the widespread agreement that the principle of Church-State separation precludes government from declaring an official church or religious denomination and that "government cannot endorse a particular religious belief" (Carter 1993: 178), the breadth and depth of what is mandated by this separation has remained the subject of debate (cf. Greenawalt 1993b: 506; Carter 1993: 255; Greenawalt 1988: 222; Perry 1988; McConnell 1992; Santurri 1992; Tribe 1988).

My own position, developed later, accords with more moderate voices, which claim that the Establishment Clause prohibits at least some types of religious influences on lawmaking (see Frankel 1993; Richards 1986: 140; Dworkin 1993: 161–62). However, before turning to discuss several important reasons why the Establishment Clause should be interpreted to require the exclusion of religious influences on lawmaking, let us examine whether the Supreme Court's interpretations of the Establishment Clause clearly establish what meaning the clause should have.

The Supreme Court's Interpretations of the Establishment Clause.
The Supreme Court's Establishment Clause cases are not terribly illuminating
on the issue of the Establishment Clause's relevance to religious lawmaking because most of these decisions have involved institutional relations between
government and religion, such as public aid to religious schools or religious influences on public schools, rather than government endorsement of or hostility toward religious beliefs, doctrines, or teachings per se. However, some of
the Court's decisions do speak to the question of how the Establishment Clause
should apply to religious lawmaking.

As an initial matter, the language in several Supreme Court decisions is
broad enough to encompass religious lawmaking, even if the subject matter of
the central issue in the case was institutional Church-State relations. For example, in the case of *Walz v. Tax Commission* (397 U.S. 664, 668 [1970]), the Court
characterized the three main evils against which the Establishment Clause was
intended to protect as "sponsorship, financial support, and active involvement
of the sovereign in religious activity." The latter is especially pertinent to religious lawmaking, which involves government in religious activities. In *Lemon
v. Kurtzman* (403 U.S. 602, 622–23 [1970]), the Court added that the Establishment Clause was also designed to protect against "political division along religious lines" (see Conkle 1988: 1124), another danger presented when laws are
based on or influenced by religious considerations. The *Lemon* case established
the Supreme Court's test for determining the constitutionality of legislation
under the Establishment Clause (which was applied by all federal courts, at
least until recently) and contained three criteria, or prongs:

1. The primary purpose of the legislation must be secular (secular purpose).
2. Its primary effect must neither advance nor inhibit religion (primary effect).
3. It must avoid "excessive entanglement" with religion (entanglement).

The Court in *Lemon* described the secular purpose requirement as designed
to ascertain whether "the legislative intent was to advance religion" (613).
Legislation having a religious purpose would violate the first prong. However,
in another decision, the Court clarified that "even though a statute that is motivated in part by a religious purpose may satisfy the first criterion . . . the First
Amendment requires that a statute must be invalidated if it is entirely motivated by a purpose to advance religion" (*Wallace v. Jaffree*, 56 [1985]). In other
words, having some religious influence does not necessarily invalidate a law as
long as it is not completely motivated by a religious purpose. In *Wallace*, the
Court further specified that in applying the secular purpose test, it is appropriate to ask "whether government's *actual* purpose is to endorse or disap-
prove of religion" (emphasis added; see also *Lynch v. Donnelly*, 456 U.S. 668,
690 [1984; O'Connor, J., concurring]).

Unfortunately, the Court has not been consistent in its rulings on whether
such mixed-motive cases, where both religious and secular purposes are involved, violate the Constitution. In part, this results from the difficulties in determining the primary legislative purpose or intent. Although the impetus behind the secular purpose requirement is a sound one, as I argue, its potential

infringements on the free exercise rights of religious lawmakers counsels an alternative approach to determining the violation of the Establishment Clause, one focused on whether the law can be fully justified on the basis of secular reasons, regardless of its actual purpose or intent.

The second and third requirements of the *Lemon* test clearly encompass the concerns presented by religious lawmaking. Regarding the second requirement that the primary effect of a law cannot be to either advance or inhibit religion, the Court stated that "Government may not promote or affiliate itself with any religious *doctrine* or organization" (*City of Allegheny v. American Civil Liberties Union*, 492 U.S. 573, 590 [1989]; emphasis added) and that the clause, "at the very least, prohibits government from appearing to take a position on questions of religious belief" (593–95). The third requirement, prohibiting the government from "excessive entanglement with religion," has usually been found in situations where government has delegated its own authority to a religious group[3] but could also be interpreted to prohibit religious lawmaking.

The Court's current Establishment Clause jurisprudence appears to be in flux because the Court has failed to apply the traditional *Lemon* test in recent cases,[4] yet it also has refused thus far to expressly reject *Lemon*. Instead, in recent decisions, the Court has applied standards such as "coercion" (*Lee v. Weisman*, 507 U.S. 557, at 557–58 [1992]) and "endorsement" (*Board of Education of Kiryas Joel v. Grumet*, 114 S. Ct. 2481 [1994]) to determine whether a challenged law violates the principle of government neutrality held to be central to the meaning of the Establishment Clause.

These more recent pronouncements about the scope of the Establishment Clause also support my claim that religious lawmaking is constitutionally suspect. In *Lee v. Weisman*, the Court stated: "The First Amendment Religion Clauses mean that religious beliefs and religious expression are too precious to be either proscribed or prescribed by the State. The design of the Constitution is that preservation and transmission of religious beliefs and worship is a responsibility and a choice committed to the private sphere, which itself is promised freedom to pursue that mission" (507 U.S. 557–58).

An Interpretation Based on the Historical Record.   In chapter 7, I more fully develop the argument that the Establishment Clause should be interpreted to prohibit religiously based or influenced laws that infringe on Citizenship Rights when those laws cannot be fully justified on the basis of secular reasons or by a compelling State interest. A few of the reasons for that conclusion should be mentioned at this juncture, however.

First, although "the intentions" of the Constitution's framers have been used to support narrow as well as liberal interpretations of the scope of the religion clauses (see, e.g., Carter 1993; Handy 1991; Levy 1985; Cord 1982),[5] the history of the debates over the Bill of Rights indicates that some of the Framers were concerned about the religious tyranny that could result from religious institutions having access to the reins of government. The Framers of the Establishment Clause were aware that closely affiliated Church and State institutions in seventeenth-century Britain resulted in political destabilization (see Karst 1993: 147). They, therefore, advocated religious tolerance.

Jefferson, in particular, viewed any State support for the promotion of religious belief as the usurpation of an inalienable right (see Richards 1986: 112). Madison echoed this perspective, stating in his famous *Memorial and Remonstrance against Religious Assessment* (1785) that the right of conscience is inalienable, dependent not on the dictates of other men but only on duties owed to "the Creator" (Meyers 1981: 5–13). James Madison recognized the problems of alienation and exclusion in asserting that the establishment of religion "degrades from the equal rank of Citizens all those whose opinions in Religion do not bend to those of the Legislative authority" (quoted in Meyers 1981: 10–11, cited in Richards 1986: 161). These views counsel a broad reading of the Establishment Clause that would extend to religious infringements on lawmaking and not simply apply to conflicts between government and religious institutions.

Establishment Concerns versus Establishment Clause Violations

Because specific instances of religious lawmaking may abridge Establishment Clause rights to greater and lesser degrees, different levels of infringements on Establishment Clause interests should be recognized by adjudicators of this constitutional provision. Less severe infringements include religious lawmaking that results in the alienation, exclusion, and coercion of nonbelievers and in the fostering of political divisiveness, referred to collectively as *Establishment Concerns*. Justice O'Connor's oft-quoted statement in *Lynch v. Donnelly* recognized that "direct government action endorsing religion or a particular religious practice is invalid . . . because it sends a message to nonadherents that they are outsiders, not full members of the political community, and an accompanying message to adherents that they are insiders, favored members of the political community" (668, 687–88).

This danger is acute when religion provides the basis for public laws. Minority religious groups may feel particularly vulnerable because government policies that endorse religious or irreligious beliefs may be interpreted by religious adherents of other faiths as an attack on or disregard for their citizenship or even their very selves, not only their beliefs (see Davis 1993: 113, citing Silberman 1985: 348; Nahmod 1993; Marshall 1993; Conkle 1993, 1992).

Even if lawmakers promote no particular religious agenda, a generalized religious message can effectively exclude those who are nonbelievers. This was the situation at issue in the Supreme Court case of *Lee v. Weisman* (507 U.S. 557 [1992]), which involved a challenge to a clergy-led prayer at a public high school graduation ceremony. The Court recognized the alienating potential of religion "to divide societies and to exclude those whose beliefs are not in accord with particular religions" (citing *Grand Rapids School District v. Ball*, 473 U.S. 373, 385–86 [1985]). Justice Blackmun's concurring opinion expresses the view that government's imprimatur on a particular religion conveys "a message of exclusion to all those who do not adhere to the favored beliefs" (*Lee v. Weisman*, 507 U.S. 570).

The Court in *Lee* repeated the principle established in earlier precedents that "the Constitution guarantees that government may not coerce anyone to support or participate in religion or its exercise, or otherwise act in a way which 'establishes a [state] religion or religious faith or tends to do so'" (507 U.S. 577–78, citing *Lynch v. Donnelly*, 465 U.S. 668, 678 [1984]). As noted in chapter 1, in addition to its potential to alienate and coerce nonbelievers, religious lawmaking also has a tendency to be divisive for the political community as a whole. The Supreme Court has recognized this problem in several cases. It has noted that "political division along religious lines was one of the principal evils against which the First Amendment was intended to protect" (*Lemon v. Kurtzman*, 602, 622 [1973]). Even Justice O'Connor, who argues that political divisiveness should not be an independent ground for finding a violation of the Establishment Clause because of the problems with substantiating such a speculative claim, nonetheless agrees that "political divisiveness is admittedly an evil addressed by the Establishment Clause" (*Lynch v. Donnelly*, 465 U.S. 668, 689; see Wenz 1992: 92; McConnell 1992: 130).

Although the Supreme Court has often refused to invalidate laws which (merely or simply) raised Establishment Concerns, finding the infringement too minimal or indirect to constitute a full-scale violation of the Establishment Clause, it has recognized all of these possible effects of religious lawmaking as factors to be considered in assessing Establishment Clause claims. As I discuss further in chapter 7, the existence of such Establishment Concerns should be considered as evidence that religious lawmaking has violated either the Establishment Clause or other Citizenship Rights. Recognizing and responding to Establishment Concerns as well as to full-fledged Establishment Clause violations is necessary to give adequate respect to and protection for the religious convictions of all Americans in a morally and religiously pluralistic culture.

Free Exercise Rights

In addition to raising Establishment Concerns, and potentially violating the Establishment Clause's core requirement of government neutrality toward religion, religious lawmaking often infringes on rights protected by the First Amendment's Free Exercise Clause. The principle underlying this constitutional provision is that citizens should not be disadvantaged by government on the basis of their religion. This principle is directly applicable to protecting citizens against the disadvantaging effects of religious lawmaking, although it has seldom been applied by the Court to this end.

In an oft-quoted passage, the Supreme Court declared that the Free Exercise Clause means that "no official, high or petty, can prescribe what shall be orthodox in politics, nationalism, religion, or other matters of opinion or force citizens to confess by word or act their faith therein" (*West Virginia Board of Education v. Barnette*, 319 U.S. 624, 642 [1943]). More recently, "the Court has unambiguously concluded that the individual freedom of conscience protected by the First Amendment embraces the right to select any religious faith or none at all" (*Webster v. Reproductive Health Services*, 492 U.S. 490, 572 n. 17 [1989; Stevens, J., dissenting]; see *Wallace v. Jaffree*, 38, 52).

Any government policy that promotes, endorses, or disadvantages religion or involves an excessive entanglement in religious matters may infringe on the free exercise rights of nonbelievers and disbelievers in addition to running afoul of the Establishment Clause (see, e.g., *Larson v. Valente*, 456 U.S. 228 [1982], discussed in Rotunda and Nowak 1992: 447–50). The Court has invalidated legislation under the Free Exercise Clause for imposing a burden on the exercise of a sincerely held religious belief without compelling justification for doing so (see, e.g., *Sherbert v. Verner*, 374 U.S. 398 [1963]; *Wisconsin v. Yoder*, 406 U.S. 205 [1972]).

Whether government involvement with religion is sufficient to violate the Free Exercise Clause according to long-established Supreme Court decisions depends on whether it burdens the free exercise rights of citizens and, if so, whether government can demonstrate that it has a compelling State interest for imposing such burdens. Despite recognizing the importance of protecting the religious identity of citizens, the Court's Free Exercise jurisprudence increasingly has become less sensitive to government infringements on the free exercise of religion. This insensitivity is exemplified by the unduly narrow standard the Court has applied in recent years to determine free exercise violations. Whereas earlier decisions had held that indirect burdens were sufficient to show that free exercise rights had been infringed on,[6] plaintiffs in recent cases have been required to demonstrate that the government regulation directly "burdens" their religious belief or practice.[7]

The Court in *Employment Division v. Smith* (484 U.S. 872 [1990]) determined that the Free Exercise Clause does not invalidate generally applicable laws that do not single out religion for different treatment, even if they burden the free exercise of religion (496 U.S. 877–83). Only laws failing to meet the requirements of neutrality and general applicability that cannot "be justified by a compelling governmental interest . . . narrowly tailored to advance that interest" are invalid under this revised standard (*Church of the Lukumi Babalu Aye v. Hialeah*, 508 U.S. 520, 531–32 [1993]). Thus, showing that a law stigmatizes individuals is not enough to satisfy the Court that a Free Exercise violation has occurred.

The Court's recent interpretations of the Free Exercise Clause significantly have restricted the scope of religious belief deemed to be constitutionally protected and, thus, significantly limited protections for religious minorities disadvantaged by religious lawmaking. However, because these cases generally involve burdens on the free exercise rights of citizens rather than lawmakers, it is unclear to what extent the Court would permit restrictions on religious lawmaking that burden the free exercise rights of lawmakers.

One indication of how the Court might choose to rule on the constitutionality of religious lawmaking under the Free Exercise Clause if it chose to do so is provided in the line of federal cases involving the 501(c)(3) tax exemption accorded to charitable and religious nonprofit organizations. These cases indicate that Congress and lower federal courts do not consider legal limitations on an organization's religious involvement in politics as a condition of receiving federal benefits to violate free exercise rights.

In *Regan v. Taxation without Representation of Washington* (461 U.S. 540, 544 [1983]), the Supreme Court upheld the constitutionality of Congress's decision to condition eligibility for a charitable or nonprofit tax exemption on an organization's lack of involvement in politics. Although the Supreme Court did not rule explicitly on whether this restriction violated the free exercise rights of religious organizations, lower federal courts have determined that it does not (e.g., *Christian Echoes National Ministry v. U.S.*, 470 F.2d 849 [10th Cir. 1972]). These cases thus provide some support for the position that restricting religious lawmaking would not violate First Amendment rights.

As we saw with respect to the Establishment Clause, despite the narrowness of the Court's actual interpretations, the Free Exercise Clause could legitimately be applied to religious lawmaking if the Court chose to do so. That the Court *should* choose to do so should be clear from chapter 1's discussion of the centrality that religion has in the lives of many citizens and lawmakers and the consequent importance of according vigorous protection to the free exercise rights of both.

The Supreme Court's View of Religious Lawmaking? The McDaniel v. Paty Decision

The closest the Court has come to ruling directly on the constitutionality of religious lawmaking under the First Amendment is a case involving both religion clauses. In *McDaniel v. Paty* (435 U.S. 618), the Court invalidated a Tennessee statute barring ministers from serving as delegates to the state's constitutional conventions. The Court found that the statute violated ministers' free exercise rights by forcing them to sacrifice either their religious roles as clergy (to hold public office) or their public office (to maintain their positions of religious leadership), despite Tennessee's rationale that the regulation was necessary to prevent violations of the Establishment Clause.

Justice Brennan's concurring opinion in *McDaniel* argued that the Tennessee statute might violate the Establishment Clause as well as the ministers' free exercise rights by manifesting "patent hostility toward, not neutrality respecting, religion" (636). In this case, both the majority opinion and Brennan's concurrence privileged free exercise interests over those protected by the Establishment Clause. The Court's decision lends itself to the conclusion that protection for the free exercise rights of lawmakers takes precedence over protection for the free exercise and nonestablishment rights of other citizens that may be infringed on by religious lawmaking.

In chapter 7, I indicate why such an outcome would be inappropriate, even though *McDaniel* can also be interpreted to support the valid principle that government efforts to avoid Establishment Clause problems may need to be moderated where free exercise interests are also at stake. Despite the actual outcome in *McDaniel*, however, the Court left open the possibility that the kind of religious influence that a minister might exert in lawmaking might be invalid under circumstances where Establishment Clause interests are directly threatened (see Tushnet 1991: 193).

The *McDaniel* decision is also significant to our discussion insofar as it reveals the Court's liberal assumption that members of the clergy are able and willing to separate their roles as religious persons from their roles as public officials. By rejecting Tennessee's position that clergy in public decision-making roles will necessarily rely on their religious convictions, the Court implied that such a presumption is unwarranted with respect to religious persons, even those occupying roles as clergy, because they are able to distinguish their political activities from their religious ones. This interpretation is reinforced by the Court's statement that "the American experience provides no persuasive support for the fear that clergymen in public office will be less careful of antiestablishment interests or less faithful to their oaths of civil office than their unordained counterparts" (*McDaniel v. Paty*, 1329). The quoted statement also suggests that the Court considers religious lawmakers to be as obligated to uphold the Establishment Clause's separation of Church and State and other constitutional guarantees as secular lawmakers, a position discussed affirmatively in chapter 7.

McDaniel and the other cases discussed in this section show that the Supreme Court has not developed a clear position on the constitutional validity of religious lawmaking. In part, this is because of the paucity of religion clause cases that the Court has heard that directly involve religious lawmaking. However, in part, it is because the Court has failed to give adequate consideration to the extent to which religious lawmaking implicates First Amendment rights, both those protected by the Free Exercise Clause and those protected by the Establishment Clause. These cases thereby demonstrate that an adequate approach to religious lawmaking needs to go beyond the Supreme Court's rulings and reassess the relevance of the Constitution to resolving this dilemma. In the next section, I consider some additional constitutional provisions that may be infringed on by religious lawmaking.

The Relevance of Other Constitutional Provisions Integral to Protecting the Rights of Citizenship

In addition to the constitutional problems that religious lawmaking raises under the First Amendment religion clauses, it may also infringe on or even directly violate Citizenship Rights protected by other constitutional provisions, especially the Fifth and Fourteenth Amendments. The relevant part of the Fourteenth Amendment provides that "No State shall . . . deprive any person of life, liberty, or property, without due process of law; nor deny to any person within its jurisdiction the equal protection of the laws." This constitutional provision contains two different types of guarantees of individual rights under the Equal Protection Clause and the Due Process Clause.

The Fifth Amendment provides analogous guarantees that are binding on the federal government. The Due Process and Equal Protection Clauses bar government from enacting laws that either infringe on fundamental rights or classify persons in certain "suspect classes" without a compelling State interest for doing so. Religious lawmaking may infringe on both of these rights, as I discuss shortly.

Religious lawmaking on issues other than abortion may implicate these as well as other constitutional provisions. For example, religious lawmaking on the environment might implicate the Fifth Amendment's clause prohibiting "takings" of private property without compensation. Religiously influenced laws concerning capital punishment would implicate the Eighth Amendment's prohibition on "cruel and unusual punishment." To demonstrate the gendered implications of the dilemma, the following discussion focuses specifically on the constitutional problems raised by religious lawmaking on abortion.

How Religious Lawmaking Infringes on the Fifth and Fourteenth Amendment Rights to Substantive Due Process

The Due Process Clause protects individual rights of liberty and privacy from unwarranted interference by government. The State must have a rational interest to justify restricting the liberty of any citizen. The "rational basis" requirement is easy to satisfy: generally, courts will accept any plausible rationale the government offers as long as it is not patently offensive or beyond the lawmaking body's jurisdiction. When regulations burden fundamental rights, however, the State must satisfy the higher standard of showing that it has a compelling interest for imposing the regulation, one which cannot be satisfied by less restrictive or burdensome means. As with the religion clause discussion, I first describe how the Supreme Court has interpreted due process rights and then point out the limitations of those interpretations for the purposes of religious lawmaking.

Interpretations of the Due Process Clauses.   The Supreme Court has on occasion held decisions regarding religious matters to be protected by the Fourteenth Amendment due process liberty right rather than simply by the Free Exercise Clause (see *Pierce v. Society of Sisters*, 268 U.S. 510 [1925]). The Supreme Court also has interpreted the Due Process Clause to provide protection for individual rights not specifically enumerated in the Bill of Rights, including procreative decisions relating to contraceptive use,[8] abortion,[9] and marriage. These cases are similar to one another and to free exercise cases in extending protection to personal decisions involving matters of integral importance to self-identity. Such personal decisions certainly also include the religious convictions of lawmakers and other citizens.

Among the most important of the personal decisions protected by substantive due process is a pregnant woman's decision whether or not to carry the fetus to term. In *Roe v. Wade* (410 U.S. 113 [1973]), the Supreme Court determined that women have a right of privacy to decide whether to terminate a pregnancy during the first two trimesters in consultation with her physician.

The Court held that this right to privacy is a fundamental constitutional right, itself an aspect of the liberty guaranteed by substantive due process. As Tribe contends, "the liberty that is most plainly vindicated by the right to end one's pregnancy is the woman's liberty not to be made unwillingly into a mother, the freedom to say no to the unique sacrifice inherent in the processes of pregnancy and childbirth" (1990: 98).

This liberty may even be necessary to sustain women's very lives, given the health risks associated with pregnancy and childbirth. More often, restrictions on privacy and liberty rights to abortion limit women's access to adequate incomes, satisfying work, and even a self-identity defined in any terms other than the maternal role (see Siegel 1992: 366–71). Although much beleaguered by criticism and opposition from a variety of fronts, *Roe's* core holding that the Constitution protects a woman's right of privacy to terminate an unwanted pregnancy was upheld in the Supreme Court's most recent major pronouncement on abortion rights in *Planned Parenthood v. Casey* (505 U.S. 833 [1992]).

The Relevance of Due Process to Religious Lawmaking.   The Court in *Planned Parenthood v. Casey* stated, "At the heart of liberty is the right to define one's own concept of existence, of meaning, of the universe, and of the mystery of human life. Beliefs about these matters could not define the attributes of personhood were they formed under compulsion of the State" (852). It further stated that "the destiny of the woman must be shaped to a large extent on her own conception of her spiritual imperatives and her place in society" (852–53).

These statements reveal the Supreme Court's recognition that religious and other deeply held beliefs of conscience deserve constitutional protection in the abortion context under the Due Process Clause's protection for liberty. Of course, abortion restrictions not motivated or influenced by religion may also violate these protections. However, where restrictive laws are based on traditional religious patriarchal understandings about the proper status and roles of women, they are especially likely to discount or ignore women's rights and interests.

How Religious Lawmaking Infringes on the Fourteenth Amendment Right to Equal Protection

In addition to implicating due process rights, religious lawmaking may infringe on constitutional rights to the "equal protection of the laws." The Equal Protection Clause applies to all government actions that classify or differentiate among individuals. This constitutional provision ensures the right of equal citizenship by invalidating "laws enacted by a dominant group which disproportionately burden a disfavored group—laws which frequently would not be passed if their burden were equally shared by all" (Calabresi 1985: 101).

If legislative action relates to general economic or social welfare concerns, the State only needs to show that there is some plausible basis for its classifications, in accordance with the rational basis standard of review. However, if such classifications burden a fundamental right or involve a suspect classification, they are subject to the compelling State interest test described previously.

In addition, religious lawmaking may violate the principle of equal protection by discriminating between citizens on the basis of their religious beliefs, privileging some while denigrating others. As noted earlier, according official legitimacy and the binding authority of law to certain religious beliefs suggests that citizens holding those beliefs are political insiders, whereas those holding different beliefs are political outsiders and unequal citizens.

The Supreme Court's Interpretations of the Equal Protection Clause.
The Supreme Court occasionally has applied the Equal Protection Clause to assess the constitutionality of legislation relating to religion (*United States v. Seeger*, 380 U.S. 163 [1965]; see Weber 1989: 30). In addition, individual members of the Court have pointed to its relevance in the context of challenges to laws bearing on religion. Religious lawmaking warrants consideration under the Equal Protection Clause because of its tendency to disadvantage religious minorities, especially in view of the Court's decisions to limit free exercise protections.

The Supreme Court has interpreted the Equal Protection Clause to prohibit sex discrimination, although it has done so under a "middle level," or less rigorous standard of judicial scrutiny, than the compelling State interest standard applied to discrimination on the basis of race and other suspect classes.[10] The Equal Protection Clause prohibits legislation that is premised on "archaic and stereotypic notions" about women, on traditional and inaccurate assumptions about proper roles for men and women,[11] or on unsupported presumptions about women's capacities and capabilities (see Siegel 1992).

The Court has recognized that restrictive abortion laws infringe on women's rights to equal protection (*Thornburgh v. American College of Obstetricians*, 476 U.S. 747, 772 [1985]), especially when they are premised on the underlying stereotyped assumption that women can be forced to accept motherhood as a natural aspect of their role (*Planned Parenthood v. Casey*, 852, Stevens and Blackmun, dissenting; see also Siegel 1992: 348–49; Tribe 1990: 135; Ginsburg 1985: 375). As Justice Blackmun recognized in his dissent in *Webster v. Reproductive Health Services*, the right to reproductive choice "has become vital to the full participation of women in the economic and political walks of American life" (557; see also *Planned Parenthood v. Casey*, 870).

Further, as Justice Stevens notes in his dissent in *Planned Parenthood v. Casey*: "Because motherhood has a dramatic impact on a woman's educational prospects, employment opportunities, and self determination, restrictive abortion laws deprive her of basic control over her life" (900). Such restrictions run afoul of the Equal Protection Clause because they impose no analogous restrictions on men. Given the physiological differences between the sexes, there is no equivalent hardship that men are forced to undergo, either in the sphere of reproduction or in other areas of social life.

In addition, restrictive abortion laws also run afoul of the principle of equal protection by imposing roles on women that have historically contributed to their subjugation, impositions to which men have never been subjected. As Karst explains, the legitimacy of restrictive abortion laws involves the issue of whether women are "to be treated by law and government as equal and responsible participants in public life, or . . . defined officially as child-bearers and child-rearers first, with non-domestic roles distinctly secondary" (1991: 727; see 1993: 180, 182). Further, restrictive abortion laws disempower and disrespect women by permitting "some government agent—whether bureaucrat, social worker, or physician—to hold such a life-affecting decision as abortion in his or her hands" (Tribe 1990: 74). Consequently, restrictive abortion laws involve a disproportionate impact based on gender by imposing State control over women's sexual behavior and maternity in ways that determine their social and political status, while not imposing comparable controls on men (see Tribe 1990: 130–31).

Restrictive abortion regulations that impose notification requirements, waiting periods, and similar restrictions on women's ability to obtain an abortion also impose a disproportionate impact on the basis of gender, which may violate the Equal Protection Clause. Such restrictions imply that women are not morally responsible beings capable of making appropriate decisions with respect to abortion on their own, while placing no analogous restrictions on decision making by men. Not allowing autonomous decision making by pregnant women concerning whether or not to have an abortion "denigrates women as moral decision makers, and it reinforces their role as sexual objects by undermining their ability to act as sexual agents" (Olsen 1989: 121). In contrast, the law generally does not hold men responsible for giving any part of their own body to another, even if necessary to save the life of one of their offspring (see *Winston v. Lee*, 470 U.S. 753 [1985]; *Rochin v. California*, 342 U.S. 165 [1952]; Johnsen and Wilder 1989: 179). In these respects, restrictive abortion laws also deprive women of their free exercise rights.

Relevance of the Equal Protection Clause to Religious Lawmaking. As discussed earlier, religious lawmaking may especially violate women's equal protection rights. The majority of the Court in *Casey* recognized the coercive function of restrictive abortion laws on women's free exercise rights by referring to the pregnant women's suffering as "too intimate and personal for the state to insist, without more, upon its own vision of the woman's role, however dominant that vision has been in the course of our history and our culture" (877). As noted, the coercion is more likely to result in women's disempowerment and disrespect when the state's decision is made by a male lawmaker based on the tenets of a patriarchal religious tradition.

As Justice Blackmun recognizes in his dissent in *Casey*, restrictive abortion laws "force upon women the physical labor and specific and direct medical and psychological harms that may accompany carrying a fetus to term," thereby forcing women to seek illegal abortions or self-abortions at the risk of physical injury or even death "all in the name of enforced morality or religious dictates or lack of compassion, as it may be" (492 U.S. 557–58 [Blackmun, J., dissenting]). As we have seen, religiously based abortion restrictions are often premised on assumptions about women as primarily or essentially mothers and child rearers, and as lacking moral agency to make responsible decisions on their own. The worldview of prolife advocates in particular tends to reflect conservative religious and political views, including traditional ideas that gender differences are intrinsic, give men and women different roles to play, and that women's proper roles are those of wives and mothers (Luker 1984b: 159–75, 195–96).

Other research studies also show close connections between "abortion attitudes, sexual moralism, and social traditionalism, value systems deriving primarily, but not exclusively, from conservative religion" (Guth et al. 1994: 46; see Schnell 1993: 37–38; Karst 1991: 683–84; Hertzke 1988: 34–35; Luker 1984b: 159–75). Subsequent studies confirm that religious Christians who attend church frequently are more likely to oppose abortion and equal rights for women than others (Himmelstein 1986; see Becker 1992: 472).

These attitudes are also evident in the decision making of religious lawmakers. For example, Benson and Williams's study revealed that the more religious members of Congress were, the more they tend to vote against abortion (1982: 752–53). These studies indicate how close the connection between religious lawmaking and violations of women's equal protection rights can be, especially in relation to abortion regulation. They confirm that the sexist assumptions embedded in traditional religious views are an invalid basis for lawmaking because of their interference with rights protected by the Equal Protection Clause.

This review of constitutional provisions pertinent to religious lawmaking has revealed that, in addition to the problems raised by religious lawmaking generally, a number of potential constitutional problems are raised when such lawmaking directly impacts on the lives of religious minorities and women. In the following section, I discuss the inadequacies of the Supreme Court's resolution of cases involving such lawmaking.

Problems with the Supreme Court's Jurisprudence on Religious Lawmaking

On several occasions, the Supreme Court has failed to take the opportunity to rule that religious lawmaking violates or infringes on Citizenship Rights. This failure can be seen clearly through the examination of the Court's response to religious lawmaking on abortion. The Supreme Court has confirmed the relevance of both the First and Fourteenth Amendments to the issue of religious lawmaking. Yet its decisions in cases involving religiously influenced abortion regulations have not adequately upheld the rights of citizens protected by these constitutional provisions. Two primary causes have contributed to this deficiency. The first is the Court's failure to recognize the distinctive harms that religious lawmaking may cause, specifically by contributing to the Establishment Concerns of alienation, exclusion, coercion, and political divisiveness among citizens, as discussed in chapter 1. This oversight is especially troublesome in cases where the law may have multiple or mixed purposes, some of which are secular and others of which are religious.

The second main oversight is the Court's failure to recognize how religious lawmaking may infringe on the Citizenship Rights protected by the Establishment and Free Exercise Clauses, as well as by the constitutional principles of due process and equal protection of the laws. This problem is especially prominent with respect to the Court's failure to recognize how religious lawmaking disadvantages certain citizens on the basis of their gender and religious affiliation. I discuss these problems using three Supreme Court cases as illustrations.

Practical Problems with the Court's Response to Religious Lawmaking: The Case of Abortion Regulation

In the first of these cases, *Harris v. McRae* (448 U.S. 297 [1980]), as already noted, religious influence is evident in the legislative history and background to the Hyde Amendment, an abortion law which touches on all four of the Citizenship Rights identified here. In the second case, *Webster v. Reproductive Health Services* (490), religious assumptions are evidenced in the language used to frame abortion restrictions in a state abortion statute. In the third case, *Bowen v. Kendrick* (487 U.S. 589 [1988]), religious influence is suggested in the provisions of the federal *Adolescent Family Life Act* (*AFLA*) statute related to religiously affiliated grantees. These decisions have been unsatisfactory in several respects, especially in failing to take cognizance of how religious influences on abortion laws exacerbate gender inequalities, as the following discussion illustrates.

These cases illustrate a range of problems in the Supreme Court's analysis. These problems can be categorized into the following types: a failure to uphold the Constitution against violations of the Establishment and Free Exercise Clauses, especially the free exercise rights of lawmakers; a failure to recognize or acknowledge the relevance of Establishment Concerns to the violation of Citizenship Rights and, consequently, a failure to protect specific constitutional rights of citizenship; and the imposition of unduly burdensome standing requirements, which has the effect of obstructing access to the courts to challenge instances of religious lawmaking when it infringes on Citizenship Rights. I discuss each of these in turn.

Failure to Uphold the Constitution against Violations of the Establishment and Free Exercise Clauses

In several respects, the Court's rulings on the religiously influenced abortion laws in cases that have come before it are inadequate: they either fail to implement the Court's own standards for interpreting cases involving religion, or they reflect the shortcomings of the Court's religion clause analysis in cases involving abortion. Among the former category is the Court's unwillingness to consider evidence that the efforts of religious institutions had a direct influence on passage of legislation, in violation of the Establishment Clause (*Harris v. McRae*, 448 U.S. 297 [1980]; *McRae v. Califano*, 491 F. Supp. 630, 691 [1980]; *Webster v. Reproductive Health Services*, 490, 572 n. 17). For instance, the Court in *Harris* should have recognized that simply because the Catholic Church lacked a monopoly on influencing the passage of the Hyde Amendment did not establish that the law was not religiously based or influenced. In fact, as the lower federal court in *Harris* concluded, an organized effort of institutional religion to influence the vote on the amendment may have been decisive (491 F. Supp. 724). The Court should have given far more weight to this fact, given the potential abridgement of Citizenship Rights risked by this law.

In addition, the Court failed in these cases to further interrogate the possible religion clause violations of laws that "happen [] to coincide or harmonize with the tenets of some or all religions" (*Harris*, 448 U.S. 319, quoting *McGowan v. Maryland*, 366 U.S. 420, 442 [1961]; *Bowen*, 622). Instead, the Court merely assumed, rather than substantiated, its position that the government's stated interest in the protection of potential life reflected a valid secular purpose rather than a religious one, as required by the Court's interpretations of the Establishment Clause (*Harris*). Contrary to the majority opinion, Justice Stevens's dissent in *Webster* found the Missouri abortion statute's preamble invalid under the Establishment Clause as endorsing "the theological position that there is the same secular interest in preserving the life of a fetus during the first 40 or 80 days of pregnancy as there is after viability" (567–68). Stevens characterized the preamble as "an unequivocal endorsement of a religious tenet of some but by no means all Christian faiths, [which] serves no identifiable secular purpose" (566–71).

These abortion cases also reflect an unduly narrow interpretation of the Free Exercise Clause, for example, that only women having religious beliefs that compel abortions have valid free exercise claims (*Harris*). This reading undermines the central meaning of the clause, to protect freedom of conscience from unwarranted State interference. The Court overlooked the potential of religiously premised abortion restrictions to prevent some women from acting in accordance with their own moral and religious views in both the *Harris* and *Webster* cases. In *Harris*, the impact of the Hyde Amendment on indigent women may obstruct their ability to act in accordance with their religious beliefs, thereby restricting their free exercise rights, even in the absence of such compulsion (see Petchesky 1990: 337), as the lower courts had found (see *Harris*, 320). In addition, the denial of abortion funding may delay the ability of indigent women to have abortions until private sources of financing can be arranged, thereby postponing the date of the procedure beyond the point of ensoulment and thus creating a conflict between abortion and pregnant women who hold religious beliefs pertaining to ensoulment.

With respect to the values protected by the Establishment Clause, in *Webster* the Court failed to examine how explicitly religious language in abortion legislation infringes on interests in maintaining secular laws (501, 506). Similarly, in *Bowen*, the Court declared a statute regulating abortion—which evidenced both religious and secular motivations—to have a "primary secular purpose" rather than investigating whether it could be fully supported on the basis of secular reasons (604). The *Bowen* Court also failed to recognize the potential of government subsidies in the federal *AFLA* for programs that include explicit religious teachings to result in entangling government with religion by supporting the dissemination of religious messages. Such entanglement is particularly problematic when members of the audience receiving those messages are impressionable youth who are less capable of discriminating government support from the religious organizations involved in the *AFLA*-funded programs themselves (see *Lee v. Weisman*, 112 S. Ct. 2469 [1992]).

In sum, the Court's approach to religion clause jurisprudence, especially in the area of abortion regulation, has been inattentive to the distinctive harms that religiously based or influenced laws may cause to the free exercise rights of women and religious minorities. At the same time, however, with the exception of *McDaniel v. Paty* (618), discussed in this chapter, the Court's decisions have failed to give due recognition and protection to the free exercise rights of religious lawmakers. Interpreting the validity of lawmaking under the first, secular purpose, prong of the *Lemon* decision may require courts to attempt to ascertain lawmakers' motivations for proposing or supporting a particular enactment.

This requirement is problematic for a number of reasons. It runs contrary to the judiciary's general refusal to inquire into legislative motivation (see *McDaniel v. Paty*, 1333 [Brennan, J., concurring], citing *Arizona v. California*, 283 U.S. 423, 455 [1931]; *Center for Reproductive Health v. Akron*, 479 F. Supp. 1172, 1194 [1979]; Feldman 1980: 970–71). This policy of noninterrogation of legislative intentions is based on the sound rationale of preventing undue judicial interference with a coordinate branch of government in violation of the constitutionally mandated separation of powers.

Second, the secular purpose standard of the Court's test for assessing Establishment Clause violations is fraught with practical difficulties, especially surrounding the determination of whether religious convictions motivated a particular law. As discussed, lawmakers frequently have mixed motivations for favoring a particular policy and may not be able to distinguish which of their reasons were motivated by religion (see Greenawalt 1988: 11–12).

It is even more difficult to ascertain whether such motivations were causally responsible for the passage of legislation. As Chief Justice Warren pointed out in *United States v. O'Brien*, "Inquiries into congressional motives or purposes are a hazardous matter. . . . What motivates one legislator to make a speech about a statute is not necessarily what motivates scores of others to enact it" (391 U.S. 367, 383–84 [1968]). As Kenneth Karst notes, it "is hard enough for a judge to unveil conscious legislative motives that are illicit; a search for the unconscious, ideology-based motivations that lie beneath a legislator's vote is a task no judge should be asked to perform" (1991: 722). Justice Scalia echoes this view in his claim that "discerning the subjective motivation of those enacting the statute is, to be honest, almost always an impossible task" (*Edwards v. Aguillard*, 482 U.S. 578, 636–37 [1986]).

Further, lawmakers are entitled to the same protections of the Free Exercise Clause as other citizens. Although, as I argue later, lawmakers have special moral obligations that require them to justify their decisions on the basis of secular reasons rather than religious ones, this need not preclude lawmakers from relying on their religious convictions in determining how to vote on a law. As Justice Stevens's dissent in *Webster* notes, "the constitutionality of legislation could [] not rest on the fact . . . that the legislators who voted to enact it may have been motivated by religious considerations" (566).

Thus, the appropriate focus of constitutional inquiry for religious lawmaking should be on the postdecision rationale or justification for an enactment, not on the subjective purposes or motivations of the lawmakers involved in its passage. These oversights suggest the necessity of amending *Lemon's* secular purpose requirement, or at least its interpretation, so that it is understood to apply only to objectively discernible religious influences rather than to lawmakers' subjective motivations and only in situations where the enactment under consideration would raise Establishment Concerns and adversely affect Citizenship Rights.

Failure to Acknowledge Establishment Concerns and Their Relevance to Citizenship Rights

A second main difficulty with the Court's decisions in cases involving religious lawmaking is its failure to consider how the presence of Establishment Concerns may have infringed on plaintiffs' other Citizenship Rights. As discussed in chapter 1, although Establishment Concerns of alienation, exclusion, coercion, and political divisiveness may not rise to the level of full-scale violations of the Establishment Clause, these concerns often exacerbate violations of either the religion clauses or other Citizenship Rights.

In particular, the Court's decisions in the cases I have considered thus far have failed to recognize Establishment Concerns in several respects. First, they overlook the risk of alienation of nonbelievers in connection with legislation enabling religious organizations to receive grants and encouraging grant applicants to involve religious organizations in their provision of services to adolescents, especially those alleged to be teaching religious values under the auspices of a federally funded program (*Bowen*). This potential problem is especially high if the program is not administered on a completely nonpartisan basis (*Bowen*), contrary to the Court's decisions in other cases (see *Larson v. Valente*, 456 U.S. 228 [1982]).

The Court also has ignored the Establishment Concerns of alienation and exclusion created when the religious character of legislation is linked to a specific religious tradition, such as with those of the Roman Catholic Church underlying the Hyde Amendment (*Harris*). These cases are inconsistent with the Court's earlier decisions on public funding of religious schools, which held that the Establishment Clause prohibits "government-financed or government-sponsored indoctrination into the beliefs of a particular religious faith" (487 U.S. 611–12, citing *Grand Rapids School District v. Ball*, 373, 385).

Third, the Court also has ignored the symbolic link created between government and religion (and, thus, the potential for political divisiveness and other Establishment Concerns) when legislation is directed to or involves specifically religious organizations (*Bowen*, 617 n. 14) or is coercive of pregnant women who do not share the state's religiously defined views of fetal life (*Webster*), especially given the Court's recognition of symbolic linkages between government and religion as a ground for invalidating laws in other Establishment Clause cases (see *Grand Rapids School District v. Ball*, 373). As Justice Stevens's dissent in *Webster* recognizes, "the preamble read in context threatens serious encroachments on the liberty of the pregnant woman" (563).

By endorsing a particular religious view of when human life begins, in connection with provisions significantly restricting abortion, the preamble communicates the state's opposition to all abortion, with the likely effect of deterring some pregnant women from exercising their constitutional rights. The Court's failure to adequately take account of the damaging effects of religiously influenced legislation signals a need to revise how religious lawmaking is assessed under the Constitution.

Failure to Protect Other Citizenship Rights

A third problem with the Court's decisions in cases involving religious lawmaking is its failure to protect the Citizenship Rights protected by constitutional provisions other than the religion clauses. In the cases I have considered, the Court has ignored how religiously motivated legislation may violate pregnant women's liberty and privacy interests, protected by the due process guarantees, in deciding whether to terminate their pregnancies (*Webster*; *Harris*). In addition, the Court has refused to recognize the equal protection violations in statutory prohibitions on funding abortions for indigent women (*Webster*; *Harris*, 448 U.S. 315, 324–25). At the same time, the Court in these cases did not inquire into the difficulties that restricting the religious aspects of the legislation at issue would raise for the Citizenship Rights of lawmakers, especially their free speech and free exercise rights as protected by the First Amendment.

Imposition of Unduly Burdensome Standing Requirements

A final problem with the Supreme Court's decisions on religiously influenced abortion laws is their imposition of unduly restrictive requirements for the determination of who has standing to challenge such laws in federal court. This is starkly evident in the *Harris* case, where the Court mandated that a pregnant woman show "that she sought an abortion under compulsion of religious belief" while pregnant and eligible to receive Medicaid to be eligible to claim that her free exercise rights had been violated (*Harris*, 448 U.S. 320).

In general, to establish standing in federal cases, plaintiffs must show an "injury in fact" that was caused by the challenged action and that the injury is likely to be redressed by a favorable decision. Even if the stated requirements are met, the Supreme Court has sometimes imposed other "prudential" limitations to avoid hearing cases. Such limitations apply to "generalized grievances pervasively shared" that the Court determines are best addressed by the representative branches of government, cases that are brought on behalf of third parties, and claims that are not within the "zone of interests" to be protected by the challenged regulation (see Tribe 1988: 110).

The Court's decisions on religious lawmaking hold that stigmatization alone, without further injury, is not sufficient for standing in cases alleging violation of Citizenship Rights (see *Allen v. Wright*, 468 U.S. 737, 755 [1984]; *Moose Lodge No. 107 v. Irvis*, 407 U.S. 163, 166 [1972]; McConnell 1992: 165). In *Larson v. Valente* (456 U.S. 228, 238 [1982]), the Court announced its standard for assessing standing in Establishment Clause cases as "whether the persons seeking to invoke the court's jurisdiction have 'alleged such a personal stake in the outcome of the controversy' as to assure that concrete adverseness which sharpens the presentation of issues upon which the Court so largely depends for illumination of difficult constitutional questions." The Court's application of this standard in cases analogous to those involving religious lawmaking has rendered differing, even inconsistent, results.

In *Flast v. Cohen* (392 U.S. 83 [1968]), the Court allowed a taxpayer to bring an Establishment Clause challenge to a federal program that granted aid to religious and public schools, despite the Court's general denial of standing to taxpayers (see *Frothingham v. Mellon*, 262 U.S. 447 [1923]). Standing in other Establishment Clause cases challenging laws relating to education has been granted to plaintiffs whose only connection to the case was as residents, where they were able to show that the challenged laws impacted on them directly and concretely (e.g., *Abington School District v. Schempp*, 374 U.S. 203 [1963]). However, in *Valley Forge Christian College v. Americans United for Separation of Church and State* (454 U.S. 464 [1982]), a case brought against the Secretary of the Department of Health, Education, and Welfare for transferring public property to a religiously affiliated college, the Court held that standing requirements had not been met because the plaintiff organizations could not "identify any personal injury suffered by them *as a consequence* of the alleged constitutional error" (485).

In the case of *In re United States Catholic Conference* (885 F.2d 1020 [2nd Cir. 1989]), the federal circuit court refused to grant standing to a group of clergy, taxpayers, and citizens suing to revoke the tax-exempt status of the U.S. Catholic Conference. The Court rejected the plaintiffs' claim that the Conference had violated the conditions for its tax-exempt status by involvement in anti-abortion political activity, finding that none of them had "been injured in a sufficiently personal way to distinguish themselves from other citizens who are generally aggrieved by a claimed constitutional violation" (1024).

Judicial decisions on standing have been especially mixed in cases involving challenges to abortion lawmaking. As we have already seen, in *Bowen*, the

Court upheld the plaintiffs' standing to challenge the *AFLA* both "on its face" and "as applied" (618–19). Yet in *Harris*, the Court denied standing to plaintiffs to challenge the Hyde Amendment on free exercise grounds because none of them could show "that she sought an abortion under compulsion of religious belief" (448 U.S. 320).

Such stringent requirements for standing such as those the Court imposed in *Harris* present an unwarranted obstacle to the protection of the constitutional rights of citizens, especially those of religious minorities and women. The fundamental importance of Citizenship Rights, and the potential risks that they will be infringed by religious lawmaking indicate the desirability of liberalizing standing requirements in this area. As I discuss further in chapter 7, plaintiffs who can make a plausible showing that their Citizenship Rights have been infringed by religiously based or influenced laws should be granted standing to pursue challenges to the validity of such laws.

Theoretical Problems with the Court's Approach to Religious Lawmaking

The problems with the Supreme Court's approach to religious lawmaking described previously reflect several assumptions that have contributed more generally to the failure to develop a satisfactory resolution of the dilemma. These include assumptions that are shared with others who have offered potential solutions to the problems raised by religious lawmaking, among them, liberal assumptions about religion and moral identity, communitarian assumptions about religious pluralism, and traditional assumptions about gender relations. I discuss these assumptions again and explore them further in later chapters. Here, I discuss only the Court's liberal assumptions about religion and moral identity, as these bear directly on the discussion of the moral identity of religious lawmakers in the following chapter.

The Justices' blindness to the problems with religious lawmaking may be in part a consequence of their liberal assumptions that religious convictions are not central to a person's moral identity. Their failure to protect religious believers against Establishment Concerns suggest that they do not consider that harms to a person's religious beliefs cause harm to the person himself or herself and, thus, cause no harm to their constitutional rights. In other words, their decisions reflect a lack of concern with the role that religion may play in the constitution of moral identity and the implications of Citizenship Rights for protecting the religious aspects of that identity. Such assumptions may have contributed to the Court's imposition of unduly restrictive standing requirements that severely limit the ability of aggrieved citizens to challenge religious lawmaking, while ignoring the centrality that religion may have in the decision making of lawmakers.

The decisions discussed previously suggest that the Supreme Court assumes a *voluntarist* conception of religion, that is, a view of religion as freely chosen or rejected by its adherents (see Sandel 1992; Williams and Williams 1984: 1468–69). Like liberal views generally, this voluntarist conception is closely related to and follows naturally from what I call a liberal view of moral selves as voluntary choosers (to distinguish it from a more communitarian view of selves as relational and socially constructed). The liberal view assumes that religious convictions can be adopted or discarded at will and, thus, are not central to moral identity. This view thereby fails to acknowledge that many religious adherents understand their beliefs to be integral to their moral identity and, thus, held involuntarily rather than as the result of free or deliberate choice (I examine understandings of religious identity held by religious lawmakers in chapter 3).

Such voluntarist assumptions are clearly reflected in many of the Supreme Court's religion clause decisions. In invalidating Tennessee's law barring ministers from legislative office in *McDaniel v. Paty* (618), as discussed earlier, the Court implicitly assumed the capacity of lawmakers to refrain from exerting a sectarian influence. The Court's validation of *AFLA* against claims that the religiously affiliated grantees would exert a sectarian influence on the content of the programs at issue in *Bowen* is similarly premised, at least in part, on an assumption that grantees are able to moderate such influence. In these later cases, the assumption behind the Court's rulings appears to be that the religious beliefs of the subjects of the legislation were not sufficiently fundamental to their moral identity to warrant any cause for concern that they would exert a religious influence on others.

The Court's voluntarist assumptions have also contributed to its failure to consider how religious beliefs embodied in coercive abortion restrictions may conflict with the religious beliefs of those subject to obeying them. Such assumptions are particularly evident in the *Webster* Court's decision that the Missouri abortion statute's preamble is benign because it has no operative effect, the *Harris* Court's determination that religious influences on the Hyde Amendment were constitutionally insignificant, and the *Bowen* Court's finding that *AFLA* does not run afoul of the free exercise rights of adolescent female clients on its face.

Decisions premised on voluntarist assumptions that consider religious selves capable of freely adopting or discarding religious convictions are problematic as a premise for constitutional interpretation because they tend to place the burden of separating religious and other citizenship roles on those subject to government regulation rather than on the authors of those regulations. Because this capacity may not be recognized or even intelligible to religious believers, laws premised on voluntarist assumptions may infringe on their free exercise rights.

Such assumptions simultaneously fail to acknowledge that lawmakers and other public officials have special responsibilities to ensure that their religious beliefs do not infringe on the constitutional rights of their constituents. If, as will sometimes be the case, public officials are unable or unwilling to take steps to ensure that their religious convictions do not infringe on these rights without a compelling purpose for doing so, the Supreme Court, which is vested with the power of judicial review, final interpretive authority over the Constitution, should be responsible for ensuring that Citizenship Rights are protected.

Given the harms to religious freedom that may result from voluntarist assumptions, a preferable approach to judicial review would recognize the centrality that religious beliefs and practices have to the moral identity of many citizens. This alternative would impose the burden of separating religious convictions from actions, where necessary to ensure public accessibility, on the lawmakers responsible for creating the conflicts, rather than on the citizens whose free exercise rights have been infringed on.

Summary and Conclusions

In this chapter, we have seen that in addition to the general problems with religious influences on lawmaking, the activity of religious lawmaking raises a number of constitutional issues and may violate a number of fundamental constitutional rights. In particular, we have seen how religious lawmaking raises Establishment Concerns and infringes on constitutionally protected Citizenship Rights. These problems are starkly evident in the case of religious lawmaking on abortion.

Contrary to the view that abortion is not a religious issue but merely a matter about which most religious organizations have expressed a position, the material presented here demonstrates that abortion has been a religious issue for many of the lawmakers who have been involved with abortion regulation. Many abortion laws have been proposed, adopted, or adjudicated on the basis of, or with a view to, religious considerations. Yet neither the religious groups attempting to influence lawmakers, nor the lawmakers themselves, have acknowledged the negative impact of religiously influenced abortion restrictions on women's Citizenship Rights.

Further, the Supreme Court has failed to recognize the extent to which religious lawmaking may exacerbate or constitute violations of the religion clauses or other Citizenship Rights, especially those to due process and equal protection rights. I have examined in some detail how the Court has permitted religious lawmaking on abortion to violate the constitutional rights of women. Consequently, it has failed to apply a heightened scrutiny to those laws which raise Establishment Concerns to ensure that they do not contribute to the violation of Citizenship Rights.

The Court has also failed to find violations of constitutional rights where citizenship protections were clearly infringed by religiously motivated laws that government was unable to justify on the basis of either publicly accessible reasons or a compelling State interest. In addition, the Court's decisions on religious lawmaking have imposed unduly restrictive standing and burden of proof requirements, thereby limiting the ability of aggrieved citizens to protect their Citizenship Rights.

In the specific context of abortion lawmaking, the Court's voluntarist assumptions about religion have validated abridgements of the Citizenship Rights of pregnant women, yet at the same time have failed to fully respect the religious identity and First Amendment rights of lawmakers. In this regard, there are important countervailing reasons for not invalidating all religious lawmaking under the Constitution. These include the important role that religion may play in the moral identity of many citizens, including lawmakers.

In the following chapter, I examine the centrality of religion in the lives of a representative sample of lawmakers and the inadequacy of the Court's analysis of their free exercise rights. Having detailed the considerations on both sides of the dilemma, I will then assess the merits of scholarly proposals to resolve it in chapters 4 and 5.

THREE

Religious Lawmakers on Moral Identity and Abortion Law

Chapter 2's description of abortion legislation and case law revealed specific ways that religious lawmaking infringes on the constitutional rights and interests of pregnant women. The discussion also pointed to problems with religious lawmaking more generally, especially for the citizenship rights and interests of women and religious minorities. At the same time, however, it showed how the constitutional rights and interests of religious lawmakers are also implicated in religious lawmaking, thereby warning against a solution to the problem that would simply prohibit religious influences on lawmaking.

In this chapter, I first describe more fully the moral identity and constitutional rights of religious lawmakers and their implications for any adequate resolution of the dilemma posed by religious lawmaking. Considering how several lawmakers describe their own relationship to religion and political decision making will help to clarify the actual role of religious faith in moral identity and the range of ways that religious convictions may influence the decision making of lawmakers, especially in regard to abortion. The diversity of views articulated by these political leaders about the role that religious convictions should play in government and lawmaking more generally will provide an empirical basis on which to evaluate the feasibility and fairness of the liberal and communitarian proposals for addressing the dilemma that is discussed in the following two chapters. It also points out the oversights of the Supreme Court's interpretations of the free exercise rights of lawmakers in its treatment of cases that involve religious lawmaking.

The Place of Religion in the Lives of Lawmakers

Religion indisputably holds a central place in the lives of many Americans, including lawmakers. Not surprisingly, then, religion has had an impact on political life as well. It has been a significant factor influencing voting patterns, for example. Historically, Americans have tended to vote on the basis of their religious affiliations on certain public policy issues, including gambling, liquor, contraception, and marriage laws. Religion is especially likely to influence voting "when the church provides unambiguous clues for its membership" (Wald 1992: 192–93, 204; see *McDaniel v. Paty*, 435 U.S. 618, 642, n.25 [1979; Brennan, J., concurring]).

Correlations between an adherent's religious denomination and his or her political party affiliation continue to the present decade (Kosmin and Lachman 1993: 192). Even stronger associations have been located between the depth of an adherent's religiosity and his or her political views. For example, data indicate that regular attendance at religious worship influences many people to the conservative side of the political spectrum, regardless of whether they are Jewish, Catholic, or Baptist. This influence is even more pronounced for Americans who are affiliated with fundamentalist denominations (Kosmin and Lachman 1993: 196–97). The "nature and motivation of religiosity" also influences how religious faith influences citizens' politics (see Wald 1992: 349–50).

Studies also indicate that religious affiliation influences the voting behavior of lawmakers (see Guth and Green 1989: 333; Regens and Lockerbie 1993; Duke and Johnson 1992: 326; Benson and Williams 1982). Benson and Williams's study indicates that religion has an influence on the thoughts and actions of approximately 75 percent of congresspersons and is related to specific voting issues by "substantial and significant relationships." Twenty-four percent of the congresspersons in the study described religion as having a major influence on their voting, and another 56 percent said it had a moderate influence (Benson and Williams 1982: 73). Even more pertinent to the subject of religious lawmaking, 31 percent of the study sample stated that they were aware of a conscious effort to apply their religious beliefs to voting decisions, and another 36 percent thought there was a "likely influence" (143).

Further, the religious affiliations of members of Congress tend to be linked to specific political outlooks. For example, members who are Southern Baptists, Mormons, Episcopalians, and Presbyterians tend to be politically conservative, whereas those who are Jews, Catholics, Unitarians, Congregationalists, or are nonreligious tend to vote in accordance with a liberal agenda (see Duke and Johnson 1992: 326). Allen Hertzke's study of the influence of religious lobbies on members of Congress found that the most salient religious differences among congresspersons were not due to the particular religion members subscribed to but rather "to the different ways congressional members experience or express their faith" (78; see Fowler and Hertzke 1995: 124–25). Given that many lawmakers consider themselves to be seriously religious persons, requiring them to bracket their religious convictions, even if restricted to their policy-making roles, may be untenable.

Abortion is one of the key issues for which religious convictions play a key role in determining how Americans, including legislators, will vote (see Regens and Lockerbie 1993: 30; Wald 1992: 194; Granberg 1991: 266; Page et al. 1984). Page et al.'s study found that of a number of issues surveyed, "abortion provides the closest example of . . . legislators likely to be voting in accordance with their own consciences, interest group pressures, or their ethnic loyalties" (752). Their research indicated that Catholic membership is a significant factor in Congressional voting on abortion (see Page et al. 1984: 752–53; cf. Hanna 1979: chap. 3).

Similarly, based on a limited survey, Mary Hanna's study showed that Catholic members of Congress supported anti-abortion regulations in significantly greater percentages than their non-Catholic colleagues (1979: 189), in part because of the intensive lobbying and pressure they received from their church (72). Benson and Williams's study suggests that the more congresspersons believe that God is or should be a significant influence on the nation, the more they vote against abortion and other traditionally liberal causes such as civil liberties for gays and lesbians and government spending for social programs (Benson and Williams 1982: 142). Religion may also influence the public policy positions of members of the executive branch, including the president (see, e.g., Hutcheson 1988). The few studies of judges that have been conducted also indicate that the religious affiliations of members of the judiciary influence their views on Church-State issues (see Sorauf 1976, discussed in Wald 1992: 196; Carter 1989). Thus, religion has demonstrably influenced the political decision making of many lawmakers.

Because of the centrality that religion has had to the moral and political decision making of many lawmakers, it would seem unfair, if not futile, to attempt to restrict all reliance on religious convictions in public policy making. Further, because lawmakers are entitled to the same constitutional rights as other citizens, it would be legally problematic under the Free Exercise Clause to attempt to compel them to excise religious considerations from their deliberations on political and legal matters. Yet, as the prior chapters have described, religious lawmaking may infringe on the Citizenship Rights of other citizens.

Little empirical research has been conducted on how lawmakers reconcile their religious convictions with their public decision making, however (see Cook, Jelen, and Wilcox 1982: 162). The Catholic lawmakers Hanna interviewed articulated a range of different perspectives on the particular role religion played in their public lives. Although some responded that their religious convictions were inextricably tied to their political judgments, others made a deliberate effort to consider the public interest separately from their religious views (see Hanna 1979: 83, 178). Further, most of them had a serious commitment to maintaining the boundaries between Church and State (Hanna 1979: chap. 3; see Fowler 1985: 130). Although some applauded the Church's effort to influence public policy, others objected (see, e.g., Hanna 1979: 100, 175).

Most Catholic congressmen had relatively little motivation to conform their voting in accordance with the pressures of Catholic lobbies or their own personal commitment to the Church. The differences in the studies may result from the circumstance that religious influence on lawmakers' voting behavior is more a matter of the intensity of religious convictions rather than the bare fact of having a religious affiliation. This interpretation would be consistent with the difference between commitment to religious beliefs and commitment to a particular religious institution.

To help clarify more precisely what role religion has played in the lives of actual lawmakers, the following section describes six public leaders who have articulated their views about the influence of religious convictions in shaping their moral identity and their lawmaking, especially on abortion. To consider the influence of gender and religious affiliation on religious lawmaking, I carefully examine the extent to which each lawmaker considers the needs and interests of pregnant women and religious minorities, respectively, in describing his views on abortion policy.

Contemporary Lawmakers Speak on Religion, Politics, and Abortion

The group of political leaders discussed here represents a broad cross-section of American lawmakers. It includes members from all three branches of the government—legislative, executive, and judicial—as well as those from both state and federal levels. The common Christian, male, and mostly Caucasian profile of the six was not deliberate but neither was it merely coincidental. Relative to the American citizenry at large, lawmakers are disproportionately male, Caucasian, and of socioeconomically and educationally privileged backgrounds. In addition, the vast majority of lawmakers in the United States are Christian, with a large Protestant majority, a moderate number of Catholics, a small Jewish minority, and an even smaller number of members of other faiths. There are still relatively few women or men of color in positions of high public office. Pertinent to this study, an even smaller minority of lawmakers has publicly addressed whether or how their religious convictions bear on their politics.

Although Catholic legislators compose only approximately one-quarter of the members of Congress, lawmakers from Catholic backgrounds have attracted a disproportionate amount of public scrutiny regarding the relative independence of their decisions from church teachings. The controversy surrounding John F. Kennedy's fitness for the office of president is a well known example of this type of scrutiny. As we will see, despite their shared religious faith, the three Catholic lawmakers described here do not hold similar views about either abortion law or the appropriate place of religious convictions in politics and lawmaking.

The first Catholic lawmaker discussed here, former New York governor Mario Cuomo, a liberal Democrat, has given one of the most articulate explanations of how personal religious convictions and public responsibilities are (and should be) related in the life of a government official. The second Catholic lawmaker, Representative Henry Hyde, a conservative Republican, has been one of the most active national lawmakers in the effort to reverse the *Roe v. Wade* decision and to ban legalized abortion. Although he describes his religious convictions as having no influence on his lawmaking, his political activities reflect a strong religious impetus. The conservative scholarship on abortion law written by the third Catholic lawmaker I discuss, federal Ninth Circuit Judge John T. Noonan, Jr., during his tenure as a law professor, influenced former president Reagan's decision to appoint him to the federal judiciary. Noonan has been far less abashed than Hyde about revealing the religious roots of his decisions on abortion, yet he also contends that his views are not necessarily religious.

The second set of lawmakers are all Protestants, in keeping with the predominantly Protestant character of American religiosity. Again, despite a similarity of religious denomination, the views of Senator Mark Hatfield, an evangelical Baptist, and the Reverend Jesse Jackson, a Baptist minister and the first African American candidate to run for U.S. president, reflect distinctive orientations with respect to the role religious convictions should play in public decisions and in regard to abortion laws. Finally, the views of former president Reagan, a member of the Disciples of Christ, are significant in revealing how a public official, who seemingly is lacking deep personal religious commitments, may nonetheless advocate religious lawmaking as appropriate, even beneficial.

I also correlate the views of each of these political leaders with the different types of religious influence described earlier: Motivation, Justification, or Guidance. Again, these styles of religious influences are ideal types. That is, they do not necessarily fully or accurately reflect any particular lawmaker's self-understanding or approach to the issue of religious lawmaking but instead represent tendencies or styles of influence. Although one type will usually be dominant, more than one frequently will be evident in an individual lawmaker's approach. Classifying the statements of the lawmakers surveyed in this chapter by these styles or types of religious influence facilitates an assessment of how problematic each of their approaches is for the Citizenship Rights of their constituents. It also points out the limitations of the Supreme Court's approach to the constitutional rights of religious lawmakers in relation to those of other citizens.

Governor Mario Cuomo

Mario Cuomo served as governor of New York from 1982 until 1994. He describes himself and is described by others as a deeply religious man (see Cuomo 1984b; McElvaine 1988).

Views on Regulating Abortion

Cuomo has come under fire from American Catholic bishops on several occasions for his view that despite his personal opposition to abortion he does not believe that, as a public official, he should impose his views on others. In 1984,

John O'Connor, then the new archbishop of New York, alluded to Cuomo in a television interview, saying: "I don't see how a Catholic in good conscience can vote for a candidate who explicitly supports abortion" (quoted in Krauthammer 1984: 15). Cuomo replied by characterizing the archbishop's position as one requiring that no Catholic can vote for anyone who disagrees with O'Connor on abortion (Krauthammer 1984; see generally Byrnes 1991: 142).

In an address at the University of Notre Dame in the fall of 1984, Cuomo responded to the bishops in a now famous speech. In it, he opposed legislation against abortion on two grounds: first, that it would be contrary to the spirit of religious tolerance in our system of government and, second, that it would be unworkable, much as Prohibition was. Elaborating on the first reason, Cuomo explained that "The Catholic public official lives the political truth which most Catholics through most of American history have accepted and insisted on: the truth that to assure our freedom we must allow others the same freedom, even if occasionally it produces conduct by them which we would hold to be sinful" (1984b: 16).

This does not require religious legislators to be silent, however. Cuomo insisted that such lawmakers are not precluded from the "right to articulate our personal views in the public forum and to seek to persuade others of the rightness of those views—even to the point of seeing them enacted into public policy" (quoted in Segers 1990c: 164). In fact, Cuomo accepts that "my church and my conscience require me to believe certain things about divorce, birth control and abortion. . . . As a Catholic, I accept the Church's teaching authority" (Cuomo 1984b: 21). Here, Cuomo clearly expresses his understanding of the difference between the public and the political. He recognizes that the type of religious influence that is appropriate in the former is not in the latter because of the risk of coercion and oppression of nonbelievers that it entails.

Regarding the second reason against legislating abortion, Cuomo asserts that morality only becomes the proper object of lawmaking when it is supported by a consensus view (1984b: 18; see Segers 1990c: 164–65). Moreover, he believes that efforts to develop such a view should be based on common values and reasoned debate, not on the intrinsic authority of religious values. Because a consensus view is clearly lacking in the context of abortion, it is not a proper object of legislation.

Cuomo also objects to the Church's position on abortion on other grounds, including inconsistencies between Church teaching with respect to abortion, on the one hand, and divorce and birth control, on the other (1984b: 20; see also Byrnes 1991; Segers 1990c). Further, he notes that individual Catholics support the right to abortion in equal proportions to the rest of the population (1984b: 26). Based on these arguments, Cuomo rejects the position of the Catholic Church that abortion should be outlawed (24).

Consideration of Gender and Religious Pluralism

More recently, Cuomo has also acknowledged the relationship of women to the abortion issue: "[Earlier,] I said I felt presumptuous talking about the terrible, hard judgment women make with regard to abortion. I do. I am very uncomfortable with having to make decisions about abortion. I do think there is an element of the absurd or incongruous in men making laws about something they can never experience—pregnancy" (1989: 265). Nonetheless, soon after expressing this opinion, he stated that "If it were my judgment that theoretically doable legal restrictions on abortion (for example, limitation of medicaid funding) were fair and would engender a greater respect for life in our state, then I would have to be disposed to advocate for such change" (1990c: 170). This latter statement suggests that the basis for Cuomo's opposition to a prohibition on abortion is moral (fairness) and prudential (the inability to effectively enforce such laws), not, as his earlier statements suggest, because of an opposition to legislating religious morality per se.

This sentiment has not been followed by consistent action, however. In this speech, Cuomo concludes that because such actions would not have desirable effects, they should not be implemented. Nonetheless, in 1989, Cuomo acted against including abortion among Medicaid services paid for by the state of New York when it extended eligibility to persons 185 percent above the poverty level (1990b: 70). Such inconsistencies suggest that Cuomo has attempted to walk a very fine line between adherence to the Church's position on abortion and the liberal perspective that religious considerations are an inappropriate basis for public policy decisions.

Views of Religion's Place in Lawmaking Generally

Cuomo also addressed the relationship of religious convictions to public office more generally in his Notre Dame speech. He stated that "my politics is, as far as I can make it happen, an extension of . . . [my Catholic] faith and the understanding [my faith gives me]" (1984a: 464). Nonetheless, he recognizes that the existence of a large diversity of views, both religious and nonreligious, necessarily will "determine our ability—our realistic, political ability—to translate our Catholic morality into civil law, a law not for the believers who don't need it but for the disbelievers who reject it" (quoted in Segers 1990c: 166). In fact, he characterizes the argument that America is a Christian nation as appropriately frightening to both "non-Christians and thinking Christians" (1984b: 19). These comments reveal that Cuomo is both deeply religious and deeply sensitive to the problems presented by religious lawmaking in a pluralistic society.

Cuomo's awareness of pluralism is further evidenced in his rhetorically questioning of whether he is obliged "as a Catholic governor who was elected to serve Protestants, Jews, Moslems, Sikhs, deists, animists, agnostics and atheists" (1984a: 16) to attempt to impose his personal morality on others. Despite his claims about his politics being an extension of his faith, Cuomo finds the answer to this question not in his church's teachings but in the Constitution. This document, he says, was deliberately designed not to impose a specific religion or formal morality as "an article of civic duty" but instead to ensure "that no group has the right to insist that the rest of the community follow its religious views" (1984a: 16).

Cuomo's policy making bears out his fidelity to these principles in areas besides abortion, including the death penalty (1993: 163) and contraception (1990a: 198). These statements reflect a strong commitment to the separation of Church and State and a heightened public awareness that religious and cultural pluralism make the legislation of religious views inappropriate.

In other comments, however, Cuomo has suggested that religion more generally has a valuable role to play in government. For example, he claims that Christian obligation extends not only to individuals but also through government, creating a duty for the State to also do "good works" (1993: 70). He affirms the view that *as we hear God*, he tells us it is our moral obligation to be our brother's keeper, all of us, as a people, as a government, that our responsibility to our brothers and sisters is greater than any one of us" (1993: 227; emphasis added). Public decisions are to be assessed by the standard of the common good, which for Cuomo is not only a theological principle but one publicly intelligible on the basis of reason (see Lawler 1990: 179). Such comments suggest elements of the kind of Catholic natural law thinking that we see evident in Perry's views in chapter 5. Both assume (incorrectly) that the common good is both publicly accessible and hegemonic, despite cultural and religious pluralism.

Cuomo also alludes to the role of religion in shaping his own moral identity by asserting that "those of us who believe that we cannot separate our religion from the rest of our lives, . . . are presented with a further question: if we want to impress our convictions of rightness on the whole society, how do we go about it?" (1993: 71). He answers by suggesting two solutions. The first, which he characterizes as a strategy employed by the bishops and which he rejects, seeks to "insist that people agree with us as a moral proposition." The second strategy, which he endorses, is "to convince our brothers and sisters that even if they don't believe they are required to love as a matter of moral obligation, that helping the poor and the disadvantaged and those who need a bit of a start makes common sense, even in the most practical terms" (72).

Summary of Cuomo's Style of Religious Lawmaking

The comments just mentioned are consistent with the consensus view that Cuomo articulated in his Notre Dame speech. Religion may play a role in government but only to the extent that it can be articulated in commonly understood terms on which consensus can be reached. In this respect, Cuomo's approach to the role of religion in lawmaking is best described as embracing the third, Guidance model of religious influence. By arguing that religious views are inappropriate grounds for public policy in the absence of a consensus and by understanding lawmakers to be capable of separating their personal religious convictions from the grounds of their public decision making, Cuomo implicitly rejects the Authority and Justification models of religious influence on politics.

Unlike most of the other lawmakers described here, Cuomo clearly recognizes the distinction between religion in the public or sphere of civil society and in the political, or lawmaking, sphere. In these respects, Cuomo's views bear marked similarities to the liberal approaches discussed in chapter 4. On the specific issue of abortion, Cuomo's position is based on his recognition of and respect for both religious pluralism and the moral conscience of pregnant women. Although religious faith is fundamental to Cuomo's articulated self-identity, it has not inhibited his ability to make public policy decisions using a broader set of considerations that are based on publicly accessible reasons.

Judge John T. Noonan, Jr.

Ninth Circuit Judge Noonan was appointed to the bench by President Reagan in 1986, presumably in part because of his conservative views on abortion.

Views on Regulating Abortion

Noonan has written extensively on reproductive matters, including abortion and contraception (see, e.g., Noonan 1979, 1970). Noonan testified before Congress in support of the Human Life Amendment in 1981. His view that *Roe v. Wade* was wrongly decided and could be effectively reversed by Congress returning the power to regulate abortion to the states (see Noonan 1979: 186) has been influential in the strategies of prolife lawmakers to reverse the effect of *Roe v. Wade* (see Paige 1983: 119–20). Needless to say, Judge Noonan has a significantly different view of the appropriate role of religion in politics than his fellow Catholic Mario Cuomo.

Although Noonan holds a traditional Catholic view of abortion as wrong and morally impermissible because the fetus is a human life worthy of protection from the moment of conception, he denies that his views are necessarily religious. Rather, he holds that the foundation of Catholic teaching in natural law distinguishes it favorably from other religious teaching. He claims that "in its basic assumption of the equality of human lives," the teaching of the Catholic Church "depends on a stoic, democratic contention which any man might embrace and Western humanism has hitherto embraced" (Noonan 1970: 3). Despite general public accessibility, however, Noonan admits that Catholic "teaching in its totality cannot be detached from the religious tradition which has borne it" (3). Nonetheless, he insists that "the teaching in its fundamental questions about the meaning of love and humanity cannot be disregarded by those who would meet the needs of man humanly" (3).

In other words, the Christian (singular) view of abortion is an acceptable basis for public policy because as it originated, it "did not depend on a narrow theological or philosophical concept" (Noonan 1970: 51). Instead, it "could easily be translated into humanistic language by substituting 'human' for 'rational soul,' [because] the problem of knowing when a man is a man is common to theology and humanism" (Noonan 1970: 51). Yet, Noonan assumes his conclusion in his argument. He admits that aspects of the abortion issue are publicly unresolvable because they involve "assumptions and judgments about what human beings are and about what human beings should do for one another" (1979: 175). Thus, Noonan is inconsistent in his claims about what is distinctively religious as opposed to readily available through reason alone (natural law).

With reference to the specific case of abortion, Noonan argues that "belief in a transcendent source of authority and sanctity may be required for reverence toward those regarded as the image of God; but simple coexistence with other humans demands that the lives of some not be open to sacrifice for the welfare and convenience of others. . . . One person's freedom to obtain an abortion is the denial of another person's right to live" (1970: xvii). His claim that abortion is wrong because it discriminates among human beings "on the basis of their varying potentialities" (1970: 51)[1] is based on his assumption that the moral status of the fetus is equivalent to that of "other humans" and thus is entitled to equal rights to life.

Yet these assumptions rest on highly controversial normative claims that he is forced to defend on theological grounds. For example, Noonan supports his views about the appropriate legal status of abortion with the theological rationale that according to the biblical love commandment, "the fetus was a neighbor; his [sic] life had parity with one's own" (1970: 58).[2] From this rationale, he argues that "in these terms, once the humanity of the fetus is perceived, abortion is never right except in self-defense" (1970: 58). The problem with this argument is that his assumption about the personhood of the fetus cannot be demonstrated on the basis of publicly accessible reason alone.

To further support this view, Noonan claims that abortion is analogous to killing animals, which we must not harm because "we who are called to imitate God" must love them out of charity, as God does; that "we" are bound to the fetus by a common experience of pain in the womb, a "common destiny" to "share eternal life" (1986: 367). These arguments against abortion suggest that Noonan's views in opposition to abortion are fundamentally religious, despite his articulated natural law rationale.

In Noonan's estimation, the only occasion on which law validly cannot mandate moral views with respect to abortion is where the life of the mother can only be saved by terminating the life of the fetus. Historically, Noonan claims, only in this instance "no legal obligation could be imposed on the mother to prefer the child's life to her own; if she made the choice of self-sacrifice it was in obedience to a higher law of love than common morality or law could enforce" (1970: xi). The Christian love commandment and Jesus' "self sacrifice carried to the point of death" are the basis for Noonan's claim that "preference for one's own interests to the life of another seemed to express cruelty or selfishness irreconcilable with the demands of love" (59). Judge Noonan's implicit suggestion that a truly moral woman would sacrifice her own life on behalf of the fetus, such as his view that abortion in non-life-threatening cases can never be moral, is also based on theological presuppositions that are widely disputed in our society.

Consideration of Gender and Religious Pluralism

Noonan's position on abortion lawmaking ignores religious pluralism and moral considerations outside of Roman Catholicism that may inform pregnant women's decisions regarding whether to terminate their pregnancies. Consistent with traditional Catholic teaching, Noonan gives scant consideration to the burdens that restrictive abortion policies place on women forced to carry unwanted pregnancies to term. This is evident in his characterization of "the most fundamental question involved in the long history of thought on abortion" as "how the humanity of a being is to be determined" (Noonan 1970: 51; see, e.g., Noonan 1984: 679, 1979). This characterization glaringly omits any reference to the pregnant woman carrying the "being," or to the possibility that her humanity might still take priority even if the humanity of the fetus were to be incontrovertibly established (see Thomson 1971).

In addition to ignoring the relevance of women's needs and interests to determining the morality of abortion, Noonan also devalues women as moral agents by ignoring their human rights. For example, he describes the prochoice position simply in terms of "the desire of many women to be free from restraints imposed by men" (1970: 2), without recognizing how denying women the ability to control their reproductive destiny and coercing them to remain pregnant by denying them access to safe, legal, and affordable abortions constitutes a denial of their basic human rights.

In a coauthored essay, Noonan rejects the prochoice argument that abortion rights are necessary for women's self-determination. His conclusion is based in part on the view that pregnancy is the voluntary result of the woman's choice not to refuse sex or to use contraceptives (Noonan and Louisell 1970: 235–36). This assumption ignores not only rape but many other forms of sexual coercion that make sex for many women less than voluntary in a still sexist and patriarchal society.

When Noonan does consider whether an exception to the prohibition on abortion should be allowed in cases of rape, his affirmative conclusion to the question of whether a woman should "suffer the psychological trauma of bearing and giving birth to offspring literally forced upon her?" (Noonan 1970: xi),[3] reflects the insensitivity and arrogance of many male lawmakers who lack direct experience of pregnancy attendant on rape (or the benefit of consultation with those who have had such experience) in deciding whether women should be forced to undergo this "psychological trauma."

Noonan further devalues the significance of women as moral agents in his moral analysis of abortion. By considering the fetus to be a separate individual (1970: 236), he ignores the biological reality that the fetus is completely and totally dependent on the pregnant woman's physical body for its survival and continued growth. Attributing separate personhood to the early fetus ignores its utter dependence on the pregnant woman and reinforces traditional Catholic views of women as reproductive vessels or wombs, valued only because they carry human life, not because they are themselves human and thereby entitled to human rights.

In addition, Noonan impugns the moral virtue of women who do have abortions, such as in his statement that "a mother's love for her child is a central paradigm of human fidelity. If the object of the operation is her child and the end of the operation is the child's death, it is hard to reconcile what is done with the basic cultural norms of love and fidelity" (1979: 174). This statement lacks any attention to the particular circumstances that may have led to the abortion and, thus, leaves no place in his analysis for compassion and empathy for the pregnant woman. In the same vein, prior to *Roe v. Wade*, Noonan's assessment that "the law as it has stood on abortion has asked the sacrifices and proclaimed reverence for each life" (Noonan and Louisell 1970: 259), suggests that women should be bound to a supererogatory standard. Noonan does not propose any strategies for minimizing the disproportionate burden that such sacrifices impose only on women nor how this burden avoids running afoul of the constitutional principle of equal protection of the laws.

Noonan also devalues the human worth of women in rejecting the argument that the male dominance of the legislatures that originally enacted abortion prohibitions in the nineteenth century (when women were not allowed to vote) is a reason for liberalizing abortion restrictions. His response to this argument—pointing out that some states enacted abortion restrictions "with electorates composed of both men and women" (1979: 48; Noonan and Louisell 1970: 236)—ignores the states where this was not the case, as well as overlooking the constraints on women's actual, as opposed to merely theoretical, political power to influence male-dominated legislatures, the election of those legislators, or the content of legislation. More generally, it shows a lack of sensitivity to the inequities engendered by male-dominated legislatures mandating the legal behavior of women who, as a class, have been systematically excluded by a sexist and patriarchal society from participating in the formulation of those laws.

Views of Religion's Place in Lawmaking Generally

Noonan's views on abortion are consistent with his larger views about the relationship of religious morality to lawmaking. He asserts that the "American instinct" has correctly linked the moral and the constitutional tightly together. In his view, laws like "the Civil Rights Act . . . are merely prominent examples of the normal process of legislators enacting their moral ideals into statutory prescriptions" (Noonan 1970: x). Contrary to Cuomo, Noonan would not require a consensus to enact religiously influenced moral values or principles into law. From his point of view, lawmakers should act on the basis of their personal moral convictions, regardless of how widely shared or publicly accessible those values are and without regard for whether they infringe on Establishment Interests or Citizenship Rights.

Implicit in Noonan's defense of legislating morality is an assumption that legislators inevitably will base their decision making on their personal moral norms. For religious lawmakers, these moral norms will reflect their religious convictions. Noonan also assumes that religious influences are inevitable and appropriate in judicial decision making, regardless of whether they are widely shared or publicly accessible (see Noonan 1970: x; 1987: 1126). Noonan's view lacks any recognition of the potential of religious lawmaking to raise Establishment Concerns and infringe on Citizenship Rights where lawmakers' religious views differ from those of their constituents.

Summary of Noonan's Style of Religious Lawmaking

In sum, Noonan sees little problem with lawmakers relying on their religiously based moral convictions to provide the rationale or justification for their decisions, at least where those convictions are based on natural law, which he erroneously assumes is publicly accessible. His own views on abortion lawmaking appear to be informed primarily by a view of religion as a source of Justification but also by the idea of religion as Motivation. He does not recognize that lawmakers have any special obligations by virtue of their roles as public officials to make their decisions on the basis of a set of considerations broader than their personal religious views.

Because Judge Noonan neglects religious pluralism, he fails to consider whether religious lawmakers are morally obligated to take the attitudes and interests of their nonreligious constituents into account in their public decision making on morally controversial issues such as abortion. In these respects, Noonan's views are much closer to communitarian perspectives than liberal ones. He understands Catholic moral teachings based in natural law to be publicly accessible and, therefore, appropriate grounds for lawmaking.

Representative Henry Hyde

The Honorable Henry Hyde has been a member of the U.S. House of Representatives since 1974. He is a Catholic, a Republican, and a political conservative. Hyde's views are similar to his fellow Catholic John Noonan's in several respects.

Views on Regulating Abortion

As we saw in chapter 2, Representative Hyde has been an ardent supporter of the movement to legally prohibit abortion. He authored the so-called Hyde Amendment, which prohibits federal welfare funding for all non-life-saving abortions. Hyde first introduced the amendment in 1974, the same year he was elected to office and has continued to introduce it each year since then. He has also supported a number of other proposed constitutional amendments and legislative initiatives to outlaw abortion.

For Hyde, like Judge Noonan, the fundamental issue involved in the abortion debate is the "humanity of the unborn" (Hyde 1982: 1098). Hyde vehemently insists that his anti-abortion stance is justified exclusively on the basis of scientific and biological evidence of when human life begins (e.g., Hyde 1982: 1078, 1083, 1091) and need not engage religious considerations. For example, he maintains that "abortion is not a Catholic issue, nor a Mormon issue, nor a Lutheran issue. It is an ethical issue that the Supreme Court . . . has specifically found is 'as much a reflection of traditionalist values toward abortion, as it is an embodiment of the view of any particular religion'" (1984: 39, citing *Harris v. McRae*, 448 U.S. 297, 319 [1980]). Similar to Noonan, Hyde indicates that the natural law tradition of American Catholicism eliminates the problems that members of other religious traditions have in expressing their faith in politics. He explains that natural law "provides a means for mediating religious values into the public arena in a publicly accessible way" (1984: 44), including the Church's position on social issues such as abortion.

However, as was the case with Judge Noonan's views, some of Representative Hyde's other statements indicate that his religious beliefs in fact play a significant role in determining his views. He admits that "one's religious views can have an impact on whether the pre-born ought to be protected or not" (1982: 1099). In a barely disguised attack on Cuomo, who preceded Hyde's own address to the Notre Dame community by two weeks, Hyde argues against the "favorite ploy of the 'I'm personally opposed to abortion but . . .' school of politician," by characterizing its "dilemma" as wanting to maintain Catholic "credentials" while remaining liberal enough for the Democratic Party. In Hyde's characterization, this requires being feminist, which in turn requires being in favor of abortion (Hyde 1984: 39). In addition, Hyde contends that

> The duty of one who regards abortion as wrong is not to bemoan the absence of a consensus against abortion, but to help lead the effort to achieve one. Catholic public officials have . . . a moral and civic obligation to clarify precisely what is at stake in the abortion controversy . . . we have a moral and civic obligation to help disentangle this fundamental question of constitutional protection from the confusing sound of rhetoric involved when separation of Church and State and feminist ideology are brought into the debate; and we have a moral and civic obligation to create structures in society that make the first resort to abortion in the case of unwanted pregnancy less likely. (1984: 47)

These criticisms of his fellow Catholic lawmaker Mario Cuomo highlight how starkly different Hyde's views are about the propriety of religious influences on abortion lawmaking.

Consideration of Gender and Religious Pluralism

Like communitarian theorists, Hyde clearly would allow a larger role for religion in government than more liberal lawmakers such as Cuomo would. For example, although he argues for the right of Catholic bishops to engage in public instruction and persuasion about policy issues, he insists that they do so "in language and imagery that is accessible to a pluralistic audience, and not just to Catholics" (1984).

In contrast to Noonan's stance, however, Hyde appears to accept the criticism that religion, and Catholicism in particular, is inappropriate in politics.

Speaking of Catholics generally and their reaction against the "secular-separa-tionist agenda," he asserts that "we were accused of 'trying to impose our reli-gious values on others.' One can only absorb so much of this falsification, and then one reacts" (Hyde 1984: 39). Perhaps this sensitivity to criticism helps to explain Hyde's reluctance to admit that his beliefs on abortion are derived from or influenced by his Catholic faith.

Notwithstanding this awareness of religious pluralism, in a telling state-ment Hyde demonstrates his limited vision of what respect for pluralism means. In contending that "public officials must take all possible precautions to avoid even the appearance of giving the state's favor to one expression of the Judeo-Christian traditions over others" (1984: 42), he completely ignores the existence of or need to accord respect for religious traditions outside of the Judeo-Christian ones. This insensitivity to religious pluralism is also evident in Hyde's proposal to make churches "the primary channels for federal nutri-tion programs, community health services, and other programs" (1994: 31) rather than continue federal provision of these services.

His argument that giving churches this responsibility would not mean "re-quiring church attendance," for "so long as no doctrinal preferences are made as to which institutions can participate, there should be no constitutional ob-jections" (1994: 31), ignores the serious risks of alienation, exclusion, coer-cion, and political divisiveness entailed in making religious institutions pri-marily responsible for the provision of vital social services. It also fails to acknowledge the likelihood that such a policy would run afoul of the Estab-lishment Clause—even on Hyde's own "institutional" interpretation—as well as other Citizenship Rights protected by the Constitution.

Like Noonan's, Hyde's views on abortion reflect scant consideration of the interests of pregnant women. His response to the question of whether women can achieve true equality without control over their reproductive lives is that "women have control over their reproductive lives—the answer is just don't get pregnant" (1988: 32). This attitude reflects a gross insensitivity to the coer-cive or otherwise involuntary circumstances that may result in women becom-ing pregnant.

Also like Noonan, Hyde ignores the responsibility of males in contributing to unwanted pregnancies. Instead, he takes a traditional family values stance to solving the problem of unwanted pregnancy, suggesting the need for a "serious and careful reconsideration of a welfare system that currently re-wards pregnancy out of wedlock, and that has contributed to the erosion of the family structure among the poor" (Hyde 1984: 46; see Hyde 1994: 31). In fact, Hyde's family values agenda includes several measures that would signif-icantly hinder women's efforts to obtain independence, autonomy, and equal treatment in society, including proposals to "maximize the role of religious in-stitutions in distributing assistance," (1994: 31) make it more difficult to obtain a legal divorce (especially where there are children or an objecting spouse), limit the legal status of nonmarital living arrangements, and require Congress to "affirm the traditional family" (1994: 31).

Views of Religion's Place in Lawmaking Generally

On the relationship of religion and politics more generally, Hyde's views make a sharp contrast with Cuomo's. Hyde affirms the American Catholic Bishops' statement that "a Catholic public official cannot finally sunder personal conscience and civic responsibility" (1984: 45). He asserts that it is "awfully hard to go anywhere in the world without your soul tagging along" (50). These statements suggest that Hyde holds a view of the self similar to the communitarian conception (which is discussed in chapter 5), in which the self cannot be divided into separate religious and political roles but is a unity. Consequently, one's religious convictions entail both moral and civic obligations. Occupying a role as a political leader does not alter these obligations. The Catholic public official has the same obligations as other Catholic citizens.

In keeping with the views just stated, Hyde claims that "religious values, particularly the Judeo-Christian tradition's insistence on the inherent dignity and inviolable worth of each individual human life, lie at the root of . . . the 'American Proposition'" (1984: 36). He contends that "religion and politics have thus always 'mixed' in America, if what we are talking about is religious values and public policy" (36). Thus, in Hyde's view, religion has a natural and historically accepted place in politics, at least in the United States.

Part of Hyde's strategy for arguing that religion should play a larger role in government is to interpret the Establishment Clause narrowly. He would limit its effect to preventing religious institutions from becoming excessively entangled with government. He insists that the Clause "was never intended to rule religiously-based values out of order in the public arena" (1984: 37).

Hyde also attacks Cuomo's opinion that a consensus is required to impose religious values on the society at large. He contends that this view is inconsistent with the Civil Rights Act of 1964 and the codification of civil rights, which preceded and cultivated a consensus rather than being the products of one (1984: 39–40). Yet Hyde's own conduct in proposing the Hyde Amendment and other religiously influenced laws designed to restrict, if not prohibit, abortion are inconsistent with his proposed accessibility standard. He appears not to recognize that the legal imposition of religious views on a controversial issue such as abortion, regardless of whether such views represent several religious traditions or only one, still runs a risk of violating the Free Exercise and Establishment Clause rights of those who do not share those religious views.

Summary of Hyde's Style of Religious Lawmaking

Because he identifies himself as a specifically Catholic public leader, with moral obligations based on that status, Hyde's approach is best characterized as following the Authority or Motivation model of religious influence. He has clearly articulated his belief that Catholics have moral and civic responsibilities by virtue of their faith, responsibilities that take precedence over moral obligations based on social roles as political leaders and government officials. Representative Hyde would go even further than Judge Noonan in legislating moral values derived from Catholic religious teachings. However, like Noonan, Hyde's approach to religious influences on lawmaking also manifests aspects of the Justification model.

Although his principle of public accessibility as a limitation on religious influences on politics is a sound one, Hyde fails to acknowledge the respects in which even natural law perspectives bear theological assumptions and, thus, may raise Establishment Concerns and infringe on the Citizenship Rights of nonbelievers. In addition, Hyde's views about abortion do not entail a sensitivity for or appreciation of how laws severely restricting or prohibiting abortion, including a human life amendment and his own sponsored Hyde Amendment, impose hardships and disadvantages on many pregnant women by forcing them into unwanted childbearing.

Senator Mark Hatfield

Mark Hatfield served in the U.S. Senate for three decades, starting in 1966. He is an evangelical Baptist whose statements (as well as the statements of others about him) suggest that his religious faith is integral to his self-identity and to his conduct as a lawmaker.

Views on Regulating Abortion

Hatfield has generally taken a prolife position on abortion. As an early sponsor of a Human Life Amendment to prohibit abortion, he stated: "There is no single characteristic of our society that troubles my inner self more than the degradation, the cheapening, the dehumanization of life that we see all around us today" (1974: 4). This dehumanization is not limited to abortion for Hatfield but includes the Vietnam War, the suppression of the Attica prison riots, capital punishment, the alienation of urban life, corporate growth, and the materialistic and consumptive orientation of society (see Hatfield 1982: 17).

Senator Hatfield characterizes abortion as a form of violence that is condoned by a society that has become callous and indifferent to the ultimate value of human life (Hatfield 1974: 5; see Craig and O'Brien 1993: 135; Noonan 1979: 62; Pippert 1973: 75, 77). The theological basis for Hatfield's views on abortion is evident from his statements that "our country was founded on the principle that human rights—the most fundamental of which is the right to life itself—are not given by government, but by God" and that "our task is to insure that rights endowed by God are not denied by the State" (Hatfield 1974: 6, 7). For Hatfield, then, the religious immorality of abortion is a legitimate basis for mandating its illegality.

He contends that the "belief in life's fundamental right to be has inevitable corporate consequences," and that refusing to act in accordance with those beliefs by proposing, "as a legislator, that society embrace this view" (Hatfield 1974: 9), would be hypocritical. His testimony in support of the Human Life Amendment indicates that his position was clearly motivated by his religious convictions, at least in part: "I have wrestled with my beliefs about abortion—

morally, legally, biologically, sociologically, and theologically. In doing so, convictions that I find totally compelling have been deeply affirmed" (9).

Like Hyde and Noonan, however, Hatfield insists that abortion is not only a religious issue but also a scientific one, for which science "proves" that life begins at the moment of conception (Eells & Nyberg 1979: 95). Similar to natural law proponents, Hatfield also argues that this view is not unique to any particular religion but is based on universally accepted understandings.

Consideration of Gender and Religious Pluralism

Like the views of the Catholic lawmakers we have discussed, Hatfield's comments similarly assume the existence of a universal standard of morality. He expresses hope that returning the abortion issue to the states and to direct citizen participation will bring about a national moral consensus on the issue (see Craig and O'Brien 1993: 147). These remarks reflect a lack of awareness of or concern about moral and religious pluralism.

Hatfield's statements reveal a mixed picture regarding his consideration of women in relation to the abortion issue. On the one hand, some of his comments suggest a lack of awareness of the significant hardships for women that may accompany an unwanted pregnancy. For example, he characterizes the prochoice position as part of a "whole moral climate that elevates selfish personal convenience to a supreme status in human decision-making" and as elevating "self-seeking personal prerogatives as the ultimate norm" (1974: 5). On the other hand, both in 1973 and several years later in speaking in support of the "Hatch Amendment," a proposed constitutional amendment stating that "A right to abortion is not secured by this Constitution," Hatfield recognized that

> An issue marked by such intensity and divisiveness invites public neutrality on the part of the politicians, quite candidly; it usually seems pragmatically imprudent to become strongly and unapologetically committed on either side of this controversy. . . . The reason why it has become so difficult and even perilous to discuss the issue of abortion is because of the growing realization by women that they have inner gifts to express, and roles in society to explore, that have previously been disregarded and resisted by society—or more specifically by men. . . . Many women today believe deeply that their worth is defined in ways that far transcend their ability to bear children. . . . They reject the notion that the only normal, worthy, and respectable role they should play is that of being a mother. . . . I believe they are right. (1983: S9089–92; quoted in Craig and O'Brien 1993: 146–47; see Hatfield 1974: 13–14)

This statement suggests some awareness that the result of restrictive abortion laws is to coerce pregnant women to become mothers, regardless of their own desires and interests.

Hatfield also concedes that women who have abortions have often been "dehumanized by relationships lacking either commitment or responsibility" (1974: 6). In addition, he recognizes that whereas society allows males responsible for causing pregnancy to avoid any obligation "the mother faces the emotional and physical demands of a nine month pregnancy, plus the psychological pain that can result, and then the guilt from a judgmental society" (1974: 6).

Unlike the prolife agendas of many religious lawmakers, Hatfield's proposals for abortion reform include a plan for government action that would reduce the hardship of pregnancy on many women's lives. Hatfield characterizes these measures, which include sex education, birth control information, and availability and support for family planning clinics, day care centers, reforms in adoption laws, foster-parent plans, and rape treatment centers, as actions that "must be taken as part of a commitment to the protection and nurturing of all life" (1974: 7).

Hatfield's sensitivity to the hardships faced by unwed mothers and women with unwanted pregnancies does not convince him of the validity of legalized abortion, however. He claims that such hardships "do not exempt an individual from moral responsibility. . . . Sociological tragedy does not alter the biological reality of a life's existence" (1974: 4). Thus, Hatfield would compel a pregnant woman to carry a fetus to term, regardless of the circumstances surrounding conception.

These comments, although undoubtedly sincere in their effect to be compassionate to all forms of life involved, reflect a naivete in assuming that society will provide measures necessary to ensure that women bearing unwanted children will suffer the least hardship possible and failing to adequately mitigate the coerciveness involved in forcing women to carry unwanted pregnancies to term.

Views of Religion's Place in Lawmaking Generally

Hatfield has written extensively about the relationship between his religious faith and politics. He believes that "the wisdom and compassion demanded to solve any of today's personal or societal problems cannot be found in any person or place other than in the power of God, working through a man" (1971: 12). He contends that "the greatest need of our times is for men who will give of themselves and who will serve unselfishly in a position of public trust. The call is for leaders who will be led by God" (161).

Hatfield believes that Christians in politics should be guided by the New Testament (e.g., Hatfield 1971: 25; 1976: 47) and should exercise a prophetic role (e.g., Hatfield 1976: 29): "As Christians . . . one of the urgent avenues for personal action is to influence public attitudes and values. . . . We must attempt to mold public attitudes so they will become attuned to God's purposes" (1971: 47). In particular, he believes that Christian lawmakers can find guidance for deciding how to relate to political power in the narrative of Jesus's life (see Hatfield 1976: 49).

Despite these strong statements affirming the acceptability, even moral responsibility, of Christians to promote their religious views in the public arena, Hatfield's statements reflect an unacknowledged inconsistency about where a political leader's ultimate loyalties must lie. On the one hand, he clearly considers public service to be a calling (e.g., Hatfield 1982: 14; 1976: 216). He asserts that one of the challenges of the citizen-Christian "is to be willing to serve God in politics and government if that is where God wants him" (1971: 161). He also claims that government is structured in a manner which "recognizes, in a general way at least, that God rules in the affairs of men" (156). In addition, he contends that "if the Christian faith is to have any effect on the mechanics of government, it must be through the lives of public officials coming together in God" and suggests prayer groups as one model of such "coming together" (see p. 165).

On the other hand, he asserts that "we recognize that a public official is a servant of the people and a trustee of their delegated sovereign power. We acknowledge the need for loyalty to common goals and ideals of government by both officials and citizens of the nation" (1971: 156). These latter comments suggest that the public official's primary obligation is to his or her constituents, not to God. Hatfield's recognition of the need for loyalty to common goals and ideals may be an implicit acknowledgment that pluralism may prevent religious convictions from satisfying this standard. In this regard, Hatfield asserts that "as a public official, I have as much responsibility to the Christian as to the non-Christian. I firmly support the full separation of church and state. Yet Christ asks each of us to involve ourselves with mankind. This includes a very real responsibility to the institutions of our secular life. The responsibility of the public servant is not to Christianize the institutions of government but to bring the influence of Christ to bear upon them" (165).

Summary of Hatfield's Style of Religious Lawmaking

The statements just quoted clearly show Hatfield's affirmation of the Guidance model of religious influence, whereas he rejects the Justification model. Other comments noted earlier, such as that expressing the view that leaders should be "led by God," indicate more of an affinity with the Authority type of influence, however. These statements also suggest that Hatfield does not distinguish the responsibilities of the moral self *qua* Christian from those of the moral self *qua* citizen or recognize that the two roles may be in tension, if not in outright conflict.

Yet elsewhere, Hatfield's comments acknowledge this distinction. For example, he says that "our heresy today comes in believing that the spheres of Caesar and God are equal, or that they can never make conflicting claims on the Christian" (1976: 52). In fact, "our fundamental allegiance and loyalty is always to another kingdom" (1976: 52). Hence, "we can expect a tension, a clash, between the calling of that kingdom and those purposes to which societies and nations want to give themselves" (1982: 17). On this interpretation, the Christian owes primary obedience to God such that "whenever the state and God come into direct conflict, the Christian has only one choice: Render to God, not to Caesar" (quoted in Pippert 1973: 77). Similarly, Hatfield asserts that "the revelation of Jesus Christ, and his triumph and love, must be seen as the final judge and authority over all government" (Hatfield 1976: 66).

Despite this stated position, obligation to the State sometimes has taken precedence over adherence to Christian teachings in Hatfield's own life, especially with respect to issues other than abortion. For example, after Hatfield contemplated withholding a proportion of his income tax to protest the Vietnam War in 1971 (a war he considered immoral on religious grounds), he ultimately decided not to do so on the rationale that he had taken an oath as a U.S. senator to uphold the Constitution (see Pippert 1973: 77). He also has refused to vote on behalf of prohibiting pornography, an issue to which he has religious objections (see Eells and Nyberg 1979: 87). Similarly, as governor of Oregon, he made a decision not to commute the death penalty of a defendant, despite his religious opposition to capital punishment, on the basis of his oath of office to uphold the state's constitution and laws (see Hatfield 1976: 109). These instances show that in his conduct, even if not in his rhetoric, Hatfield has imposed limitations on the extent to which he uses his religious beliefs to determine his political positions.

Hatfield's statements about religious lawmaking specifically are similarly inconsistent. On the one hand, with respect to "the relationship of a leader's personal spiritual life to his public service" (1971: 161), Hatfield claims to oppose religious lawmaking on the ground that "whenever we are successful in institutionalizing a particular article of our faith by enacting it into law, we seem to lose the vitality, spirit, and freshness of it. . . . We cannot capture great spiritual truths in concrete, or in law. Both statues and statutes can become forms of idolatry" (165).

On the other hand, as noted earlier, Hatfield's own conduct reveals an effort to legislate his religious views on abortion. For example, when voting, he claims to "have prayerfully considered each issue and [be] persuaded that my stand is the one demanded by my convictions. At times I have used biblical references to support my views but with full acknowledgment that each one is subject to interpretation and personal experience" (12). These statements also suggest that Hatfield does not consider it necessary to justify or rationalize his religiously based decisions on grounds that would be publicly accessible to his non-Christian constituents.

In sum, Hatfield's statements, as well as his conduct, suggest that he is a deeply committed Christian whose faith is integral to his politics. Similar to Hyde and Noonan, Hatfield believes that religion is central to legal decision making on moral issues and that his personal religious convictions are integral to his moral identity as a lawmaker. He appears to be most comfortable with promoting the Guidance or Authority forms of religious influence on lawmaking, by which he seeks God's assistance through prayer to determine the morally correct action to take.

However, Hatfield's actual practices, especially on the abortion issue, suggest a more determinative role for religion in lawmaking. Although Hatfield publicly acknowledges the need for a constitutional separation of Church and State, ultimately, it seems, religion takes priority over loyalty to government and fidelity to oath of office. Consequently, Hatfield's views reflect more of the Motivation type of influence. They also have elements of the Justification model to the extent that he uses religious rationales and imagery to support his views. Hatfield's views overall more closely reflect communitarian rather than liberal assumptions about the significance of religion to moral identity and the appropriateness of religion in lawmaking.

President Ronald Reagan

Ronald Reagan served two terms in office as president of the United States (1980–1988). He describes himself as a religious man guided by God. Although he was not actively involved either in the churches of his inherited religion (Disciples of Christ) or in any other religious group, he closely aligned himself to the "religious Right" during his administration.

Views on Regulating Abortion

President Reagan's prolife views are stated in his book *Abortion and the Conscience of the Nation* (1984). In it, he asks whether "that tiny human life has a God-given right to be protected by the law—the same right we have" (1985: 102) and asserts that "every legislator, every doctor, and every citizen needs to recognize that the real issue is whether to affirm and protect the sanctity of all human life" (Reagan 1986: 106; see also Reagan 1984a, 1: 119).

The grounds for Reagan's prolife position are explicitly religious. He speaks of "respect for the sacred value of human life," the "sanctity of human life," the value of prayer in directing the American people to the "right" answer on the abortion question, and the guidance of "faith." In this regard, he opines that "As a nation today, we have *not* rejected the sanctity of human life. The American people have not had an opportunity to express their view on the sanctity of human life in the unborn. I am convinced that Americans do not want to play God with the value of human life. It is not for us to decide who is worthy to live and who is not" (1986: 103). Reagan's religious orientation also is evidenced in his statements about the sanctity of unborn life and the "God-given right" to life of every person, whether born or unborn (see Reagan 1986).

Although Reagan supported legalized abortion during his tenure as governor of California, he attempted to legislate his opposition to abortion by supporting several prolife measures proposed during his White House administration. For example, in 1984, Reagan sent a delegation to the U.S. World Conference in Mexico City to oppose abortion. That same year, he approved the 1984 Hyde Amendment, which prohibited federal funds to international family planning organizations involved in abortion counseling or services. He also introduced *The President's Pro-Life Act of 1988* designed to overturn *Roe v. Wade* and prohibit "any Federal dollars from being used to fund abortion unless a mother's life would be physically endangered by carrying the fetus to term" (Reagan 1988: 1). Reagan also met with a group of prolife leaders in 1983 during their annual "March for Life" (see Ginsburg 1989: 52).

While President, Reagan also banned the importation of the contraceptive RU-486 into the United States and banned federal funding for scientific research involving the use of fetal tissue (because of its close connection with and potential to promote nontherapeutic abortions; see Blanchard 1994: 33), he also refused to define bombings and arson against abortion service providers as terrorism, which precluded the investigation of these incidents by the Federal Bureau of Investigation and the Bureau of Alcohol, Tobacco, and Firearms (see Blanchard 1994: 74). Reagan's views about abortion fail to acknowledge that perspectives different from his own may be a result of a difference of opinion rather than the result of sin (see *New Republic* Editorial Staff 1983: 7).

Consideration of Gender and Religious Pluralism

Reagan's record generally reveals a lack of support for women's rights. He opposed the Equal Rights Amendment and adopted the rhetoric of family values without regard to its impact on the lives of women, especially those subject to domestic violence and poverty. Although he appointed Sandra Day O'Connor as the first female Supreme Court justice, he appointed far fewer women to government offices than the preceding Carter administration. His prolife stance reflects no consideration of how restrictive abortion laws impact the lives of pregnant women.

Reagan's lack of consideration for religious pluralism or the negative impact that legislating Christian morality may have on the free exercise rights of religious minorities[4] is evident in his comment that "We have respected every other religion. They're free to practice in our country" (Lear and Reagan 1984: 17). (In reply, Lear notes that "there are no 'other' religions in 'our' country. America belongs to all citizens, no matter what their religion" [Lear and Reagan 1984: 17].)

This Christo-centric bias is also revealed in Reagan's proposed constitutional amendment "to restore . . . prayer in our public schools and institutions" in 1982. The interest of the Reagan administration in returning religion to the schools was articulated in speeches made by then education secretary William Bennett to the effect that religious training would be reintroduced in schools by "legislation . . . judicial reconsideration and constitutional amendment" (quoted in Edel 1987: 157). A letter from the president accompanying the proposed amendment states that "the public expression through prayer of our faith in God is a fundamental part of our American heritage and a privilege which should not be excluded by law from any American school, public or private" (Reagan 1982: 1). The viewpoint reflected in the letter ignores the potentially alienating, exclusionary, coercive, and politically divisive effects of legally mandated prayer on nonbelievers and students whose religious faiths do not involve a God.

Views of Religion's Place in Lawmaking Generally

During his term of office, Reagan made a number of public statements in which he freely discussed his views about the role of religion in politics (see Hutcheson 1988: 170). Perhaps his best known views were expressed at the 1984 annual prayer breakfast in Dallas, where he stated: "I believe that faith and religion play a critical role in the political life of our nation and always have, and that the church . . . has had a strong influence on the state, and this has worked to our benefit as a nation. Those who created our country . . . saw the state, in fact, as a form of moral order, and felt that the bedrock of moral order is religion" (1984: 7).

He also contends that "politics and morality are inseparable. And as morality's foundation is religion, religion and politics are necessarily related. . . . And our government needs the church because only those humble enough to admit they are sinners can bring democracy the tolerance it requires in order to survive" (Reagan 1984: 10; see Tipton 1984: 1013).

Reagan also made a number of revealing comments about his views of religion and politics in a speech to the National Association of Evangelicals in Orlando in 1983. Here he stated that "modern-day secularism" is the enemy within the country and that political struggles are spiritual in nature. Policy decisions must have religious reasons. The Founding Fathers designed the First Amendment to protect churches from government interference, not the reverse. "They never meant to construct a wall of hostility between government and the concept of religious belief itself," he claimed (quoted in *New Republic* Editorial Staff 1983: 8).

In an interchange of letters with Norman Lear in *Harper's* in 1984, in reply to Lear's endorsement of a strong separation of Church and State to protect public debate, Reagan stated that the First Amendment is distorted when it is misinterpreted to "make freedom *of* religion into freedom *from* religion" (Lear and Reagan 1984: 15) and that the First Amendment "says the government shall not establish religion, but it also just as plainly says the government shall not interfere in the practice of religion" (15).

On a number of occasions, Reagan suggested that religious beliefs were significant to his political decision making. Reagan explicitly asserted that personal moral decision making in public life is inseparable from his religion. In his words, "If you practice a religion . . . then your private life will be influenced by a sense of moral obligation. So, too, will your public life. One, you see, affects the other. . . . [Thus] those who believe must be free to speak of and act on their belief to apply moral teaching to public questions" (Reagan 1984: 10; Pierard 1983: 1183). Similarly, in a television interview following his governorship, he "committed himself to reclaim the principles in the Judeo-Christian tradition by turning America back to God" (Pierard 1983: 1183). In introducing his new budget in 1985, Reagan argued that his efforts to increase military spending had "the Scriptures" on his side (see Castelli 1985: 526).

Summary of Reagan's Style of Religious Lawmaking

Compared with the other lawmakers discussed here, Reagan's views about the relationship between religion and government seem unsophisticated. His simplistic conflation of religion and morality contributes to his (unfounded) perspective that religion is necessary to government and politics. His statements also reflect a lack of consideration for religious pluralism and the constitutional rights of and moral respect owed to non-Christians. He sees little, if any, difficulty in legislating Christian morality in society, especially with respect to issues such as abortion and mandatory prayer in public schools.

Reagan's public statements that politics requires morality, that policy decisions must have religious reasons, and that morality is religious align his views most closely with the Justification type of religious influence. However, his references to America as a Christian nation dependent on God, along with his personal reliance on God, suggest the Authority model. Reagan's stated views on the role of religion in his own life clearly place him in the communitarian camp, next to those who assert that religion is inseparable from moral identity and, thus, from political decision making.

Reverend Jesse Jackson

The Reverend Jesse Jackson, the last public figure to be considered in this survey, was the first African American presidential candidate in U.S. history, running as a candidate for nomination on the Democratic ticket in both 1984 and 1988. In addition to being a political leader, he is also an ordained Baptist minister who regularly preaches in churches across America (see Jackson 1987: xi). Religion, particularly the support of the Black Church, has been central to his political life (see Hatch 1988: 3).

Views on Regulating Abortion

Jackson's views on abortion appear to have shifted over time. In 1974, Senator Hatfield cited Jackson as analogizing abortion to genocide, quoting him as condemning "the moral emptiness and aloofness that comes when protecting human life is not considered sacred" (Hatfield 1974: 7). Consistent with this perspective, Jackson sent an "Open Letter to Congress" in 1977, requesting that government funding for abortion be diverted to "meet human needs" of caring for children rather than supporting a "federal policy of killing" (quoted in Noonan 1979: 66–67). In recent years, however, Jackson has supported a prochoice platform, arguing that decisions about family size and timing are private. He advocates additional government support for family planning, the reduction of infant mortality, and unintended adolescent pregnancy. Although all of these strategies are designed to reduce poverty and the need for abortion, Jackson opposes any attempts to repeal women's right to choose. He also favors public funding for abortion to ensure that poor women have the same access that wealthier women have (see Clemente 1989: 166).

Jackson's prochoice stance does not mean that he approves of abortion, however. To the contrary, his disapproval is indicated by a confession made to the American Student Association that he personally abhors abortion because his mother would have aborted him had it not been for the intervention of his grandmother (quoted in Paige 1983: 101). In the same talk he argued that "The idea that says it's alright to conceive a baby, but unpolitical to have it—there's something shallow about that. I'm contending that unless we put human life second only to God in our lives, we're becoming a Sodom and Gomorrah-ethic oriented people. . . . I'm thinking that we have an obligation to take sex and life as a far more sacred event than we do now" (quoted in Paige 1983: 101). In addition, Jackson has asserted that "many girls stoop to the distortion of abortion because they are not educated to appreciate life. . . . We fail to deal with the ramifications of the devaluation of human life" (Jackson 1987: 155–56). Like Cuomo's, these views reveal a separation of Jackson's personal religious views about abortion from his views about appropriate public policy measures on the issue. They suggest his awareness of a distinction between his roles as a private citizen and as a political leader.

Consideration of Gender and Religious Pluralism

Also similar to Cuomo, Jackson seems to appreciate the unfairness of cultural assumptions that pregnancy and children are women's sole responsibility. To those who object to abortion on religious grounds, he says, "Some even suggest that having babies is a woman's role. Women can't make babies by themselves, nor can men—though they can be irresponsible when they've planted the seed. Life must be maintained as the highest value in this cosmic order, and when abortion chairs and convenience become more basic than children, even the religious objectors become extensions of the decadence. . . . No man can become pregnant. No man can have a baby. Most probably couldn't stand the pain" (Jackson 1987: 155–56). This passage demonstrates how distinctive Jackson's views on abortion are. Unlike many religious political leaders (including some of those discussed here), who oppose abortion without considering the coerciveness of restrictive laws on women carrying unwanted pregnancies, Jackson seriously considers gender in his conclusions about reproductive policy. More generally, Jackson has included women's rights in his political platform, speaking out for the need for the Equal Rights Amendment and equal pay for equal work for women (e.g., Jackson 1987: 8, 14; see Colton 1989: 82, 93).

Jackson's acceptance of religious pluralism and ecumenical spirit is evident in his comments about his Rainbow Coalition "making room for Arab-Americans" as well as Hispanic Americans, Native Americans, and Asian Americans (Jackson 1987: 6–7). He says that "our nation is a rainbow—red, yellow, brown, black, and white—and all are precious in God's sight" (5). Of course, this does not include nontheistic religions or nonreligious views, but it is nevertheless more inclusive than, say, Reagan's "Christian nation" rhetoric. When Jackson does appeal to religious principles, he regards them as public rather than private. Jackson believes that people of many faiths can share his vision, whether or not they share his particular beliefs in God (see Jackson 1987: xvi; Hatch 1989: 98).

Views of Religion's Place in Lawmaking Generally

Jackson's dual roles as minister and political leader have resulted in a good deal of reflection about the relationship between his politics and his religious convictions. Jackson has stated that "my religion obligates me to be political, that is, to seek to do God's will and allow the spiritual Word to become concrete justice and dwell among us. My politics do not make me religious. Religion should *use* you politically to do public service. Politics should not *misuse* religion" (1987: ix). This quote suggests that Jackson's religious convictions act as Motivation in his politics. Similarly, early in Jackson's 1984 campaign for president, he stated to a newspaper interviewer that "the main thing is that I do God's will to the best of my ability, if He can use me as an instrument of His peace, for some purpose" (McTighe 1990: 585–86).

The Judaic and Christian religious traditions are clearly an important source for Jackson's public values (Jackson 1987: 6; Hatch 1988: 37). Jackson frequently draws from the prophetic tradition, especially Isaiah (e.g., Jackson 1987: 3; see Hatch 1988: 38). He uses biblical language and imagery in many of his speeches (e.g., Jackson 1987: 6–7; Hatch 1989: 87, n. 1) and does not hesitate to refer to God and other religious themes in his public pronouncements. His speeches often refer to the redemptive value of suffering (Jackson 1987: 78; see Hatch 1988: 81). He has also called for the creation of "new covenants" between the Democratic Party and those who are lacking in social, political, and economic power in society (see Hatch 1987: 381).

It is evident that Jackson sees a clear and direct interaction between religious beliefs and political responsibility. For example, he began his speech to the 1984 Democratic National Convention as though he were beginning a sermon: "Tonight we come together, bound by our faith in a mighty God . . . we are called to a perfect mission: to feed the hungry, to clothe the naked; to house the homeless, to teach the illiterate, to provide jobs for the jobless, and to choose the human race over the nuclear race" (1987: 3). Similarly, in speaking to a joint session of the Alabama legislature in 1983, Jackson used religious terms to describe the momentousness of an African American addressing the lawmaking body which had formed the Confederacy in 1861: "Our presence here today is not accidental, it is providential—it is God's will. We serve a God who hears and answers prayer. . . . Now that we're here together—because of God's investment in us and the stewardship that he has entrusted to us—we are obligated to give back to God a return on his investment. We must be faithful to our sworn duty. . . . Our faithfulness is all that we have with which to impress God. But if we are faithful over a few things—even the least of these—God will promote and elevate us and make us rulers over many" (1987: 138). Although these statements suggest a direct relationship between religion and politics, they do not necessarily suggest one in which the former properly directs or determines the latter.

However, some of Jackson's statements definitely express a theistic bias. For example, he contends that "at the center of every political, economic, legal, and social issue is the spiritual, moral, and ethical dimension" (Jackson 1987: 152; see McTighe 1990: 594–95) and that part of society's current ills can be attributed to "a publicly godless generation" (Jackson 1987: 152) and the exclusion of prayer from public schools (Jackson 1987: 153).

Notably, however, Jackson has not translated these views into prescriptions for legislating morality such as mandating prayer in public schools or outlawing abortion, as other religious lawmakers such as Hyde, Reagan, and Hatch have. In addition, Jackson is aware of the significance of a separation between religion and politics. On one occasion, he stated that "as black people, we have only varying degrees of access to the Republican and Democratic vehicles. But we can't ride to freedom in Pharaoh's chariot" (Jackson 1987: xxii). He characterizes himself as living "on the boundary" with the inevitable tension that comes from trying to synthesize and put in their proper relationship, in a pluralistic society, the "religious and the secular," the "spiritual and the material" (Jackson 1987: ix).

Despite the emphasis on religious themes and imagery animating Jackson's politics, he rarely referred to the name of God in his 1984 campaign speeches, nor does he, like President Reagan did, claim a God-like status for the nation (see Hatch 1987: 382). In fact, he rejects the rhetoric of civil religion that Reagan drew on so heavily. In addition, Jackson advocates his views using a model of cultural pluralism that appeals to widely shared values and in which the distinctive elements of Christianity do not dominate (see McTighe 1990: 595–96; Hatch 1988: 38). In effect, Jackson uses religion in the public sphere but not in the political one. Hatch observes this distinction in noting that Jackson "consistently appeals to people as fellow citizens, not as adherents of a common Christian religious tradition" (Hatch 1989: 98). He does not claim that Christian doctrine provides definitive answers to public policy issues or eliminates the need to consider secular approaches but, rather, that religious commitments can provide general guidance and principles for political decision making (see Hatch 1988: 38).

However, like Hatfield and unlike Cuomo, Jackson appears to place God's authority above Caesar's. For instance, in a speech on civil disobedience and conscience at a Bicentennial Conference on Religious Liberty in 1976, Jackson stated that "the appointments of government may lead to rebellion for selfish reasons, but the annointment of God may lead to authentic civil disobedience or objection to the state" (Jackson 1987: 146–47). In other words, religious motivations for opposing government and law may be more appropriate because they are more genuine and well intentioned than political motivations for doing so.

These comments and observations suggest that Jackson considers religion and politics to be fundamentally interrelated. Jackson biographer Roger Hatch in fact argues that Jackson's views are essentially religious and "grow out of a consistent way of looking at reality that is deeply rooted in the black church and in the Civil Rights Movement," the core of which is a "religious-political vision for America" (Hatch 1988: 4, 7, 1989: 92; see Jackson 1987: 116; Hatch 1988: 79, 81). Jackson expressed this religious vision in his speech to the 1984 Democratic National Convention, in which he charged: "We must seek a revival of the spirit, inspired by a new vision and new possibilities. We must return to higher ground" (Jackson 1987: 3).

These statements assume that religion and politics are interrelated, but they do not suggest that Jackson favors religiously sanctioned laws. Indeed, Jackson's prochoice stance in the face of his personal conviction that abortion is wrong exemplifies his recognition of the inappropriateness of religious lawmaking. Whether this is a deliberate strategy like Cuomo's not to legislate his personal moral views in the absence of consensus or, more pragmatically, a political strategy that will have greater appeal to his liberal, progressive constituency is difficult to ascertain, because Jackson does not appear to have directly addressed this issue. In any event, his position is similar to Cuomo's in illustrating the possibility that religious lawmakers can make public policy decisions on grounds different from or broader than their personal religious convictions.

Summary of Jackson's Style of Religious Lawmaking

In sum, Jackson's statements reflect the perspective of a deeply religious political leader whose worldview is shaped by his religious faith and commitments. He draws on religious themes and imagery for many of his political positions yet is also able to articulate these positions in secular terms. He plainly offers religious faith as relevant to politics and the resolution of social problems. This conclusion is supported by similar findings of two Jackson biographers, who claim that "unlike the moral majority and the fundamental right, Jackson does not use biblical presuppositions to take public policy positions. . . . He simply views circumstances through a moral lens of what is right and wrong" (Clemente and Watkins 1989: xv). In these respects, his statements indicate a strong affinity with the Guidance model.

There is also evidence of the Motivation model in Jackson's claims about having certain obligations to God, being "used by God to do his will," and so on. Nonetheless, Jackson's religious views are broadly ecumenical rather than sectarian. They do not indicate that he would do God's will by making political decisions that conflicted with his obligations as a public leader. His awareness of the distinction between personal convictions and appropriate public policy, along with his awareness of cultural and religious pluralism, align his views more closely with liberal than communitarian perspectives about the appropriate influence of religion on politics.

Summary and Conclusions: Implications of Religious Identity for Religious Lawmaking

The foregoing accounts have provided us with a stronger foundation for understanding the role of religion in shaping the moral identity and political perspectives of some of America's political leaders. It is extremely difficult to imagine that any of these lawmakers, especially Hatfield and Jackson, could renounce all reliance on their religious faith in making public policy decisions, as liberal proposals would advocate.

Even Cuomo, Hatfield, and Jackson, who have demonstrated at least some distance from their personal religious convictions in making public policy pronouncements on abortion, still indicate the deep relevance of their faith to their public perspectives. Thus, even if it is theoretically possible for lawmakers to separate their religious convictions from their decisions as public officials, it is unlikely as a practical matter that many lawmakers could be convinced that they either could or should do so.

However, neither does the foregoing substantiate the communitarian view that religion is inextricable from the moral decision making of lawmakers. To the extent that some of the political leaders discussed here—Cuomo and Jackson in particular, and Hatfield to a lesser degree—have demonstrated the ability and/or the desirability of limiting the definitiveness of their religious views in their public policy making, they undermine the accuracy of communitarian assumptions that separating religious convictions from one's moral identity is effectively impossible. The ability of these lawmakers to distance themselves, at least to some degree, from their religious convictions suggests that religion need not be the Motivation or Justification for the political decisions of religious lawmakers.

In addition, if the communitarian approach were correct, we would expect the positions of religious lawmakers to reflect not only their Church's teachings about abortion but also their perspectives about the status of women. Yet as the preceding survey indicates, this is not necessarily the case. For example, although the views of two of the three Catholic lawmakers considered here might be characterized as reflecting traditional Catholic views of women as primarily childbearers and mothers, Cuomo's views are sharply divergent. Similarly, the views of Senator Hatfield and the more recent views of the Reverend Jackson about women's roles differ significantly from traditional Christian views.

This survey of selected political leaders also suggests that there is no necessary or direct relationship between a lawmaker's religious affiliation and the type of influence, if any, that religion will have on his or her lawmaking. Among the Catholic lawmakers, Noonan's views reflect more of a Justification model, in contrast to Hyde's predominantly Authoritarian type, and Cuomo's Guidance-oriented style. Among the Protestants, all three have elements of the Authority model, and both Hatfield and Jackson, the two Baptists, also have strong elements of the Guidance type in their statements.

Further, these political leaders suggest that there is no necessary correlation between the type of influence religion has on one's lawmaking decisions and the type of public office held. Former governor Cuomo is the only lawmaker of the group who clearly recognizes that applying his religious views in his political decision making is problematic because of the coercive power of his public office and, consequently, attempts to limit the influence of his religious views on his political decisions. Although Jackson's prochoice approach may be a manifestation of the same view, it has not been publicly articulated on these terms.

Senator Hatfield expresses a recognition of the problem but basically adopts the communitarian view that his religion is inextricable from his moral identity. Representative Hyde's rhetoric recognizes the need for lawmakers to use publicly accessible reasons in their political decisions, but his own policy making fails to adhere to that standard. Judge Noonan sees religious morality as foundational to public decision making even in relation to lawmaking. Former president Reagan's position generally does not acknowledge any problem with religious influences on politics.

This exploration of how religion has influenced actual lawmakers' political and public policy decisions suggests that an adequate approach to religious lawmaking must consider the centrality that religion may have to the moral identity of lawmakers in addition to the risks that religious lawmaking poses to the citizenship rights and interests of women and religious minorities. The views of several of the political leaders included here, especially Hyde, Noonan, and Reagan, fail to take into account religious pluralism in their decision making. Most lawmakers are Christian and assume their constituents are as well.

The Christian presuppositions of many lawmakers are especially problematic when the lawmaking at issue includes a gender dimension, as do abortion laws. The views of the political leaders examined here reflect varying degrees of sensitivity to and consideration of unwanted pregnancy, an event of which most lawmakers, because they are male, have no direct experience. Unfortunately, the views of some of the lawmakers included here reflect traditional patriarchal and sexist religious assumptions about women's moral agency and appropriate social roles. Because women and religious dissenters have generally been excluded from the formulation and interpretation of religious morality, it is unlikely that political issues decided on the basis of traditional religious rationales, especially Christian ones, will include their perspectives and interests.

Even lawmakers who attempt to be more sensitive to gender differences and religious pluralism often fall short of providing adequate protections against infringements on the constitutional rights and interests of women and religious minorities. For example, Hatfield's proposals for making abortion unlawful are premised on unrealistic assumptions about social provision for a "common good" that rationalizes depriving women of their constitutional rights to control their reproductive lives. Even Cuomo's liberal views for supporting abortion restrictions are problematic because they still risk raising Establishment Concerns or burdening Citizenship Rights.

To a large extent, the foregoing investigation indicates the validity of Karst's observation that "when a male-dominated legislature considers an issue that touches the interests of women, it would be extraordinary if the legislators were to think consciously about the origins of their own personal definitions of woman and to find the ability to transcend those definitions during the process of legislative decision" (Karst 1989: 112). Although certainly some of the lawmakers discussed in this chapter have been able to take women's status and interest into consideration in their deliberations on abortion, notably Cuomo, Hatfield, and Jackson, others, especially Hyde, Noonan, and Reagan, seem oblivious or even hostile to how restrictive abortion laws limit women's Citizenship Rights and may restrict or even endanger their lives. Allowing predominantly socially and economically privileged Christian male lawmakers to determine how women are to conduct their reproductive lives, even if their mandates are accompanied by social services to reduce hardships, perpetuates women's subordinate social status.

Nevertheless, when they provide a source of Guidance rather than Authority or Justification, religious influences on lawmaking are less likely to raise Establishment Concerns or violate Citizenship Rights. As we have seen, the two lawmakers who best manifest the Guidance approach, Cuomo and Jackson, both have refrained from attempting to legislate their personal religious convictions regarding abortion. In contrast, the perspectives of the other four lawmakers, who exemplify either or both the Authority or Justification models, have attempted to engage in religious lawmaking on abortion. This is not to suggest that the correlation is a necessary one, but it is, nonetheless, suggestive of the impact of different types of religious lawmaking on Citizenship Rights and interests.

Having provided the background on both sides of the dilemma of religious lawmaking in the first three chapters of this book, in the next three, I look at theoretical approaches to resolving the dilemma. In chapters 4 and 5, I describe and assess the predominant approaches as formulated by liberal and communitarian theorists. In these chapters, I consider the gender dimensions of the issue by examining specific liberal and communitarian proposals for religious lawmaking on abortion. These two chapters confirm that the problems with religious lawmaking raised in this and the preceding chapters have not been addressed satisfactorily by either liberal or communitarian theorists, leaving us in search of alternative approaches.

FOUR

Liberal Approaches to Religious Lawmaking

As we have seen, the Supreme Court's jurisprudence fails to recognize a range of constitutional problems presented by religious lawmaking, particularly for the liberty and free exercise rights of women and religious minorities. At the same time, however, the Court has also failed to recognize how central a role religion may play in the moral identity of citizens, especially that of religious lawmakers. In this and the following chapter, I explore alternative theoretical approaches to the dilemma of religious lawmaking. The most prominent of these proposals have been forwarded by theorists who use predominantly either liberal or communitarian political theory. Unfortunately, neither liberal nor communitarian theorists have offered an alternative to the Court's jurisprudence that is able to account for both primary constituencies that are influenced by religious lawmaking: lawmakers and citizens.

In this chapter, I describe liberal proposals for addressing the dilemma of religious lawmaking, focusing on Kent Greenawalt's work. Among the several liberal theorists who have addressed the issue of what role religion should play in law and politics—including John Rawls (e.g., 1997, 1996, 1993, 1989, 1988, 1987, 1971), Robert Audi (1997, 1993, 1990, 1989), Bruce Ackerman (1980), Kathleen Sullivan (1992), William Galston (1991), Ronald Dworkin (1989, 1986), and David A. J. Richards (1989, 1986)—Kent Greenawalt's (1997, 1996b, 1996a, 1993a, 1993b, 1990, 1988, 1985) represents one of the most thoughtful and sympathetic to the concerns of religious believers. In contrast to more mainstream liberal approaches, which find little place for religious convictions in politics, Greenawalt takes seriously arguments favoring an expanded role for religion in political decision making, as evidenced in his claim that "reliance on religious convictions is appropriate under any plausible model of liberal democracy much more often than is claimed by those who would have the good liberal citizen restrict himself in political decisions to shared nonreligious premises and common forms of reasoning" (1988: 203).

To illustrate Greenawalt's distinctiveness among liberal approaches, I compare his views to those of Robert Audi and John Rawls. Whereas Audi offers one of the most restrictive approaches to permitting religious lawmaking, Rawls, at least in *Political Liberalism* (1993, 1996 [paperback]), as supplemented by a more recent article entitled "The Idea of Public Reason Revisited" (hereafter, "Public Reason"; Rawls 1997), permits a much greater role for religious lawmaking outside of carefully delimited areas.

I discuss Greenawalt's understandings of moral identity and religious pluralism, two of the most pronounced issues in formulating an adequate approach to religious lawmaking, and how Greenawalt proposes to resolve the tension between these two concerns with respect to religious lawmakers. This background provides the context for a discussion of how Greenawalt proposes to address the specific case of religious lawmaking on abortion and its differences from more traditional liberal approaches. I conclude the chapter by pointing out the inadequacies of Greenawalt's proposal in particular and liberal proposals more generally for addressing the dilemma presented by religious lawmaking.

In the next chapter, I follow the same general approach in analyzing communitarian approaches, focusing on the work of Michael Perry. As Perry and Greenawalt's views have evolved in their subsequent writings, they have increasingly addressed the concerns and criticisms raised against their own position by others and have become increasingly similar in their overall recommendations regarding religious lawmaking. Despite this seeming convergence, however, as well as their common failure to adequately recognize or provide for the significance of gender differences in their proposals, their approaches retain elements that are distinctively liberal (in the case of Greenawalt) or communitarian (in the case of Perry) and that bear important implications for their overall adequacy.

Liberal Approaches to Religious Lawmaking

Although liberal theorists are by no means a unified or uniform group of thinkers, their theories generally share several elements in common. These include an emphasis on moral pluralism, the individual and justice, and associated principles of autonomy, liberty, freedom, equality, toleration, and limited government (see Delaney 1994: vii; Rosenblum 1989: 2–4). Traditional liberal understandings of how citizens and legislators should deal with their religious convictions in making political decisions are based on a conception of moral selves as autonomous, independent individuals with capacities for rationality that entitle them to rights; on a distinction between public and private spheres; and on the conviction that government should maximize the liberty of citizens. Because liberal theorists tend to ignore or at least to discount the potential difficulty, inability, or unwillingness of citizens, including lawmakers, to separate their public political identities from their private, religious ones, their theories lack an account of moral identity that satisfactorily accounts for the role of religion in the lives of believers.

Overview of Liberal Proposals for Addressing Religious Lawmaking

In this section, I provide a brief overview of the major elements of liberal theory that are relevant to religious lawmaking. First, I describe Greenawalt's views and then compare them with those of Rawls and Audi. To provide a solid basis for comparison, I describe each thinker's views of religion, moral identity, pluralism, and the appropriate place of religious convictions in lawmaking, including those ideas applied to the specific matter of abortion regulation.

Greenawalt's Approach to Religious Lawmaking

In attempting to provide a more expansive role for religion in politics than traditional liberal theory has permitted, Greenawalt shares with several communitarian theorists the regret that religion has been marginalized in "our culture's intellectual life and in public media" (1990: 1035). He contends that conventional liberal opposition to the influence of religious convictions in politics is not grounded on some fundamental opposition to religion itself but instead on the view that "the grounds of decision should have an interpersonal validity that extends to all members of society" (1988: 58). This perspective is embodied in Greenawalt's own proposals, which are premised on his views of the character of religion, especially in relation to nonbelievers; the proper role of government in a liberal society; and fairness to citizens holding religious convictions.

Greenawalt defines religion somewhat analogously to that adopted here, that is, as "having to do with beliefs or institutional embodiments that involve a number of the features of traditional religions" (1988: 156). He defines "religious bases for decision" as "connected to theistic belief or other belief about a realm of ultimate value beyond, or deeper than, ordinary human experience, or to forms of life or institutions understood to be religious" (1995: 39). Greenawalt accords all religious views the same validity for purposes of his argument (1988: 72). Similarly, on the presupposition that there is no legitimate basis for singling out religious convictions for exclusion from political decision making (1988: 158–60), he accords religious convictions the same status as other "personal bases of decision" (1988: 156).

In this respect, Greenawalt diverges from traditional liberal thinkers, who distinguish religion from other personal bases of decision, such as Audi's distinction between religious and secular convictions. Somewhat more akin to

Greenawalt, Rawls would exclude all "comprehensive doctrines," not just religious ones, from political decisions regarding principles of justice and other "constitutional essentials" of social cooperation (1993: 13, 58–59). On this point, Audi's view that religion should be distinguished from other "personal bases for decision" has the strongest constitutional basis, given the explicit consideration given to religious belief in the First Amendment religion clauses, as noted in chapter 2.

In spite of his affinity with communitarian theory on this point, Greenawalt restricts the application of his proposal in *Religious Convictions and Political Choice* to "good, liberal citizens" in our "liberal, democratic" society (e.g., 1988: 4), in which individual autonomy (conscience) and diversity (pluralism) are central values. It is a crucial premise of our liberal society, Greenawalt argues, that "citizens of extremely diverse religious views can build principles of political order and social justice that do not depend on particular religious beliefs" (1993b: 513; see also 1988: 16–17). Thus, respect for religious pluralism is central to Greenawalt's theoretical approach to religious lawmaking.

Greenawalt's views on pluralism are consistent with those of other liberal theorists. Robert Audi's concerns about religious influences on lawmaking arise out of his awareness of the potential for injustice in a situation of religious pluralism. In his view, "Any governmental religious preference creates some tendency for greater power to accrue to the preferred religion, particularly if it is that of the majority (1997: 40)."[1] Even if the existence of certain disproportionate powers does not necessarily (or at least does not directly) restrict anyone's liberty, concentration of power in a religious group as such is problematic. It easily impairs democracy, in which citizens should have equal opportunities to exercise political power on a fair basis, and it may impair religious freedom in particular.

Rawls's framework for limiting the role of religion in lawmaking also emanates from his recognition that "the political culture of a democratic society is always marked by a diversity of opposing and irreconcilable religious, philosophical, and moral doctrines" (1993: 3–4). According to Rawls, this "fact of reasonable pluralism . . . means that the differences between citizens arising from their comprehensive doctrines, religious and nonreligious, may be irreconcilable" (1997: 765; see also Griffin 1997: 300). Thus, Rawls places pluralism at the center of analysis, framing the problem as one of establishing "a stable and just society of free and equal citizens profoundly divided" by such divergent doctrines (1993: xvii; see also 58–61, 127–28, 146).

Consistent with other liberal thinkers, who are pessimistic about the likelihood that political argument in a pluralistic society can result in agreement about controversial moral issues, especially when those arguments are religiously influenced, Greenawalt urges citizens to restrict their reliance on their religious beliefs in their public discourse. He determines that the severity of restrictions should be determined in accordance with a hierarchy intended to reflect the different levels of persuasiveness that various kinds of reasons have in lawmaking. Realist reasons are least problematic because their "truth or falsity must be available to common human understanding" (1995: 26). "Widely shared premises" can be used when realist reasons offer incomplete grounds for decision making but may be overridden if they are shown to be unjust or misguided (29–30). Moral reasons based on authority, especially religious authority, have even lower priority, but they are not ruled out of bounds, as in some liberal proposals, including Audi's.

Greenawalt thus would require using publicly accessible reasons, which he describes as "shared understandings" or "ordinary modes of thought" in "public discourse about political issues with those who do not share religious premises" (1988: 216–17). Contrary to (some) traditional liberal theory, Greenawalt argues that the grounds for public choices under liberal democracy cannot be validly limited to those that are "exclusively rational." Nevertheless, he claims that "what are publicly accessible reasons in a society will overlap very greatly with what are widely regarded as canons of rationality in that society" (1988: 57).

Requiring people to use publicly accessible reasons "when these lead to solid factual conclusions . . . is owed to others of diverse convictions in a pluralist society" (Greenawalt 1988: 204), because "it is fundamentally unfair to coerce people, or to use the corporate authority and power of the state, when the grounds for doing so are not ones that all those affected could be expected to accept if they made reasonable judgments [and that] the political life of a society will be healthiest and most stable if political issues are resolved on premises and grounds that are fully available to everyone in society" (Greenawalt 1995: 72). In other words, "if I am going to coerce others, I should have reasons that I think are fairly applicable to them" (Greenawalt 1995: 37).

In Greenawalt's view, reliance on religious convictions is generally inappropriate in political decision making when publicly accessible reasons are available to provide "conclusive" or "decisive" answers or "solid factual conclusions" (e.g., Greenawalt 1988: 204, 207; 1990: 1022). He provides several interrelated reasons to support his view. One reason is that "claims about religious truth are outside the domain of publicly accessible reasons" (1988: 75) and are "not consonant with reliance on shared reasons" (58).

Another reason is that because people's religious convictions rest partly on elements such as personal experience that are not subject to "reasoned interpersonal evaluation" (Greenawalt 1990: 1032; see also Greenawalt 1993a: 649), they are relatively exclusive to a particular group of religious adherents and, consequently, inaccessible to others. This situation is enhanced in a religiously pluralistic society such as our own, where "significant numbers of people dissent from even the most widely held religious beliefs, such as belief in the existence of God" (Greenawalt 1988: 58; see also Greenawalt 1993a: 672). In addition, religions tend to be based on inflexible and uncompromising tenets (Greenawalt 1988: 158–59). Thus, religiously based arguments are often founded on intractable differences among religious views that foster separation between those of different religious faiths (or of no faith).

Greenawalt contends that "religion is something people feel so strongly about that it will inevitably be a source of tension that will be aggravated by reliance on religious grounds in political decision and arguments" (1993a:

674). In the specific context of lawmaking, he is concerned about the negative effects of coercive lawmaking based on views that are anathema to some religious views. Among these effects are constraining those holding such religious views, implicitly "'disapproving' the views" (1995: 59), being religiously and politically divisive (1988: 219), and having exclusionary effects (1995: 157–58, 1990: 1035, 1993a: 675).

Despite these concerns, however, Greenawalt rejects the view that the "bare presence of an impermissible aim to impose or promote a particular religion" is sufficient to invalidate legislation (1988: 245). To determine whether religious convictions played a fundamental role in a particular decision (Greenawalt 1988: 36; see Audi 1990: 391–92), he proposes that a "systematic reconstruction" be conducted. If abandoning religious convictions would cause a person to reconsider seriously his or her position, then religion should be viewed as fundamental to the decision and, thus, invalid.

In his earlier work, Greenawalt argued that the *"actual debate* of political issues in terms of competing religious convictions is disturbing in a pluralist society because religiously-based or influenced decisions impose dictates upon nonbelievers based on grounds they cannot be expected to share" (1993b: 517; emphasis added). From this perspective, even *public advocacy* should "be conducted in the nonreligious language of shared premises and modes of reasoning" (Greenawalt 1990: 1022; see also Greenawalt 1993b: 669; emphasis added). More recently, however, Greenawalt has shifted to a view that favors "greater restraints on discourse than on judgment" (1996a: 636).

In this more recent view, "no problem is raised if religious belief has led someone to a position he now thinks he can fully and persuasively defend in nonreligious terms. The issue is not about the causal relation between religious belief at some earlier time and one's present position; instead, the issue concerns one's present dependence on religious convictions to support his position" (Greenawalt 1990: 1021). Thus, reliance on religious convictions in making political decisions need not be problematic so long as those decisions can be justified ultimately on nonreligious grounds. Greenawalt defends this modified view on the eminently sensible basis that it is much easier to determine whether someone is justifying their decision on religious grounds than it is to tell whether their judgment is based on religious grounds. Also well taken is his additional rationale that it is easier to refrain from engaging in discourse that relies on religious grounds than it is to bar such grounds from one's considered judgments.

Part of Greenawalt's justification for allowing some reliance on religious convictions is that religion may provide important "sources of insight" for religious persons (1988: 43) and may "bear pervasively on people's ethical choices, including choices about laws and government policies" (1988: 30, 34). In addition, as a practical matter, Greenawalt contends that "most religious persons could hardly decide what personal perspectives they would have but for their religious beliefs" (1990: 1022; see also 1988: 180).

Indeed, contrary to traditional liberal perspectives, including those of Rawls and Audi, Greenawalt contends that the underlying assumption that people can generally distinguish the influence of religious reasons and other non-publicly accessible reasons from that of reasoned convictions "is in fact highly misleading." This is "because of psychological impediments to detached independent judgment, difficulties in disentangling the threads of publicly accessible reasons from other considerations, and the inherent inter-relatedness of the two sorts of considerations" (1988: 152). In his estimation, religious convictions "may be inseparably interwoven with other grounds of moral decision making" (1988: 30).

Based on these assumptions about the way moral selves are constituted, Greenawalt believes that requiring people to set aside their religious convictions is to ask them to make decisions on the basis of only part of what they regard as relevant (1988: 40). Even further, he believes that religious beliefs are paramount for those who hold them and may take precedence over a conflicting model of liberal democracy (1988: 201). Thus, he concedes that complete independence of moral identity from religious convictions is probably impossible (1993b: 508). In this sense, Greenawalt accepts the communitarian premise (to be discussed in chapter 5) that it is impossible to prohibit people from relying on their religious convictions in making political decisions.

Based on this analysis of the role religious convictions play in the political decision making of believing citizens, Greenawalt concludes that "nominal regard" for their "wholeness and integrity" requires that government cannot demand that legislators or other citizens "systematically expunge all religious conviction as a guide to action" (1988: 237; see also 1988: 225, 155). Another reason for Greenawalt's position that religious convictions should be a legitimate basis for decision making when publicly accessible reasons are absent or indecisive is based on the practical consideration that "citizens will revert to their own preferred theories, including whatever religious and metaphysical convictions underlie them," when shared premises are unavailable (Greenawalt 1988: 184; see also 1988: 258). In this respect, he believes that the "strict secularist" approach of traditional liberalism "invites religious persons to displace their most firmly rooted convictions about values and about the nature of humanity and the universe in a quest for common bases of judgment that is inevitably unavailing" when publicly accessible reasons are not available (1988: 258). He hypothesizes that sometimes people will be "thrown back" on their personal moral convictions even when they attempt to rely exclusively on publicly accessible reasons (1990: 1040–41).

Further, for Greenawalt, it simply is not feasible to forego making decisions on certain controversial issues for which publicly accessible reasons are unavailable. In his words, it is "misleading to suggest that when common grounds are inconclusive, the state can comfortably leave people free of restrictions on individual behavior" (1990: 1045). On some occasions, such as when determining whether to protect an endangered species, a political decision for which there are not adequate publicly accessible reasons is necessary. In addition, limiting the appropriate grounds for decision to publicly accessible reasons in such cases tends to maintain the status quo and relies too heavily on inertia and tradition (Greenawalt 1988: 236).

In the circumstance that religious convictions and common forms of reasoning are both relied on and cannot be disentangled, Greenawalt believes
that "people should not have to try to slice their understanding into pieces, attempting to guess what they would think were it not for religious convictions" (1988: 208).[2] Expecting people in such situations to disregard what
they believe are relevant considerations would be asking a great deal (1988:
150). In this respect, Greenawalt differs from both Audi and Rawls who, as we
see shortly, assume people have the capacity and motivation to engage in such
disaggregation.

With respect to lawmakers in particular, Greenawalt argues that religion is
a problematic basis for lawmaking because a liberal society requires legislation
to "rest on *a* proper secular objective" (1988: 87), that is, on "*some* justification
. . . beyond its conformity to religious doctrine" (1988: 249; emphasis added).
Because "the common currency of political discourse is nonreligious argument
about human welfare" (Greenawalt 1988: 216–17), "laws should seek to promote *some* good that is comprehensible in nonreligious terms" (21; emphasis
added; see also Greenawalt 1990: 1022). Further, Greenawalt argues that "a liberal society should not rely on religious grounds to prohibit activities that
either cause no secular harm or do not cause enough secular harm to warrant
their prohibition" (1988: 90–91).[3]

Thus, Greenawalt concludes that "a dominant motive to impose or promote
a particular religious view [by legislators] could be relied upon by courts as
evidence to invalidate a statute if that motive were readily apparent" (1988:
245). Such a motive would be evident "if religious grounds figure prominently
in a statute or committee report" (1988: 245). In such a case, "the statute may
well violate the establishment clause" (1988: 245). He adds that "a similar conclusion applies if the executive branch issues regulations with legislative
effect, or an agency proposes legislation, or the president issues an official
message explaining his signing or veto of a bill" (1995: 153).

Other Liberal Approaches to Religious Lawmaking

The views of other liberal thinkers point out some sharp divergences with
Greenawalt's approach to religious lawmaking. Here, I consider the approaches
of Robert Audi and John Rawls.

Robert Audi's Approach to Religious Lawmaking.   In marked contrast
to Greenawalt, Audi would allow religion to play a role only in the "discovery"
and "framing or supporting" of political decisions (1989: 292–93), weak forms
of the Guidance and Justification types sketched in chapter 1. He recommends
a secular resolution principle that requires political decisions to be "fully warranted by secular considerations, and promulgated in that light" (1989: 280).
Religious considerations can play "an important heuristic role" or even some
motivational role in answering public policy questions (the Motivation type of
influence), but they are "neither necessary nor sufficient" bases for the deci-

sion, especially those concerning coercive laws "where direct restriction of human freedom is at stake" (Audi 1990: 396–97).

Audi also advocates adoption of a principle of secular motivation, according to which "one should not advocate or promote any legal or public policy restrictions on human conduct unless one not only has and is willing to offer, but is also *motivated by*, adequate secular reasons" (1989: 284; 1993: 691–92). According to Audi, a religiously motivated decision that includes a secular rationale but lacks a secular motivation is disingenuous because it does not accurately reflect the decision maker's real motivations. It also is manipulative because it involves "using a reason [the secular rationale] that carries potentially coercive effects on others when that reason is in some sense not good enough for oneself" because one has actually relied on religious reasons (Audi 1991: 73). In his view, it therefore lacks respect for other citizens.

Thus, Audi argues that the secular rationale requirement is necessary to protect religious freedom and to mitigate the resentment that may result when persons are coerced on grounds that cannot motivate them. In his view, excluding religious reasons as sufficient justifications for political decisions does not provide enough of a limitation on religious influences on public policy because it demands only the presence of some secular rationale to allow religious convictions to remain the actual grounds for a person's decision. This enables religious believers to use these grounds to determine how others (who may not share these commitments) should behave in civil society (Audi 1989: 283).

Contrary to Greenawalt's assumptions, religiously based policies will breed resentment by members of other groups, according to Audi, even where good secular reasons could be offered. To his way of thinking, where coercion is involved, it is necessary to have appropriate motivation, not merely secular rationales (Audi 1997: 57–58). (Although Greenawalt also claims to be troubled by a lack of correlation between the grounds of reliance and the grounds for public justification, he defends the distinction by claiming that it leads to a less divisive and exclusionary result and is more achievable at a practical level than other alternatives [Greenawalt 1990: 1046].)

Audi also claims that a failure to adhere to the principle of secular motivation will undermine respect for democratic principles of freedom and liberty that the separation of Church and State are designed to protect. He concludes that a "compromise model" such as Greenawalt's, in which religious considerations may take priority as long as one brings adequate secular considerations to the debate, does not adequately protect "public civility" (1989: 280–81). Of the three liberal theorists considered here, Audi's proposal by far provides the most restrictive and limited role for religion in lawmaking.

John Rawls's Approach to Religious Lawmaking.   John Rawls's liberal theory in some respects falls between those of Greenawalt and Audi, being more permissive concerning the role religion should play in politics and lawmaking in some respects but more restrictive in others. In Rawls's more recent political theorizing, which he terms *political liberalism*, he argues that "even though our comprehensive doctrines [including religious ones] are irreconcilable and cannot be compromised, nevertheless citizens who affirm reasonable doctrines may share reasons of another kind, namely, public reasons given in terms of political conceptions of justice" (1997: 895). Thus, although recognizing the problems that pluralism of religious (and other) beliefs presents for political agreement, Rawls claims that public reason can provide the basis for shared public discourse.

Rawls defines *public reason* as "citizens' reasoning in the public forum about constitutional essentials and basic questions of justice" (1993: 10). Reliance on such public reasons rather than comprehensive doctrines is required by a political conception of justice. Because public reasons are general and minimal enough to be accepted by the different reasonable comprehensive doctrines on the basis of an "overlapping consensus" yet not so broad or extensive as to conflict with the varying positions taken by different reasonable comprehensive doctrines (Rawls 1993: 38), they can provide the basis for political agreement in a morally and religiously pluralistic society.

According to Rawls's account of the overlapping consensus, "all those who affirm the political conception start from within their own comprehensive view and draw on the religious, philosophical, and moral grounds it provides" (1994: 143). He assumes that because the political conception is so minimal and basic, citizens will be able to view it "as derived from, or congruent with, or at least not in conflict with, their other values" (1993: 11). Consequently, points of view other than those of public reason, which include religious and individual moral views, "are generally not to be introduced into political discussions of justice" or regarding "constitutional essentials" (Rawls 1993: 15–16; see also 1985: 231; 1993: 12).

Further, the comprehensive doctrines that participate in the overlapping consensus must be reasonable, that is, they must allow us to have tolerance for comprehensive doctrines different from our own (e.g., Rawls 1993: 247). As far as possible, fundamental political issues should be resolved by "principles and ideals acceptable to common human reason" (136–37). Because there is "no shared public basis to distinguish the true beliefs from the false" (127–28), persons "must reason only from general beliefs shared by citizens generally, as part of their public knowledge" (69–70). In Rawls's framework of political liberalism, then, religious beliefs are unreliable and inappropriate grounds for determining the fundamental foundations of government and lawmaking.

According to Rawls's "principle of reciprocity," "our exercise of political power is proper only when we sincerely believe that the reasons we offer for our political action may reasonably be accepted by other citizens as a justification of those actions" (Rawls 1993: xlvi). Because no religious view of the meaning of life is accepted by most citizens, the use of political institutions to pursue one's religious agenda is inappropriate and unsuited to be the focus of an overlapping consensus (Rawls 1993: 180).[4]

Contrary to his earlier views, Rawls now allows that "reasonable comprehensive doctrines may be introduced in public reason at any time, provided that in due course public reasons, given by a reasonable political conception, are presented sufficient to support whatever the comprehensive doctrines are introduced to support" (1993: li–lii). Similar to Greenawalt's shift in perspective, Rawls is not adverse to citizens relying on their religious views in making public decisions as long as they can then justify them on the basis of public reasons. This shift enables religious persons to rely on their religious convictions to a much greater extent than stated in Rawls's earlier theories.

As I argue in chapter 7, however, this modification in Rawls's approach still does not go far enough in recognizing the centrality that religion may have to moral identity because it still requires proponents of the comprehensive doctrines to introduce public reasons themselves. In other words, rather than simply requiring that public reasons be available to justify a given position, Rawls would require that such public reasons actually be offered by proponents of what are, in fact, religious views.

This requirement may be unfairly burdensome on religious lawmakers (or other citizens), whose reasons for making a political decision are indeed religious and who do not have publicly accessible reasons at their disposal. It discriminates against religious citizens, arguably in violation of their Equal Protection Clause rights, by requiring them to forward additional rationales to substantiate their views, when citizens who rely on secular reasons are not required to do so. (As discussed in chapter 7, however, finding an infringement on equal protection rights would depend on whether the State had a compelling State interest for the differential requirements.)

As the previous summaries illustrate, liberal theorists share the view that religious convictions are problematic in public lawmaking. They are more concerned about respecting the rights of all religious citizens by forbidding religious doctrines from determining public policy. They diverge, however, in terms of the extent to which they believe that religion is problematic in the public sphere and the level of burden that should be placed on citizens to restrain them from using religious rationales in their public decision making. In addition to the general elements of liberal approaches to religious lawmaking just described, further clarification of the differences, both among liberal perspectives and between liberal and communitarian views, may be obtained by considering liberal perceptions of the status of religious lawmakers in relation to that of other citizens.

Liberal Views about Religious Lawmakers

As in the previous section, I first summarize Greenawalt's views of the status of religious lawmakers and then compare these with the views of Audi and Rawls.

Greenawalt's Views of Religious Lawmakers

Greenawalt differs from other liberal theorists in the extent to which he would permit lawmakers to rely on their religious convictions in public policy making. In his earlier writing on this topic, he argues that citizens and legislators should be governed by similar principles of restraint because it would be unfair if legislators could not themselves rely on their religious convictions to the same extent as other citizens (1995: 127) and that "serious incongruity would arise" if public officials were held to a more restrictive standard (1988: 12). However, he did argue that legislators should give greater weight to reasons that are generally available than to those they understand are not.

More recently, Greenawalt has recognized that lawmakers' reliance on religious convictions risks more serious and controversial consequences and greater "dangers of divisiveness and exclusion" (Greenawalt 1990: 1035; 1988: 219, 235). He now claims that the most fundamental distinctions in thinking about the role of religious convictions in public policy are between citizens and public officials because the risks of damaging religious influence are greatest "when public officials explicitly rely on religious grounds" (1990: 1035). Greenawalt contends that this distinction between lawmakers and other citizens is based on an already prevalent "understanding shared by most high officials and many citizens that *serious, practical political discourse* by officials should be nonreligious," even though "it is harder to tell if there is any similar sense that a legislator's ever relying on his or her own religious convictions is inappropriate" (1995: 156).

In addition, because in Greenawalt's view "people have great difficulty trying to face particular political issues free of the push of their religious or other comprehensive views," he thinks "it is doubtful whether one should recommend to ordinary people a self-restraint that is so hard to perform" (1995: 138). Thus, the obligation of public officials to use publicly accessible reasons is greater than those of other citizens (157, 162). Whereas "private individuals should regard themselves as free to rely upon and state religious reasons; public officials acting in their official capacity should rarely state religious reasons as their bases for political decisions, and they should be more hesitant even to rely on religious reasons than private citizens" (Greenawalt 1996a: 630).[5] Instead, "legislators discussing particular issues should mainly employ public reasons" rather than religious ones, that is, "explanations that connect particular religious premises to conclusions of policy" (Greenawalt 1995: 158).

Greenawalt's conclusion that it is important to "a common, equal citizenship" that legislators provide publicly accessible reasons to justify political decisions is consistent with his view that "to demand that other people act in accord with dominant religious beliefs is to promote or impose those beliefs in an impermissible way" (1988: 247). Nonetheless, although legislators "should focus primarily on public reasons . . . we should not expect them systematically to disregard personal reasons and religious grounds" (1996a: 639). As noted earlier, the primary restraint should be on public discourse, not judgment.[6] Nonetheless, Greenawalt maintains that although members of Congress typically do not make religious arguments on the floor of Congress or before their constituents "there is, however, no accepted understanding that they should avoid giving any weight to their own religious convictions and those of constituents in the formulation of their positions" (1996b: 1419).

But whereas "on specific issues, it may be appropriate for legislators to declare that they are affected by underlying religious grounds," Greenawalt argues that they should make their arguments in other terms (1995: 158).[7] As a practical matter, he contends, requiring public reasons "involves only a minor impairment of the religious liberty of legislators" (1996a: 639). In addition, restricting legislators' reliance on their personal religious convictions also is supported by their oath of office, which prohibits legislators from relying on reasons that violate the Constitution (1995: 55, 127). Thus, Greenawalt's current view now seems to be that at a national level, legislators should not even make religious arguments because they are obligated to represent all their constituents.

The obligations of executives are greater than those of legislators, since "they speak for all the people in a fuller sense than any individual legislator" (Greenawalt 1995: 156). Judges also should be more reluctant than legislators to rely on their religious convictions, especially "when he [sic] recognizes that his premises or the positions they yield are not widely shared" (Greenawalt 1988: 241). The nonelected status of the judicial office makes it extremely difficult to remove judges for opposing public opinion or standards of public opinion.

These views about judges diverge from Greenawalt's earlier statements, where he contended that the occasional reliance by judges on their religious beliefs is not improper, especially when publicly accessible reasons are unavailable (1988: 241). More recently, however, Greenawalt argues that in rare instances when judges find public reasons to be evenly balanced and, thus, legitimately "may treat their own religious beliefs as they would other personal sources of judgement" (1996a: 638), that judicial opinions nevertheless should not contain references to their religious premises but instead should be justified solely on the basis of public reasons. He proposes similar requirements for executives performing quasi-judicial determinations (1995: 150; 1988: 239).

What appears to be missing in Greenawalt's more recent view, however, is continued acknowledgment of his original insight that, as religious persons, lawmakers are not different from other citizens. Greenawalt justifies imposing different obligations on public officials than other citizens on the less-than-persuasive ground that whereas "officials are used to making judgments and offering reasons that do not include everything they believe is relevant in their personal lives," that "ordinary citizens are not trained to restrain their judgments and discourse in the manner of judges or legislators" (1996a: 641; 1996b: 1417).

However, by concluding that "ordinary citizens should feel much freer to rely on religious grounds than public officials" and that for many citizens "religious convictions have implications for political issues, and acting to realize these implications is an aspect of the exercise of their religion" (Greenawalt 1996a: 641), Greenawalt fails to account for the reality that some lawmakers also hold religious beliefs on which it is part of their exercise of religion to act. In other words, the arguments that Greenawalt makes for why lesser restrictions should be placed on ordinary religious citizens are also applicable to religious lawmakers. He has not offered a persuasive rationale for differentiating the two categories of persons with respect to the propriety of religious influences on public policy making.

In sum, Greenawalt would allow lawmakers to rely on their religious convictions in their public decision making, but he insists that they must provide publicly accessible reasons to justify their positions, whether or not those positions are actually based on religious reasons. Some exceptions to this requirement hold when publicly accessible reasons are not available, but it is not evident in Greenawalt's most recent formulations to what extent the exceptions apply.

Other Liberal Views about Religious Lawmakers

In spite of its limitations, Greenawalt's differentiation of the obligations of lawmakers and other citizens with respect to religious lawmaking represents a significant advance over the views of Audi and Rawls. In stark contrast to Greenawalt, Audi makes almost no distinction between lawmakers and other citizens (at least those acting in some lawmaking capacity). He would apply his two principles of restraint to "legislators making law, to judges and lawyers interpreting it, and to citizens proposing it" as well as to "government officials carrying out laws and policies . . . to educators . . . and to clergy and laity alike in their activities that affect society as a whole" (1989: 289–90; see also 1993: 701).

There are two main problems with this formulation. First, it effectively leaves many religious believers, including lawmakers, without a way of participating meaningfully in politics short of the denial of their identity as religious persons. It, thereby, privileges the separation of Church and State over the free exercise of religion (see Wertheim 1991: 64). In addition, Audi's specification of those categories of persons who are subject to restrictions on religious lawmaking does not recognize that persons occupying roles as public officials have different and additional obligations from those appropriate for other citizens.

Somewhat similar to Audi, Rawls says the requirement of public reason should apply to citizens and lawmakers engaged in political advocacy, political campaigns, and elections, and "when constitutional essentials and matters of basic justice are at stake" (1993: 215). In his view, because citizens "have an equal share in the corporate political and coercive power of society," they do not have the right to use their comprehensive doctrine backed by "the state's police power to decide constitutional essentials or basic questions of justice" (1993: 61–62). Thus, Rawls also treats citizens like lawmakers for most purposes.

However, in a formulation slightly more nuanced than Audi's view, Rawls does claim that public reason applies in an especially restrictive way to lawmakers, based on their "duty of civility" (1997: 765; see also 1993: 216). In particular, public reason applies with special force to justices of a supreme court in a constitutional democracy with judicial review. The rationale Rawls provides for this distinction is that unlike members of the legislature and executive branches, the position of justices requires that they provide rationales for their decisions that are publicly available (particularly rationales based on the Constitution and relevant statutes and precedents). Thus, they must appeal only to public reason and the principles of political liberalism, and cannot "invoke their own personal morality, nor the ideals and virtues of morality generally . . . [nor] their or other people's religious or philosophical views" (Rawls 1993: 236).

Whereas Rawls would permit citizens and legislators to vote based on their more comprehensive views in other circumstances, he claims that judges, as the "institutional exemplars of public reason," are required to adhere exclusively to the principles of public reason in all of their decisions (1993: 235). And, contrary to Greenawalt, Rawls argues that when "legal arguments seem evenly balanced on both sides, judges cannot simply resolve the case by appealing to their own political views," for to do so would "violate their duty" (1992: lv).

In his essay on "Public Reason," Rawls specifies that public reason applies only in "the public political forum" (1997: 767), which makes it a duty only for those in the public political forum (judges and government officials, especially legislators, chief executives and candidates for public office and their campaign managers) to explain "their reasons for supporting fundamental political positions in terms of the political conception of justice they regard as the most reasonable" (769). In his shift from an exclusive view of public reason to an inclusive view, Rawls now requires citizens to advance public reasons in public debate on political questions but does not require them to exclude nonpublic reasons that support their position. Although an improvement on his earlier position, this standard, like Greenawalt's, continues to be problematic by disadvantaging religious citizens vis-a-vis those who would use secular reasons because they are nonreligious and would do so in any event.

In most respects, Rawls's approach to religious lawmaking is consistent with traditional liberal approaches such as Audi's, which exclude any significant role for religion in lawmaking. However, by limiting the requirement of public reason to the basic foundations of justice and constitutional essentials, Rawls permits religious convictions, along with other comprehensive views, to provide the basis for decisions in other areas. By excluding comprehensive doctrines only as public justifications or defenses of decisions and not as the actual motivation or basis for a decision, Rawls's approach permits a more expansive role for religion within certain parameters than even Greenawalt's.

In contrast to Greenawalt's view that religion is central to moral identity, in Rawls's and Audi's more traditionalist liberal approaches, religious convictions can be excluded (or discounted in the absence of public reasons) from public policy making. For example, Audi claims that persons are able to evaluate the secular or religious character of their motivations and do not need to depend on their religious convictions (1990: 396–97). As an example, he suggests that "if I discover that my religious outlook or even my religious history is responsible for my attitudes toward capital punishment, I may at least be disposed to change my position on what laws we should have, even if my private moral views remain the same" (393).

Audi's assumption that persons can adequately distinguish the religious from the secular reasons for their decisions and that both can and should be motivated to bracket the former reflects the predominant liberal understanding of moral identity as divisible into different, oppositional spheres, secular and religious, one public, the other private. The validity of this understanding is called into question by the narratives of the religious lawmakers discussed in chapter 3. These narratives reveal that the centrality of religion to moral identity varies from person to person. Whereas the views of some lawmakers, such as Cuomo, for the most part conform to liberal notions, the place of religion in relation to moral identity in the self-understandings of lawmakers like Reagan and Noonan clearly does not.

Rawls's view of the role of religion in relation to moral identity is more sympathetic than Audi's, but he still dichotomizes personal identity into public and private spheres and accords priority to the former for purposes of political liberalism (1985: 240–41). This is reflected in Rawls's definition of a person as a "free and equal citizen" (1993: 18). Rawls claims that "in order to fulfill their political role, citizens are viewed as having the intellectual and moral powers appropriate to that role, such as a capacity for a sense of political justice given by a liberal conception *and a capacity to form, follow, and revise their individual doctrines of the good"* (1992: xlvi; emphasis added). Because citizens are able, at least for political purposes, to separate or divorce themselves from their conceptions of the good, including their religious convictions, to examine and revise them, Rawls claims that reliance on one's religious identity and convictions is not necessary for determining one's basic political principles.

Indeed, within Rawls's theory of political liberalism, moral selves are citizens who are expected to divorce themselves from their private religious convictions in the sphere of public decision making, at least with regard to constitutional essentials (see Moore 1993: 132; Galston 1991: 153, 291). Rawls admits that "people do not normally distinguish between comprehensive and public reasons; nor do they normally affirm the ideal of public reason," yet he assumes that "people can be brought to recognize these distinctions in particular cases" (1993: 251).

Rawls seems unaware that many religious adherents do not hold a conception of persons as "reasonable free and equal citizens," as independent of their ends, and so will not be persuaded by his rationale. Rawls's conception of persons, as Galston points out, "tends to exclude individuals and groups that do not place a high value on personal autonomy and revisable plans of life" (Galston 1991:153). Political liberalism's requirement for public reason also has been criticized as asking too much of citizens who want a "religiously integrated existence," who want to be able to see all their actions and relationships as based on their religious commitments rather than on "what they have in common with those who do not share their commitments" (Weithman 1997: 21). Rawls's critics are rightly skeptical of his optimism that "citizens will judge (by their comprehensive view) that political values are normally (though not always) ordered prior to, or outweigh, whatever nonpolitical values may conflict with them" (Griffin 1997: 309).

Although Greenawalt's belief in the separability of religious convictions from other dimensions of an individual's moral identity is more qualified than either Audi's or Rawls's, he nonetheless still expects that citizens should rely on publicly accessible reasons to justify decisions when they are available. The priority that Greenawalt accords to the individual as citizen rather than religious adherent reflects liberal presuppositions about moral selves as able to segregate different aspects of their identities that are similar to those of Rawls and Audi. In particular, like Rawls, Greenawalt justifies according priority to the person as citizen on the grounds that without good citizens to contribute to a stable framework for government, there could be no guarantee of the free exercise necessary for persons to be good religious adherents. Although this is a plausible rationale, it is somewhat inapposite to the prior issue of the ontological construction of self-identity.

In addition, Greenawalt's position in *Religious Convictions and Political Choice* that it is unreasonable to ask persons to forego reliance on their religious convictions in political decision making where adequate publicly accessible reasons are unavailable (1988: 155–56) is somewhat weakened by the consideration that it is then also unreasonable to ask them to forego such reliance when adequate publicly accessible reasons are *present*. That is, the rationale for allowing citizens to rely on their religious convictions when publicly accessible reasons are absent is that of necessity, that decisions must be made on some basis and, if not publicly accessible reasons, then religious reasons are better than no reasons at all. However, all of the reasons for excluding religious reasons in circumstances when publicly accessible reasons are available also obtain when such reasons are absent. The basis for the distinction in the type of reasons is merely prudential and not moral. Further, the reasons for allowing reliance on religious convictions when publicly accessible reasons are not available—the close if not inherent connection between a person's moral identity and their religious beliefs—also apply when publicly accessible reasons are present. Thus, there is no persuasive basis in Greenawalt's proposal for distinguishing between circumstances when publicly accessible reaons are present or not present. Reliance on religious convictions should either be acceptable in both types of situation or in neither one.

Despite these logical problems with Greenawalt's proposal, his appraisal that it is often extremely difficult, if not impossible, for decision makers to assess the basis of their motivations and beliefs (e.g., Greenawalt 1988: 30, 152, 180) is more plausible than Rawls's and Audi's assumptions that the self is conscious and aware enough of its decision-making processes to disentangle the various strands of secular and personal motivations, reasons, and justifications that may be offered for a political decision; to separate out those that are religious; and to rely only on those that are not.

Comparison of Liberal Proposals for Religious Lawmaking Generally

By comparing Greenawalt's approach to religious lawmaking with those of Rawls and Audi, we can see that his is, overall, more attentive to the role of religion in the life of both citizens and lawmakers and less attentive to plural-ism. Because liberal approaches to religious lawmaking are primarily con-cerned with protecting the individual freedoms and liberties of an increas-ingly pluralistic and secular population from overreaching by government or other powerful interest groups, they have tended to overlook how important religion may be to the moral identity of individual religious believers. In fact, Paul Weithman observes that "liberalism has historically accommodated reli-gious diversity by mischaracterizing the role religious beliefs and organiza-tions play in the lives of their adherents" (1994: 272).

By recognizing, if somewhat erratically, the constitutive role that religious convictions may play in the moral identity of persons, Greenawalt thereby im-proves on conventional liberal assumptions about the self. He recognizes the practical problems, as well as the theoretical ones, of demanding that persons, including public officials, leave their religious convictions in the private sphere when they are acting in public decision-making roles. But he fails to en-sure that religious lawmaking will not infringe on the Citizenship Rights of others, especially of women and religious minorities, particularly in cases where publicly accessible reasons are not available. The examination of liberal approaches to religious lawmaking on abortion shows how these problems negatively impact on women's Citizenship Rights

Liberal Approaches to Abortion Lawmaking

In this part of the chapter, I examine how the liberal theorists discussed previ-ously approach abortion lawmaking in particular. This investigation shows how liberal approaches to religious lawmaking ignore the gender and power inequalities in religious lawmaking, problems that are not obvious in the gen-eral outlines of their theories.

The traditional liberal principle of maximizing individual liberty aligns most liberal theorists with a prochoice position on abortion regulation, one which requires the exclusion of religious influences that would restrict legal abortion rights. Rawls's and Audi's views of religious lawmaking about abor-tion reflect this mainstream liberal view, whereas Greenawalt's are somewhat more communitarian in character. As in the previous sections, I begin this dis-cussion by describing Greenawalt's views and then compare and contrast them to those of Audi and Rawls.

Greenawalt's Views of Religious Lawmaking on Abortion

Whereas other liberal approaches to religious lawmaking on abortion are more sensitive to moral and social pluralism and somewhat more sensitive to the gendered aspects of abortion regulation than are communitarian ones, they tend to lack adequate respect for the religious identity of lawmakers whose convictions counsel or compel them to favor restricting abortion rights. Greenawalt's proposal reflects the mirror opposite. Greenawalt's analysis of abortion in *Religious Convictions and Political Choice* (1988) is premised on his claim that abortion policy—like other "borderlines of status issues" that involve the determinations of the protection owed to nonhuman entities (animals and the environment)—cannot be determined on the basis of publicly accessible reasons alone.

For Greenawalt, the "nub of the question whether a restrictive abortion law can be justified turns on when a fetus warrants significant protection from society" (1988: 120–21). Because of the disagreement about the moral status of the fetus that has made the abortion issue "so intractable" (121), Greenawalt concludes that publicly accessible reasons are inconclusive in determining appropriate restrictions on abortion. Based on this conclusion, Greenawalt contends that "the religious believer has a powerful argument that he should be able to rely on his religiously informed bases for judgment" on this issue (136–37).

Greenawalt rejects giving common reasons precedence over religious values in the abortion debate because doing so would, in his view, privilege rationality in an inappropriate manner, "given the range and complexity of moral judgments that individuals and societies can make" (1988: 253) and would require making distinctions between these two types of reasons that "would be exceedingly difficult for legislators and courts to apply in practice" (253). Thus, contrary to his general approach to religious lawmaking, including its priority for publicly accessible reasons, Greenawalt holds that lawmakers can appropriately rely on their religious convictions to determine the moral status of the fetus.

Greenawalt defends his position against the argument that the determination of abortion regulations on the basis of religious convictions constitutes an impermissible imposition of one's own beliefs on another (1988: 168). Unlike a situation where homosexual acts are prohibited "simply because they are deemed morally wrong," he claims, a religiously based abortion restriction "informs a judgment of who counts as a member of the community. Once that judgment is made, the restriction on abortion is a protection of the most obvious and vital interest, life, that members of the community have" (168).

It is unclear whether Greenawalt would require lawmakers to justify their decisions regarding abortion regulations on publicly accessible reasons, consistent with his proposal in relation to other political decisions. Even assuming he would, however, his proposal regarding abortion favors a more expansive role for religion in political decision making than either traditional liberal approaches or even his own general proposal would permit.

Greenawalt also contends that restrictive abortion laws premised on religious convictions would not violate the First Amendment since a "political decision to protect fetuses does not establish any religious institution, practice, or doctrine" (1988: 253; see also 1993a: 506). This conclusion reflects an unduly narrow interpretation of what constitutes religion under the Constitution and is again in direct contradiction to Greenawalt's general sensitivity to the Establishment Concerns generated by religious lawmaking.

Contrary to Greenawalt's assertions, many restrictive abortion laws do in fact promote a metaphysical view of the fetus as a person that is based on religious beliefs, as the cases and statutes discussed in chapter 2 showed. Incorporating such views into restrictive abortion legislation entails enacting religious views of the person into law. The resulting laws establish a religious view in the sense of making it a governmentally endorsed and enforced policy. Greenawalt's view of religious lawmaking on abortion contradicts his own principle that it is impermissible to "demand that other people act in accord with dominant religious beliefs" (1988: 247).

Greenawalt's analysis also erroneously assumes that the only relevant issue in abortion lawmaking is the moral status of the fetus. By according primary importance to the moral status of the fetus, Greenawalt fails to consider other significant dimensions of the abortion issue in his analysis, beginning with his disregard for the moral agency of pregnant women; their religious and/or moral beliefs about the pregnancy, the fetus, and abortion; their reproductive autonomy, especially in a sexist and patriarchal society where violations of equal protection rights are likely; and the particular interpersonal and socio-economic facts relevant to any particular pregnancy.

Greenawalt's proposal regarding religious lawmaking on abortion also fails to provide protections for women's Citizenship Rights and interests. Assume that a legislator has relied on her religious convictions in voting for abortion legislation that denies the use of public funds for Medicaid abortions. Under Greenawalt's proposal, so long as the legislator can come up with *some* publicly accessible reasons, such as the need to conserve state funds for deficit reduction, her decision is acceptable, regardless of whether her *actual* motivation and/or rationale are religious.

As chapter 2's discussion of the Supreme Court's Establishment Clause cases reveals, lawmakers can easily cloak religiously motivated rationales for restrictive abortion laws in nominally secular justifications, such as the State's interest in promoting respect for human life. Because some secular defense or justification will usually be available, the religious principles of a dominant religious group may determine legislative outcomes under Greenawalt's scheme. It consequently does not go far enough to protect women from the harms that religious lawmaking on abortion may produce. Notwithstanding the carefully balanced and nuanced way that Greenawalt's proposals handle the tensions between moral identity and pluralism in the context of religious lawmaking, his approach to abortion lawmaking fails to adequately protect women's Citizenship Rights.

An additional problem in Greenawalt's analysis of abortion is his failure to consider the responsibilities of lawmakers as public officials to protect the Citizenship Rights of pregnant women. In his recent work, Greenawalt acknowledges that "most officials, especially higher officials, come from dominant groups in society. Their feelings will not usually be specially sympathetic to the oppressed or powerless. Allowing the officials to give fuller expression to their own individuality might lead to poorer treatment of those who are genuinely out of the mainstream" (1995: 37). As chapter 3 revealed, this actually does occur in religious lawmaking on abortion. Yet Greenawalt has failed to apply his observation in the specific context of abortion lawmaking. Audi's and Rawls's approaches to religious lawmaking on abortion better protect women's constitutional rights and interests.

Other Liberal Views of Religious Lawmaking on Abortion

In contrast to Greenawalt's priority for religious lawmakers at the expense of pregnant women, Rawls and Audi focus on protecting the values of respect for religious pluralism and the individual autonomy of pregnant women in their analysis of abortion. Applying his principle of secular resolution to abortion, Audi concludes that since there can be no knowledge or justified belief about the moral status of the fetus at a early stage of pregnancy, abortion is "an epistemically undecidable public policy issue," and since it is an issue involving liberty interests, it is not morally permissible to prohibit early term abortions (1990: 397). The danger of offending or alienating people if society were "colored by a religious agenda as people look to their religious views and attitudes as aids to resolving the issues" (Audi 1990: 395) is more compelling for Audi than the potential benefits of using religious convictions to resolve borderlines of status issues such as abortion. In addition, Audi is more optimistic than Greenawalt that many "borderlines of status" issues can be resolved by secular considerations "in a reasonable amount of time" (393).

Rawls's views are similar. Premised on the assumption that abortion involves "either a constitutional essential or a matter of basic justice," Rawls concludes that the issue is one for public reason to apply to, not one that should be resolved by comprehensive doctrines, including religious views (1993: 243 n. 32). For Rawls, any reasonable balance of the relevant political values, "due respect for human life, the ordered reproduction of political society over time, and the equality of women as equal citizens," results in a decision upholding woman's right to determine whether or not to have a first trimester abortion (243 n. 32). He argues that at this early stage of pregnancy, the political value of the equality of women is overriding and religious views are inappropriate considerations. For Rawls, any comprehensive doctrine that would exclude women's privacy right is unreasonable as well as "cruel and oppressive" (243 n. 32).

With respect to ignoring the potentially negative impact of religion on women's rights outside of the core issue of abortion, however, Rawls's approach to religious lawmaking is similar to Greenawalt's. Despite his prochoice conclusions on abortion, Rawls claims that a liberal conception of justice may have to allow for some traditional gendered division of labor within families, provided it is fully voluntary and does not result from or lead to injustice. For

Rawls, to say that the division of labor is fully voluntary means that it is adopted by people on the basis of their religion, which from a political point of view is voluntary (1997: 792).

The application of a voluntary standard to women without additional safeguards ignores the multiple constraints on women's autonomy that complicate the analysis of voluntariness, especially in relation to abortion. Since women have been excluded from participation in the formation of religious practices and traditions for centuries, how is it that women's acceptance of such gendered division of labor can be said to be voluntary? Thus, while Rawls's view generally is more sensitive to gender inequalities than Greenawalt's, he falls short in his analysis of the potentially negative impacts of religion on women's rights in the context of abortion.

Summary of Liberal Views on Abortion Lawmaking

Although Audi and Rawls reach conclusions about religious lawmaking on abortion that better protect against gender inequalities than Greenawalt's and, consequently, also better protect the value of respect for religious pluralism, they are also deficient in certain respects. First, although they both recognize the liberty interests of pregnant women, they fail to acknowledge the full range of women's Citizenship Rights and interests that are endangered by religious lawmaking on abortion. It does not appear that this deficiency is an inevitable consequence of liberal theory, however, but only an oversight of the particular theorists discussed here.

In addition, both Audi and Rawls assume that it is both possible and appropriate for lawmakers to put aside their religious convictions in favor of public reason when making abortion policy. In this respect, they fail to account for the central role that religion may have in the moral identity of lawmakers. Therefore, none of these liberal proposals accords due consideration to both the religious identity of lawmakers *and* the Citizenship Rights of pregnant women.

Summary and Conclusions

The liberal proposals discussed here for addressing the dilemma of religious lawmaking are concerned appropriately with the protection of religious pluralism and the rights of all citizens, especially religious minorities, to the free exercise of religion. In the process of protecting these worthy principles, however, liberal theorists tend to neglect the fundamental role that religion may play in the moral identity of the nation's lawmakers.

As we have seen, liberal approaches to religious lawmaking reflect problematic assumptions about the nature of religion as voluntarist, of religious convictions as a matter of choice rather than compulsion, of religion as a private rather than a public matter, and of the moral self as divisible into private and public aspects. Liberal theorists give inadequate consideration to the central role that religion may play in shaping the moral identity of citizens, including lawmakers. As Carter frames the issue, "the citizen whose public self is guided by religious faith might reasonably ask why the will of any of the brilliant philosophers of the liberal tradition . . . is more relevant to moral decisions than the will of God" (1993: 226). Liberal proposals for addressing religious lawmaking would be well served by greater attention to the actual significance of religion to many lawmakers, as the examples in chapter 3 have demonstrated.

In several respects, Greenawalt's approach, which permits a greater role for religion in lawmaking, is an improvement over more traditional liberal theories. His claim that certain moral issues simply cannot be decided without reliance on religious convictions presents a more realistic perspective than those of Rawls and Audi, who assume that it is both possible and desirable to avoid at least direct reliance on religious views in the political realm with respect to certain matters. Yet even Greenawalt's proposals are inadequate, especially in their failure to recognize or protect the Citizenship Rights and interests of pregnant women.

In the following chapter, we see that communitarian theorists are guilty of some of the same oversights, despite their sharp divergence from liberal perspectives with respect to their main proposals for addressing religious lawmaking. Whereas the main deficiency with liberal approaches is their failure to give due regard to the central role that religion plays in the moral decision making of some lawmakers, the main problem with communitarian proposals is their failure to accord sufficient value to religious and gender differences.

FIVE

Communitarian Views of Religious Lawmaking

In the previous chapter, we examined the limitations of the predominant liberal approaches to resolving the dilemma posed by religious lawmaking. We discovered that while liberal proposals do a fine job of protecting the values of religious pluralism and individual liberties in most areas, they fail to recognize or respect the centrality religion may have in the lives of lawmakers. It is thus not surprising to find that their proposals ignore the free exercise rights of lawmakers to practice their own religious beliefs in the context of their public decision making, at least to the extent that other citizens can. Although liberal theorists differ in their sensitivity to gender inequalities when applying their theories to abortion lawmaking, a third problem, evident in Greenawalt's proposal in particular and Rawls's to a lesser extent, is their inadequate recognition of the disadvantaging effects that religion may have on women's Citizenship Rights.

This chapter turns to examine the very different approaches to religious lawmaking taken by communitarian theorists. Just as chapter 4 focused on Kent Greenawalt's proposal as among the most sympathetic liberal approaches to concerns of moral identity as well as those of pluralism, the discussion here centers on the work of law professor Michael Perry as among the most respectful of communitarian proposals in regard to religious pluralism.

In general, whereas Greenawalt's approach to religious lawmaking showed more sensitivity to communitarian concerns for religious identity than other liberal theorists, Perry's reflects more sensitivity to liberal emphases on religious pluralism and difference. In addition, as noted previously, Perry's theories provide a particularly apt basis for comparison with Greenawalt's because both are sympathetic to religion and its importance in the moral decision making of public officials as well as ordinary citizens.[1] To show the main ways in which Perry's particular theories diverge from more traditional communitarian ones, I compare them with more traditional communitarian views, especially those of the political philosopher Michael Sandel.

To facilitate comparison of communitarian with liberal approaches, this chapter parallels the format of chapter 4, first discussing communitarian approaches to religious lawmaking, including specific views of the role of religion in relation to moral identity and the obligations of lawmakers vis-à-vis other citizens, and then focusing on communitarian proposals for addressing religious lawmaking on abortion in particular. After pointing out the main inadequacies with communitarian approaches at the close of the chapter, I summarize the main limitations of both theoretical approaches for resolving the issues posed by religious lawmaking and outline the prerequisites for an adequate alternative.

Communitarian Approaches to Religious Lawmaking

As with liberal theorists, communitarian thinkers are not a uniform group, although in general their main concerns tend to revolve around their disagreements and discontent with liberalism. In contrast to liberal preoccupations with individual rights and the principles of liberty, communitarian concerns focus on social life and the principles of community, tradition, virtue, and social cohesion. Whereas liberal thinkers tend to see the moral identity of individuals as independent of and preexisting society, communitarians envision the moral self as fundamentally a socially constructed and relational entity and envision personal identity as largely a product of social relations.

Where the liberal theorist focuses on the individual as the appropriate frame of reference for thinking about moral identity and lawmaking, the communitarian looks, as the term suggests, to the community. Whereas liberal theory discounts the significance of religion to the moral identity of believers, communitarian thought often highlights this aspect of persons in arguing in favor of according religion a significant role in politics and lawmaking. These differences with liberalism, as I demonstrate, result in a different vision of how to resolve the dilemma of religious lawmaking. The following sections examine how these ideas apply in the context of Perry's and Sandel's views about religious lawmaking.

Perry's Approach to Religious Lawmaking

Perry has developed at least four different formulations of the appropriate relationship between politics and religion, beginning with his strategy for "deliberative transformative politics," developed in *Morality, Politics, and Law* (1988). "Ecumenical political dialogue" is the subject of Perry's 1991 book, *Love and Power: The Role of Religion and Morality in American Politics*. The third approach is an "inclusive ideal," developed in an essay published after *Love and Power* (1993). Finally, in *Religion in Politics* (1997), Perry offers a fourth proposal, based on the principles of "secular support" and a "non-establishment norm." Although Perry has not explicitly stated that any of the later proposals are intended to replace or revise the earlier ones, I assume that he considers his most recent proposals to be improvements over his earlier ones to the extent that they are inconsistent.

Each of these proposals is problematic in its own way. Because Perry radically shifts back and forth in his view of what religion is and how it should relate to politics and lawmaking, describing his view of religious lawmaking accurately is something of a challenge.

The first proposal, for a deliberative transformative politics, is Perry's prescription for the problems presented by moral pluralism. Perry recognizes the problems posed by pluralism for religion in politics. He acknowledges that the United States is a "morally and religiously pluralistic" nation (1991: 86), encompassing many different moral communities and moral traditions, "each with its own set of basic beliefs about human good, about human possibilities and human satisfaction, beliefs constitutive of different conceptions of human flourishing" (1988: 37–38), and that respect for pluralism entails the recognition that visions of the good are different for different people (6). Further, he recognizes that citizens and government representatives belong to at least two different communities: their own moral community and the "morally pluralistic political community" (106).

Despite his acknowledgment that such pluralism gives rise to "competing convictions," Perry optimistically assumes, at least in his proposal for deliberative transformative politics, that shared understandings are still possible, even within morally pluralistic communities (1988: 36, 39–48). This includes the possibility of commonly arriving at a determinate conception of human "flourishing" (15–16). Using communitarian terminology, Perry claims that ascertaining what constitutes flourishing is a social enterprise based on moral beliefs framed in communities and informed by tradition (12 n. 21). Using a religious frame of reference, Perry contends that adjudication among diverse moral cultures is possible, that "any moral community for which love of neighbor (*agape*) is a constitutive ideal—and surely that includes many moral/ religious communities in the United States—should understand that ecumenical openness to the Other in discourse facilitates (as well as expresses) such love" (51–52). Indeed, he assumes the possibility that deliberative transformative politics can result in a moral consensus on controversial issues such as abortion.[2]

In this early approach to religious involvement in politics, Perry envisions politics as an ongoing moral dialogue with others based on religious conceptions of the good (1988: 153). Rather than separate religion and politics, he argues that religion should be put into dialogue with politics in the context of constitutional aspirations. He claims that "there is a need for 'a religious or philosophical preface to politics'" (87). Yet it is the Constitution that is to provide both the basis for a moral community and the standards of judgment necessary for the polity to engage in moral dialogue about issues, including determination of the good or flourishing for the political community as a whole.

I discuss the problems with Perry's proposal for deliberative transformative politics further later in connection with the general problems with his approaches to religious lawmaking. A couple of points specific to this proposal should be noted here, however. First, Perry's effort to construct a proposal that would lead to the creation of common understandings and/or consensus rather than imposing them is laudable, especially given the failure of most communitarians to adequately address the fact of moral and religious pluralism in the contemporary United States. Thus, his proposal to base deliberative transformative politics in the Constitution is most appropriate, both because it is applicable to all citizens and because of its nonreligious—and, thus, neutral—character.

However, to the extent that this early proposal for religious lawmaking proposes the use of religious convictions as the basis for arriving at common understandings, it reflects an inadequate recognition of the depth and extent of moral and religious pluralism in the contemporary United States, as well as unrealistically optimistic assumptions about the possibilities for moral dialogue and consensus on the basis of religion.

Perry's perspective on religious lawmaking in his second proposal regarding religious lawmaking for ecumenical political dialogue shifts significantly from that for a deliberative transformative politics. This second approach is foreshadowed in Perry's framing of the question as "not *whether* to mix religion and politics" but "*how* to mix them" (1991: 82). He describes this proposal as concerning the moral beliefs which representatives of a "morally pluralistic political community" should rely on in deciding public policy issues, particularly those that involve using the law to coerce persons against their own choices (1988: 77–78, 98). It is both a "dialogic and communitarian" method for finding common ground that transcends local or sectarian differences to cultivate political community (1991: 45–47).

Perry describes ecumenical political dialogue as an attempt to find a "middle ground" between the position of those like Greenawalt—who he claims "would largely exclude religious-moral discourse from political-justificatory practice"—and those who "would bring religious-moral discourse to bear in a sectarian, divisive way" (1991: 5, 48). Perry criticizes liberalism for "an especially insidious, if unintended" effort to repress the "essentially political nature of religion" and to "marginalize the role of religious (and other) conceptions of human good in political-justificatory discourse" (81–82). In his view, a politics "from which disputed beliefs about human good are excluded . . . is impossibly restricted" (29, 42).

This second proposal is premised on the claim that a moral life requires an affirmation of religious faith (Perry 1991: 36–41). Perry assumes that most people are religious in the sense of being "someone for whom life is ultimately meaningful" (75). He also defines *religion* more narrowly as "a vision of final and radical reconciliation, a set of beliefs about how one is or can be bound or connected to the world—to the 'other' and to 'nature'—and, above all, to Ultimate Reality in a profoundly intimate and ultimately meaningful way" (75).

Because religion is such an integral part of the American tradition and sense of community, Perry contends that religion necessarily plays an important role in the determination of public policy on moral issues. Religion is a necessary component of political morality, he argues, because only a religious understanding, such as the Christian concept of agape, can provide the basis for a commitment to others (1991: 140).[3]

Perry thus describes ecumenical political dialogue as a "religious politics" in the sense that "persons with religious convictions about the good or fitting way for human beings to live their lives rely on those convictions, not only in *making* political choices but in publicly *deliberating* about and in publicly *justifying* such choices" (1991: 112; emphasis added). In addition, ecumenical political dialogue is religious in the sense that it is "the religious traditions of American society, in particular the biblical heritage," that have provided its fundamental standards and continue to inform American political morality and our political institutions and practices (88). Consequently, the first of Perry's two parameters for the role for religion in politics is established by the biblical heritage that he claims is already embedded in our political and moral practices and institutions, that is, what is already part of "our tradition" (99–100).

Ignoring the non-publicly accessible character of many religious beliefs, Perry argues that because religion is inextricable from politics, politics must involve, at least in part, a determination of the credibility of our religious convictions. Ecumenical political dialogue makes provision for this determination by what Perry calls the two main "existential prerequisites" of "fallibilism" and "pluralism" (1991: 99–100). Perry contends that what is most central and critical about religion, that is, faith, is fallibilistic (because it does not necessarily involve consent to creedal propositions), even though religious beliefs may not be because they are "historically contingent," and thus "relative and provisional" (73–74, 100–101).

The prerequisite of fallibilism requires citizens to advance their religious beliefs "as something other than unchanging and unquestionable" in order to participate intelligibly in political dialogue (Perry 1991: 104–5). It requires us "to let our religious beliefs be tested by others who do not share them, and be ready and willing to revise them" (1988: 183). Seemingly without reference to any fundamentalist religious tradition, Perry claims that many moral communities "acknowledge . . . the provisional and therefore revisable character of their beliefs and thus allow for, even encourage, the exercise of self-critical rationality" (30).[4]

In addition to fallibilism and pluralism, ecumenical political dialogue involves the two "dialogical virtues" of "public intelligibility" and "public accessibility" (Perry 1991: 105). The former involves "translating one's position, to the extent possible, into a shared (mediating) language" (105–6). The latter is "the habit of trying to defend one's position in a nonsectarian or nonauthoritarian manner" (105–6). Perry asserts but fails to demonstrate that requiring public accessibility does not present "an insurmountable obstacle for religious persons who would bring their deepest convictions about the human to bear in political dialogue" (108). Perry contends that ecumenical political dialogue is fairer than Greenawalt's definition of public accessibility because it does not disadvantage controversial religious premises over nonreligious ones or privilege the rational over the nonrational (120) and because it allows religious argument that meets his standard of public accessibility (which is somewhat less restrictive than Greenawalt's) to be "admitted to the public square" (111).

Although it may be accurate that Perry's second approach would allow more religious participation in public and political dialogue, it is premised upon inaccurate appraisals of what religion is and how citizens are religious. In particular, Perry's definition of "authentic" religion in ecumenical political dialogue as public and willing to engage in self-critical rationality excludes a number of American religious groups that fail to meet these criteria, such as those that accept the inerrancy of scripture (see Smolin 1991: 1067, 1077, 1079). Traditions that fall outside of Perry's definition of religion include "theologically conservative forms of American Christianity" (Smolin 1991: 1067, 1079), Orthodox Jews, the Amish, and fundamentalists (McConnell 1989: 1509; see Levinson 1991: 2073).

Michael McConnell points out that many aspects of religion are not rational and that "it is not even clear that posing the question ('Is it rational?') makes sense for a belief system in which faith, piety, charisma, love, esthetics, mystery, or wonder plays the central role" (1989: 1506). Smolin notes that ecumenical political dialogue "requires religious believers to enter into dialogue with a willingness to renounce their most cherished religious beliefs. The process of dialogue, in other words, must mean more to them than their religious beliefs" (1991: 1075).

Besides misrepresenting the character of many religious traditions, Perry's definition of religion in terms of biblical heritage is both inaccurate and disrespectful of the non–Judeo-Christian faiths of many Americans. In addition, his assumption that religion is based on belief in God (1998: 3) excludes nontheistic and nonmonotheistic religious adherents. These problems suggest either an inadequate consideration of religious pluralism in America and/or an inadequate respect for religious minorities.

Because these definitions exclude all those citizens who are not members of "authentic" religious communities from participating in political-moral discourse, Perry's willingness to include the entirety of the American religious landscape in his proposals is questionable. In addition, if religion is an inextricable part of moral identity, as Perry claims, then it is presumably so not only for members of the "embedded" religions he chooses to focus on but for those members of less embedded religions as well, such as members of more recent religious arrivals.

Perry presents his third proposal, for an inclusivist ideal, as an alternative to the liberal "exclusivist ideal" of purported neutrality, which excludes all controversial moral beliefs (1993: 712). He shares with other communitarians the view that the liberal principle of government neutrality is an impossible fiction (1988: 57). In addition, requiring strict neutrality would be unfair because it "would exclude much of what is most important to a religious adherent's web of beliefs while allowing most of what is most important to a secularist" (1991: 10).

By unfairly privileging rationality, liberal views place persons with serious religious convictions at a severe disadvantage politically (Perry 1991: 10–14). In contrast, the inclusivist ideal "lets everyone rely on her relevant convictions," including their religious convictions (15). The inclusivist model enables citizens to make political choices that cannot be defended on a nonreligious basis.[5]

In contrast to his earlier proposals for deliberative transformative politics and ecumenical political dialogue, which imposed limitations on the types of religious justifications that might validly be offered, Perry's more recent argument for the inclusivist ideal is that there are no good reasons for excluding religious beliefs of any sort, regardless of whether they meet the requirements of public accessibility or those of fallibilism and pluralism. This shift in view appears to coincide with diminished optimism regarding the possibility of a shared perspective. Further evidence of a growing pessimism is evidenced in Perry's opinion that "the possibility that we Americans can resolve all or even many of the basic political controversies that engage and divide us solely on the basis of shared moral beliefs is very doubtful, given the indeterminacy of many shared moral beliefs" (1993: 708).

Despite the elements of a chastened realism in Perry's third proposal, his defense of the inclusivist ideal rests on the unsubstantiated basis that reliance on religious beliefs for political choices "do not inevitably deny to those who reject . . . the beliefs the respect due them as fellow citizens" (1993: 714). In contrast, he claims that the exclusivist ideal inevitably creates two classes of citizens: those whose basic beliefs are allowed in political choices as first class and those whose beliefs are excluded as second class (716–17).

Perry concludes his defense of the inclusive ideal by affirming four premises: (1) religious discourse in public should play more of a role in "public culture" than in "public argument specifically about political issues," (2) some religious claims should be rejected as bad theology, (3) "our politics and law should aspire to be tolerant of moral and religious differences rather than moralistic," and (4) some kinds of religious participation in politics are bad citizenship (1993: 726–27). He does not specify how much more of a role is appropriate for religion in public as opposed to political discourse.

Regarding the fourth premise in particular, Perry leaves unspecified what kinds of religious participation in politics would be bad citizenship. While these premises are far less radical and more liberal sounding in their tenor than either of the two earlier proposals, they are, nonetheless, embedded within an approach that provides no effective safeguards against the potential harms of religious lawmaking. After all, the inclusivist ideal itself endorses the position that at least some political choices appropriately can be based on and justified by religious beliefs, regardless of how publicly accessible or widely shared they are or whether they are made by lawmakers or other citizens.

This third proposal is, then, problematic for a number of reasons. It seems to embody a reactive stance to the difficulties of forging moral agreement in an environment of religious pluralism. Although he more clearly recognizes the problems presented by pluralism, Perry's proposed solution is a kind of free-for-all for religion in the political arena, a proposal that is especially disadvantaging for the interests of traditionally underrepresented groups, including those of religious minorities and women.

In his most recent proposal to use the principles of a nonestablishment norm and secular support to determine the appropriate role of religion in politics, Perry seems to have again turned to a more liberal approach that recognizes and accounts for the significance of religious pluralism. Like Greenawalt, Perry now appears to endorse the distinction between relying on religious arguments in public discussion and debate and justifying decisions on the basis of religious grounds. In contrast to the more expansive definitions of religion in his earlier proposals, Perry here offers a more traditional definition of religious belief as "a belief either that God exists or about the nature, activity or will of God" (1998: 3).

There are two aspects to this most recent proposal, one based in law and the other in "nonconstitutional political morality" (Perry 1998: 15). The first applies to government. The second applies to individual lawmakers and so is discussed later in connection with religious lawmakers. In the first aspect, "the nonestablishment norm *does* forbid government to base political choices on religious arguments in this sense . . . if government wants to make a political choice, including one about the morality of human conduct, it [may] do so only on the basis of a secular argument" (1997: 33). He specifies that "if the only reason or reasons that can support the political choice are religious . . . then government has undeniably imposed religion on those persons whom the choice coerces. This is so whether or not the political choice compels persons to engage in what is conventionally understood as an act of religious worship" (36). He also recognizes that even if laws do not violate the nonestablishment norm, they may still violate some other constitutional requirement (37).

In his greater respect for religious pluralism, Perry now sounds far more liberal than communitarian. Indeed, Perry argues in a 1998 essay that "Religiously based insights, values and arguments at some point must be rendered persuasive to the wider civil public. . . . It does violence to the fabric of pluralism to expect acceptance of such an argument in the wider public arena. When a religious moral claim will affect the wider public, it should be proposed in a fashion which that public can evaluate, accept or reject on its own terms" (29, see also Perry 1998: 34). Even given a greater recognition of pluralism, however, this proposal still reflects a communitarian assumption that there is a wider public which operates on the basis of "its own terms" (singular). It fails to reflect awareness that this wider public is itself plural and diverse, encompassing many different political and religious sensibilities rather than a single one. It also fails to ensure that religious influences on lawmaking will not infringe the Citizenship Rights and interests of others by requiring that secular reasons are adequate to justify the lawmaking on nonreligious grounds.

With this most recent proposal regarding religious lawmaking, Perry has apparently shifted his thinking 180 degrees, to a more liberal-sounding perspective. What he gains is an emphasis on respect for religious and moral pluralism, but what has been lost is his earlier recognition that religion may be such an inextricable part of the moral identity of lawmakers that they are unwilling or unable to offer secular rationales for their positions.

Despite the many differences among Perry's various proposals for religious lawmaking, one thread they share in common is an underlying conception of the moral self as thoroughly social. Because this aspect of Perry's proposals is shared with those of other communitarian thinkers, I postpone discussion of it until after describing them.

Other Communitarian Approaches to Religious Lawmaking

Sandel's approach to religious lawmaking is similar in several respects to Perry's. Perhaps most significantly, it is premised on a similar conception of moral identity. In his view, we begin life in interdependent relationships with others and only later develop into distinct individual selves (1982: 53). Community provides moral selves with commitments and with "a mode of self-understanding, a shared way of life that partly defines the identity of the participants" (1993: 485; see also Sandel 1982: 179). Indeed, Sandel critiques Rawls's contrary assumption that "we are distinct individuals first, and *then* we form relationships and engage in co-operative arrangements with others" (1982: 133). He contends that the assumptions of Rawls's conception of the self rules out the possibility that the good of community could be constitutive of the self or transform its identity (64–65).

Because, according to his "constitutive conception," members of a community view their identity as partly defined and constituted by that community, Sandel suggests that religious identity cannot and should not be separated from politics (1982: 183). This position is based on the view that it is not possible for individuals to conceive of themselves as independent of their aims and attachments "without great cost to those loyalties and convictions whose moral force consists partly in the fact that living by them is inseparable from understanding ourselves as the particular persons we are—as members of this family or community or nation or people" (179). For some persons, he argues, religion is not a voluntary choice but an involuntary commitment (1993: 491).

According to Sandel, the liberal perspective, which conceptualizes religion as one among the many values that an independent self may have, is shortsighted because it "may miss the role that religion plays in the lives of those for whom the observance of religious duties is a constitutive end, essential to their good and indispensable to their identity" (1993: 492–93). He claims that understanding religion as obligatory rather than voluntary is closer to the views of Madison and Jefferson (the predominant influences on the religion clauses of the First Amendment) than liberal understandings of religion as voluntarist.

Given his view of the centrality of religion to self-identity, Sandel criticizes what he characterizes as the liberal democratic "impulse to banish moral and religious discourse from public life" (1988: 23), as well as the liberal justification that government neutrality regarding religion is necessary in order to accord individual citizens the freedom to choose their own religious convictions (1993: 489–90). He rejects the view that government and law can be neutral regarding matters of morality (1989b: 529) and dismisses what he calls a liberal argument that morality should not be legislated because it "is merely subjective" (1984a: 15).

Communitarian Views about Religious Lawmakers

In general, communitarian approaches to religious lawmaking do not differentiate among lawmakers and other citizens or consider how religious lawmakers' roles as public officials give them special obligations not shared with other citizens. They ignore the greater power and authority of public officials to coerce other citizens and, thus, fail to hold them to a more restrictive standard of conduct (see Schauer 1986: 1075–76). As the following discussion suggests, however, there are some significant differences between Perry and other communitarian views of the obligations of religious lawmakers.

Perry's Views of Religious Lawmakers

As noted earlier, Perry's views about the obligations of religious lawmakers rest on his views about moral identity more generally. For Perry, self-identity is partly constituted by one's fundamental beliefs and commitments (1988: 60, 62, 152), which are the products of moral communities and traditions (11 [citing Taylor 1989a: 190–91], 29; 1991: 49). For Perry, as for other communitarian thinkers, because the identity of individuals is shaped by their communal contexts, including their religious community, a person's moral identity is partly constituted by her religious convictions.

Perry concludes that "the legislator's (and the citizen's) moral beliefs, including her religious beliefs about human good, are ultimately determinative of her politics" (1988: 102). Citizens must rely on their moral convictions, including religious ones, in political decision making because of the constitutive role of religion in the shaping of moral identity and the unity of the self. Requiring citizens to bracket these convictions would be to "annihilate" the self (72–73), Perry claims, because it precludes persons from engaging in moral discourse with other members of society as "themselves," that is, "as the self one is" (181). This applies to lawmakers as well as to other citizens (103).

Perry also assumes that authentic moral selves have a single, coherent, unitary identity that must be expressed as a whole. He claims that when a person brackets her moral convictions in reasoning about principles of justice, as Rawls recommends, it is not "she" that is reasoning but rather her playing "the role of *someone else* reasoning towards principles of justice—someone without the bracketed convictions" (Perry 1988: 61). For Perry, then, playing roles that require bracketing some of one's convictions, including religious convictions, is not an authentic expression of self-identity. From this perspective, lawmakers should not be required to engage in any bracketing of their religious convictions in their public decision making, for to do so would involve an annihilation of the religious aspects of themselves. Thus, the same type of conduct and the same obligations are appropriate for lawmakers and other citizens (see, e.g., Perry 1993: 704–5, 723–24; 1988: 101–2, 150–54; see also Foley 1992: 956).

Perry makes this position explicit in his proposal for deliberative transformative politics, where he argues that judges should rely on their own beliefs, including their religious beliefs, to ascertain what the "aspirations" underlying the Constitution counsel (1988: 149). In his estimation, "a judge's own convictions about human well-being properly, and in any event, inevitably, play an important role in guiding the judge's specification of a constitutional aspiration in the setting of a particular case" (181).

In his proposal for an inclusivist ideal, however, Perry is inconsistent with regard to whether there should be a distinction between what is appropriate for lawmakers versus other citizens in terms of assessing the moral appropriateness of their reliance on their religious convictions. At one point, Perry argues that lawmakers should be held to higher restrictions on the use of religious convictions in their decision making than other citizens. Yet, at another point, he rejects the validity of such a distinction, explicitly arguing that such a distinction is "a mistake," that it is difficult to see why limitations should be imposed on religious lawmakers if they are not imposed on other citizens (1993: 723).

Even with respect to the judicial role, Perry argues that when "legal premises and/or consensual/commonsensical premises . . . do not yield a single answer, presumably [the judge] should decide on the basis of premises she accepts, premises authoritative for her *qua* the particular person she is" (1993: 724 n. 71). Even more explicitly, he rejects "an axiomatic norm" that the judicial role requires a judge "to rely on one or more premises she rejects" because the judicial role is somehow separate from the person occupying it (724–25 n. 71).

More recently, however, Perry has apparently changed his views again. In the second aspect of Perry's most recent proposal, that calling for a nonestablishment norm and secular support, he argues that "an individual legislator should vote to support a political choice about the morality of human conduct only if, in her view, a persuasive secular rationale exists" (1997: 37). Here, he concludes that "the persuasiveness or soundness of any religious argument about human well-being depends, or should depend, partly on there being at least one persuasive secular argument . . . that reaches the same conclusion"

(1998: 26–27). Perry defends this requirement as a way of diminishing the potential for political divisiveness based on religious differences (34). This most recent formulation of Perry's views is more sensitive to religious pluralism and, thus, more akin to liberal proposals than either his earlier proposals or those of other communitarian theorists. As I argue later, this modification strengthens the merit of Perry's approach to religious lawmaking, but it is still problematic in a number of respects.

Other Communitarian Views of Religious Lawmakers

Sandel does not specify any conditions for or limitations on religious involvement in politics (1982: 183). Thus, his approach permits a larger role for religious influence on politics than Perry's. For Sandel, the liberal demand that lawmakers disengage their religious convictions when engaged in political decision making involves the unacceptable cost of denying them the ability to express who they are (1982: 179; 1993: 492–93). In contrast, he suggests that legislatures and courts should explicitly make substantive determinations when deciding moral issues (1993: 492–93).

Other communitarian thinkers are in accord. Stephen Carter denies that the Establishment Clause prohibits religiously motivated or grounded lawmaking because that would "force the religiously devout to bracket their religious selves before they may enter into politics" (1993: 255). Constitutional law scholar Michael McConnell argues that interpreting the Establishment Clause to prohibit legislatures from basing laws on religiously informed judgments "would be bizarre, for religion remains the single most important influence on the values of ordinary Americans" (1992: 144).

In general, Perry, along with other communitarian theorists, has proposed frameworks for thinking about religious lawmaking that are premised on conceptions of the moral self that more accurately reflect the self-understandings of many religious persons than do liberal conceptions of the self. As we saw with respect to liberal approaches to religious lawmaking in the previous chapter, however, the limitations of communitarian proposals become starkly evident in relation to religious lawmaking on abortion.

Communitarian Approaches to Abortion Lawmaking

In keeping with their general differences from liberal perspectives, communitarian theories about the appropriate role for religion with respect to abortion lawmaking focus more on the norms of community and tradition than on individual rights. On these matters, as I demonstrate, Perry's views are closely akin to those of other communitarian theorists and starkly divergent from liberal ones.

Perry's Views of Religious Lawmaking on Abortion

The overall position articulated in Perry's writing is that religious influences on abortion regulation are acceptable. On the basis of the standards he articulated for ecumenical political dialogue, he argues that making political decisions concerning abortion on the basis of religious considerations is justifiable because secular rationales can virtually always be found to justify religiously motivated coercive legislation, including secular rationales that restrict abortion on the basis of protecting fetal life (Perry 1991: 116). This position is unsupportable, as it rests on the natural law view that cannot be sustained without reference to theological assumptions.

Alternatively, Perry contends that "were government to choose to outlaw abortion, it would not have to rely on a religious argument about the requirements of human well-being because 'sacredness' is not religious" (1997: 70). Indeed, similar to the natural law arguments forwarded by fellow Catholics John Noonan and Henry Hyde discussed in chapter 3, Perry (erroneously) argues that "the most influential religious voice in the United States on the 'pro-life' side of the debate about what public policy regarding abortion should be—the voice of the National Conference of Catholic Bishops—does not rely, at the crucial and controversial stage of its case, on a religious argument about the requirements of human well-being" (1997: 70). If the Catholic bishops need not and do not rely on a religious argument, Perry claims, then government need not either (72).

The core of Perry's argument is that the bishops' prolife position is not religious because it rests on the proposition that "all humans are sacred." Ironically, Perry himself earlier argued that the proposition regarding human sacredness can only be supported on religious grounds because there is no "intelligible secular argument" that supports the claim that all human beings are sacred and it would be "silly to insist" that government is prohibited from relying on a religious rationale to support this proposition because it "is a fundamental constituent of American moral culture" (1997: 68–69).[6]

Indeed, it is part of Perry's basic proposal regarding religious lawmaking that matters regarding "human worth" are distinct from those dealing with "human well-being" and that "the only claim about human worth on which government in the United States constitutionally may rely and that is consistent with the international law of human rights" is the religious proposition that all human beings are sacred (1998: 20; 1997: 66). Consequently, religious arguments are acceptable in political decisions regarding matters involving human worth (as opposed to well-being, where he argues religious arguments are not necessary in the same way). Given these contradictory views, Perry cannot sustain his position that the Catholic bishops' prolife argument is not religious.

Perry also erroneously concludes that the bishops' position on abortion provides an appropriate basis for restrictive legislation because it satisfies the standard of public accessibility in not being defended "on sectarian or authoritative grounds" (1991: 119–20). Yet at least the part of the bishops' argument relying on the love commandment is supported by an explicitly religious rationale. Allowing such views as a basis for lawmaking on abortion in our religiously pluralistic society thus raises all of the Establishment Concerns and risks of the violation of Citizenship Rights discussed earlier.

Further, both Perry's and the bishops' prolife arguments are constitutionally problematic because they omit women from their considerations in determining the appropriate scope of the protection of human life and basic human rights. The constitutional rights to equal protection of the laws, liberty, and privacy are also human rights to which women are entitled. The bishops' "preferential concern for the weak and defenseless" that Perry favors as a basis for abortion lawmaking (Perry 1991: 117) also should be applied to many pregnant women, whose lack of social, political, and economic power in a sexist and patriarchal society provides them with limited options in life. Thus, the bishops' position on abortion lawmaking (and Perry's as well by implication) are suspect as being gender biased as well as expressly religious.

Earlier, in *Morality, Politics, and Law,* Perry attempted to make his case in favor of religious lawmaking on abortion by criticizing the Supreme Court's decision in *Roe v. Wade.* Although he argues that *Roe* was wrongly decided as a matter of constitutional law, his analysis suggests that the heart of his opposition lies more with the morality of abortion rather than its constitutional legality. Perry's stated rationale is that the protection of fetal life is a more compelling good than women's liberty interests as protected by the Fourteenth Amendment (1988: 174).

Perry also argues, however, that the Court would have been wrong to uphold Texas's prohibition on abortion, in part because the Texas statute ignores women's well-being (1988: 176). Were he deciding the case, he contends, he would have established three exceptions to an outright ban on abortion: where necessary to protect the physical health of the mother, in cases of rape or incest, or where the fetus has severe genetic defects (1988: 175–76). He argues that these exceptions are necessary to make the statute conform to constitutional principles of equal protection and due process (1988: 176).

However, these exceptions do not adequately protect women's well-being. They do not include exceptions for other circumstances when the pregnant woman determines that an abortion is in her best interests or, to use Perry's own terminology, will best promote her own flourishing (see Sherry 1989: 1596; Colker 1989: 1380). Thus, his proposal paternalistically determines what constitutes women's well-being rather than according respect to women's own moral agency to make this determination for themselves, in accordance with their constitutional rights to liberty and privacy. Why the religious convictions of lawmakers should take precedence over the moral convictions of pregnant women is left unanswered in Perry's analysis. Although Perry acknowledges the feminist critique that much religion has been used in the cause of oppression rather than liberation, his response is simply that much secular thought has been as well (1991: 144). This response is inadequate to justify allowing the personal moral views of religious lawmakers to trump those of pregnant women.

Other Communitarian Views of Religious
Lawmaking on Abortion

Other communitarian theorists reach essentially the same conclusions as Perry with regard to religious lawmaking on abortion, albeit by somewhat different routes. Sandel claims that the justice of laws against abortion depends on the morality of the practice of abortion itself (1989b: 521). Consistent with his conviction that the community is constitutive of the moral views of individuals, Sandel contends that the State is justified in making the judgment that abortion is immoral (1989b: 536–37).[7]

Sandel fails to specify what the relevant "community" is that should provide the basis for the State's legislative determination. As noted earlier, notions of a single, monolithic community are problematic, especially because those in power are likely to be themselves and to represent primarily the interests of elite, white, Christian males and not the communities of women who are contemplating the termination of an unwanted pregnancy, especially those comprised of women lacking in educational and other social resources and power, such as indigent women, women of color, and underage and undereducated women. Given these disparities in definitions of what the community is, Sandel's views about the appropriateness of State determinations of the morality of abortion fail to adequately protect Citizenship Rights and interests of all members of the community.

In Sandel's view, the Court in *Roe v. Wade* did not successfully avoid determining the moral issue of when life begins because its decision to allow the State to prohibit abortion only after the second trimester (the point of viability) itself contained a determination about the moral status of the fetus (1989b: 531). In addition, he argues that the Court's determination in *Roe* that the Constitution contains a right to privacy is based on a flawed liberal assumption about persons as freely choosing their moral views. These comments, in conjunction with Sandel's views about religion being an inextricable constituent of moral identity and about lawmaking being a normative enterprise requiring moral evaluation, suggest that Sandel would allow a prominent role for (at least the community's dominant, mainstream) religious convictions in abortion lawmaking.

In addition, other communitarian critics of *Roe* contend that pregnant women are not responsible to themselves alone but also have moral responsibilities to others. These others include not only the fetus but also the father of the unborn child and other family members and members of the community (see Glendon 1991; Colker 1992). For example, in contrast to the way that the Supreme Court decided *Roe*, Mary Ann Glendon praises how courts in European countries, particularly West Germany, have considered abortion in terms of the larger community and its long-range interests in attitudes toward human life (1987: 35).

Sandel's faith that there is a morality (singular) concerning abortion and that it can be ascertained by "the" community (singular) fails to adequately account for moral and religious pluralism and the impossibility of adjudicating fairly between different cultural and religious views of the moral acceptability of abortion. Sandel's analysis, thereby, fails to consider whose moral views are to be determinative when there is a plurality of different perspectives leading to radically different conclusions about the legality and morality of a practice such as abortion.

In addition, Sandel's proposal for religious lawmaking on abortion is also problematically based on an assumption that all abortion is morally alike, justifying uniform legal treatment in all cases. This reveals a simplistic view of abortion, one that ignores respect for pregnant women and gender and power inequalities in society. His assumption that legislatures can easily determine the morality of abortion fails to consider the circumstances surrounding individual pregnancies, such as the stage of pregnancy, the health of the fetus and the pregnant woman, the woman's feelings about being pregnant, and her life circumstances. All of these particular circumstances counsel against lawmakers imposing their personal religious views of abortion through restrictive abortion laws.

Summary of Communitarian Views on Abortion Lawmaking

Communitarian analyses of abortion as a (primarily) community or social concern rather than an individual matter, especially in the context of contemporary American society, are generally flawed in failing to recognize that pregnant women frequently do find themselves quite alone in the decision of whether to bear and raise a child. The kinds of "given" communities such as families, churches, and states affirmed by communitarian theorists are often oppressive to women and deny them fully participation.

In addition, the present-day reality is that many pregnant women lack any community of support, especially a husband or partner willing to share responsibility for the woman's unwanted pregnancy. Because our society, for better or worse, places a premium on individual freedom and autonomy, most pregnant women, like other citizens, have a reasonable expectation that they are primarily responsible for making the fundamental decisions about their lives, including whether to bear and/or raise a child. Given the realities of the ethos of individualism in our society, it is especially unjustly discriminatory to impose the model of communitarian citizenship on a woman with an unwanted pregnancy, especially when her community has not demonstrated its commitment to her flourishing.

In sum, communitarian proposals for religious lawmaking in the context of abortion reflect an inattention to, if not a disrespect for, the values of gender equality and religious pluralism. The radical pluralism of religious views on the abortion issue points to a fundamental weakness in the communitarian position in general, and Perry's in particular. The prochoice versus prolife political divisions among (and sometimes even within) religious groups on the abortion issue represent a fundamental pluralism of perspectives, one which has historically shown itself to be too deep and intractable to sustain communitarian assumptions about the possibility of consensus or common ground. As one study of abortion attitudes among Christians concludes, the plurality of views on the morality of abortion precludes the possibility of "a unitary religious perspective on abortion questions" (Tamney, Johnson, and Burton 1994: 55).

If such a lack of agreement exists even within Christianity, once all of the non-Christian religions are also taken into account, it becomes impossible to claim, as Perry once did, that the public debate over abortion can be resolved through ecumenical political dialogue (see Perry 1988: 36). Religious groups also disagree on a number of other issues relating to abortion: the value of fetal life, the appropriate way to determine that value, the nature of personhood, the extent to which pregnant women's needs and interests are relevant to the morality of abortion, and whether respect is owed to the pregnant woman as a competent moral agent. The lack of a publicly accessible basis for most of these views precludes the possibility of the kind of rational debate that might result in agreement or even a compromise position.

Many religious statements on abortion either ignore the status of the pregnant woman or devalue the importance of her life situation. The exclusion of women from the formulation and interpretation of religious views on the morality and legality of abortion has meant that these views generally have not reflected careful consideration of the needs and interests of those persons most significantly affected by the legality of abortion. The constitutional principles of liberty and privacy that undergird the right to choose are in conflict with conservative religious teachings that abortion should be prohibited. Similarly, the constitutional guarantee of equal protection conflicts with traditional patriarchal views of women found in many traditional religious communities.

Communitarians fail to recognize the actual pluralism that exists among persons within political communities and the disparities in power and authority that exist between lawmakers and pregnant women. Such disparities usually include differences of gender and religion and often other differences based on race, class, and educational and occupational status as well. Despite this difference with liberal proposals, communitarian theorists generally share with liberal ones a failure to take into consideration all of the relevant interests to abortion regulation. If lawmaking is to be truly representative of the needs and interests of all citizens, it must include consideration of women as well as religious minorities. As we have seen, communitarian proposals that promote reliance on religious convictions fail to recommend such representative lawmaking.

Benefits and Shortcomings of Communitarian Perspectives on Religious Lawmaking

Communitarian proposals regarding religious lawmaking resolve some of the problems we discovered in the previous chapter with respect to liberal approaches but raise others, especially given their problematic conceptions of what a community is, who its members are, and the extent to which it is constitutive of moral identity, their (varying degrees of) disregard for moral and religious pluralism as well as the risks that religious lawmaking will violate Citizenship Rights and/or raise Establishment Concerns.

Benefits of Communitarian Proposals

On the resolution side, communitarian views that selves are socially constructed and, thereby, unable to separate or divorce themselves from their religious commitments are more in keeping with the self-understandings of many religious persons, including lawmakers, than are liberal views that result in simplistic understandings of the ability (and motivation) of lawmakers to set aside their religious convictions in the realms of politics and law. Communitarian theory, thus, points to the importance of attending to the relationship of religion to moral identity in formulating a workable approach to religious lawmaking.

Limitations of Communitarian Proposals

As noted previously, there are several problems with communitarian approaches to religious lawmaking. First, communitarianism draws the connection between moral identity and community with too broad a brush, without considering the diversity and multiplicity of communities of which individuals are members. If people's identities are constituted as completely by their community and traditions as communitarians suggest, deviation by individuals from their community's norms and traditions would appear to be impossible.

Communitarian theorists generally overlook the reality that most Americans are members of multiple communities, not only one. Although the kinds of communities emphasized by communitarian theorists, such as familial and religious ones, are found or given, others kinds of communities, such as political and civic groups and friendships, are chosen or voluntary (see Friedman 1989: 289). This distinction is significant, as Marilyn Friedman suggests, since "our communities of origin do not necessarily constitute us as selves who agree or comply with the norms which unify those communities" (1989: 289).

In part because of their failure to acknowledge the multiple communities of which a person may be a member, communitarian theorists have not offered a procedure for determining which community does or should take priority when conflicts arise. Despite Perry's claim that the political community does not conflict with the more determinate or significant moral community(s) to which an individual may belong, there are inevitably points of tension and conflict between what he terms "constitutional aspirations" and the tenets of religious moral communities. For example, as noted previously, conservative religious teachings that abortion should be prohibited are in conflict with constitutional principles that undergird women's right to choose.[8]

Sandel assumes, as Perry does, that "communities have a common vocabulary of discourse and a background of implicit practices and understandings"

(1982: 172–73). Such assumptions of commonality are critical to communitarian claims that the pursuit of moral truths is an appropriate role for government in a religiously pluralistic society. However, such claims are based on false assumptions about a level of cultural homogeneity that does not exist, either between or even within many communities.

Communitarians especially tend to ignore the role of community in the social construction of gender identity. Frazer and Lacey note that "communitarians have not begun to analyze the male-dominated nature of existing political communities (or indeed to acknowledge the importance of such a project)" (1993: 159). Many traditional communities are founded on practices of exclusion or suppression of difference, whether it be on the basis of gender, ethnicity, sexual orientation, race, religious beliefs, or some other characteristic. The feminist and postmodern perspectives that are discussed in chapter 6 suggest how the parameters of community are largely defined by those in power.

Communitarians also ignore the potential of communities to be repressive, especially of women and other persons viewed as "other." As Frazer and Lacey point out, "on [the] communitarian view of personhood, the woman is peculiarly powerless. For she cannot find any jumping-off point for a critique of the dominant conception of value; her position as a socially constructed being seems to render her a helpless victim of her situation" (1993: 151). Iris Young similarly argues that the communitarian ideal of community as subjects in fusion with one another effectively operates "to exclude those with whom the group does not identify" and thus to deny or repress social difference (1990: 227, 230). This is as true for religious communities as for others.

In addition, given communities, more often than chosen ones, denigrate nontraditional roles and opportunities for women and call for a return to institutions such as the family and church that closely circumscribe women's activities (e.g., MacIntyre 1981; see Friedman 1989: 281, 284). Although given communities may be partly constitutive of our moral selves, the correlation need not be a close one, as the emergence of gays and lesbians from homophobic communities or liberals from conservative ones illustrates. This suggests both that such communities have played a lesser role in constituting individual identity than communitarian theorists would claim (Friedman 1989: 283).

A second major problem with communitarian proposals, related to the first, is their failure to adequately recognize and respect the value of religious pluralism. Although Perry purports to recognize pluralism as a positive resource, in actual practice he ignores it, discounts it, or considers it as an obstacle to be surmounted, as is evident in his definition of religion as beliefs about God. As Mark Tushnet points out, Perry supports his claim to the possibility of finding common ground by "passing reference to 'our' tradition, to the Judeo-Christian tradition, and to what most mainline religious denominations have to say in their official pronouncements" (1989: 1645).[9] Denying the existence of significant religious and moral pluralism enables Perry to deny the force of the point that religion has often been a source of civil strife. Sandel accords even less respect to religious pluralism in his proposal.

Perry also discounts the propensity of religious pluralism to make religious lawmaking result in the creation of Establishment Concerns. He rejects Greenawalt's view that religiously motivated politics may alienate nonbelievers, claiming that pluralism is not actually as much of a problem as it is often purported to be (see Perry 1991: 86). In fact, he contends that Greenawalt actively "disfavors" religious convictions and overrates the incidence of alienation of nonbelievers as well as the importance of preventing such alienation (Perry 1991: 17–19), which the discussion of Greenawalt in chapter 4 belies. As is evident in Greenawalt's writing, his sympathies for religious believers are balanced against the problems created when religious convictions are the basis for lawmaking. Perry's unjustified accusations against Greenawalt's proposals suggest that Perry has only a lukewarm commitment to ensuring that the religious beliefs of all members of our society are accorded respect, not only those of religious citizens desirous of influencing politics and law.

Communitarian proposals also provide inadequate protection against the possibility that religious influences will raise Establishment Concerns. Perry's reliance on tolerance as a means of protecting against the dangers of religious lawmaking in both ecumenical political dialogue and the inclusive ideal illustrates this deficiency. In the former approach, tolerance is the only defense Perry offers (other than pluralism itself) against the danger that State authority will be used by members of the dominant or majority religious groups to coerce those of other groups in situations where dialogue fails "to achieve agreement before a political choice has to be made" (Perry 1991: 30, 128; see Levinson 1991; Smolin 1991). His assertion that pluralism precludes the possibility that "the views of any single religious or other moral community can be determinative," thereby diminishing "the chance that truly idiosyncratic views might prevail" (1991: 136) is politically naive and ignores the disparities of political power and authority that exist among these different communities.

The standard of "aspiring to be tolerant of moral and religious differences" (1993: 726–27) in Perry's inclusivist ideal also fails to provide adequate protection against intolerance toward and coercion of nonbelievers in the sphere of lawmaking, especially where the religious convictions of religious minorities are in tension or conflict with those of socially and politically powerful religious groups. Both uses of *tolerance* fail to acknowledge the political power that coalitions of religious groups can and have had on particular moral issues. The multiple successes of the prolife alliance of Catholics and fundamentalist Protestants in promoting restrictive abortion laws provides just one example.

Inadequacies of Both Liberal and Communitarian Resolutions to the Dilemma

In this and the preceding chapter, we have seen that in several respects, liberal and communitarian approaches to religious lawmaking complement the strengths and weaknesses of one another. Whereas liberal theorists stress the importance of respecting moral and religious pluralism and undervalue the significance of religion to moral identity, communitarians stress the latter and undervalue the former. Whereas liberal concerns for individual liberty may overlook the significance of the relational and social aspects of moral identity in general and the role of religious communities and traditions in particular, in the quest to protect religious pluralism, the communitarian emphasis on the self as unified and as constituted exclusively by its community and tradition (both singular) fails to recognize the diversity of communities and traditions that comprise the individual self (as well as American society as a whole) or the capacity for the independent agency and judgment of the individuals that develop out of such communities. Whereas liberals may overemphasize the ultimate epistemological differences between religious and secular beliefs, communitarians underestimate the pragmatist and symbolic differences.

Even though Greenawalt and Perry's proposals to religious lawmaking are among the most progressive of liberal and communitarian thinkers on religious lawmaking, neither of their approaches provides a satisfactory resolution to the dilemma. Both largely ignore gender and other significant inequalities among moral selves. This deficiency is evident in how they address the issue of religious lawmaking in the abortion context. Both tend to ignore women's moral agency and constitutional rights in analyzing abortion regulation.

In addition, the variations within the group of lawmakers discussed in chapter 3 regarding their understanding of the role that their religious convictions do (and should) play in their public policy making suggests that neither liberal nor communitarian conceptions of moral identity or the centrality of religion with respect to that identity are completely accurate because neither accounts for both the self-understandings of some religious lawmakers as unable to separate their religious convictions from their public decision making and the abilities of at least some lawmakers to make such a distinction in actual practice. These problems indicate that neither liberal nor communitarian theory, considered either separately or together, is able to formulate a satisfactory approach to religious lawmaking.

The inability of both liberal or communitarian approaches to resolve the problems raised by religious lawmaking or to develop a workable alternative to the Supreme Court's approach reveals the need for a new model for dealing with the dilemma. In designing the framework for this new approach, however, several lessons from the limitations of liberal and communitarian proposals provide useful guidance. These limitations suggest that a satisfactory model for addressing religious lawmaking must have the following features:

1. It should neither assume that lawmakers can or will be motivated to separate themselves from their religious convictions in their public policy making nor that they have no capacity, willingness, or moral obligation to do so. Rather, it should be founded on an understanding of moral identity that more accurately reflects both the constitutive role that religion may play as well as the independent agency of the self to make choices other than those prescribed or even mandated by religious convictions.

2. It should neither ignore nor underestimate the reality and extent of religious pluralism nor make it the only relevant consideration for assessing the validity of religious lawmaking.

3. It should recognize that citizens and lawmakers share some rights and interests in common but that the latter have special responsibilities as a result of constitutional obligations and their roles as political leaders.

4. It should recognize that other power inequalities in society, including those stemming from gender and religious differences, may be exacerbated by religious lawmaking.

5. Finally, it should recognize that the Constitution and Bill of Rights are relevant to the issues raised by religious lawmaking, both in terms of explicit violations or infringements on Citizenship Rights and the less explicit and direct generation of Establishment Concerns.

In sum, a satisfactory approach to religious lawmaking must be able to effectively address the potential conflicts engendered by religious lawmaking in a pluralistic society, the centrality that religion may have to the moral identity of lawmakers, and the social reality of gender and other inequalities in our society.

In the following chapters, I propose alternative approaches to the dilemma of religious lawmaking. The first is an ideal proposal, in the sense that it indicates how religious lawmaking would be handled under circumstances in which lawmakers voluntarily adhered to their role-based obligations. This theoretical approach is based on George Herbert Mead's pragmatist theories of the social self and role-based morality, as supplemented by insights from feminist and poststructuralist theorists.

The second is a practical legal strategy that recognizes the limitations of proposing only an ideal theory that is unlikely to be implemented, especially by the parties who are most responsible for the harms of religious lawmaking. This legal approach is designed to be a more feasible and effective way to balance the most pronounced dangers of religious lawmaking—the Establishment Concerns and Citizenship Rights discussed earlier—with the legitimate free exercise and free speech rights of religious lawmakers to adhere to their religious beliefs than either the liberal or communitarian approaches or the Supreme Court's jurisprudence.

SIX

A Pragmatist Approach to Religious Lawmaking

As the preceding two chapters have shown, the most prominent approaches to religious lawmaking, those based on liberal and communitarian theory, are flawed. Liberal approaches privilege respect for pluralism at the expense of religiously informed moral identity, especially that of lawmakers, whereas communitarian proposals do the reverse. Both largely ignore how gender biases and disparities of power in religious lawmaking have a disproportionately adverse effect on the constitutional rights and interests of women. They therefore fail to provide a satisfactory remedy to the problems with the Supreme Court's jurisprudence on religious lawmaking.

In this chapter, I propose that an alternative conception of moral identity, based on George Herbert Mead's pragmatist theory of the social self and his concept of role-based morality, offers the basis for a more accurate and workable theory for addressing the dilemma of religious lawmaking. George Herbert Mead was an early twentieth-century philosopher associated with the school known as American Pragmatism. He described his approach to the self as one of "behavioristic psychology" to convey the message that his theories were based on observable behavior rather than on speculation or abstraction, as are many accounts of moral identity (including elements of both liberalism and communitarianism).

Although Mead's views bear certain resemblances to aspects of liberalism and communitarianism, they offer fresh ways of thinking about religious lawmaking that avoid many of the problems in liberal and communitarian approaches. Contrary to the liberal conception of the self as an autonomous, solitary "chooser," Mead places the core of the self squarely in the social process. But unlike the communitarian tradition, he does not view the self as fixed or as determined exclusively by its community and tradition. In addition, his view of morality suggests that it is a shared enterprise that transcends individual judgments and requires taking into account the attitudes of all relevant others.

Mead's theories were not designed to address the specific context of religious lawmaking. In addition, in some respects they reflect outdated ideas about society. Thus, Mead's ideas do not provide a full and complete resolution to the dilemma. However, as I argue in this chapter, insights from feminist and poststructuralist theory can be used to modify Mead's account. So modified, this "Meadian" framework provides a sound ethical strategy for resolving the dilemma of religious lawmaking. After describing the elements of this framework, I conclude the chapter by sketching the practical limitations of a theoretical approach to religious lawmaking and suggest the need to supplement a Meadian approach with a more pragmatic, legal strategy.

Mead's Theory of the Social Self

Mead's model of moral identity includes a number of distinctive features that avoid many of the deficiencies of liberal and communitarian approaches. These include the character of the self as at once thoroughly social and yet active, fluid, and self-reconstituting and as having a multiple yet unified character. After describing these features, I assess both the strengths and weaknesses of Mead's account for purposes of offering an alternative approach to religious lawmaking.

Characteristics of the Social Self

The central principle of Mead's theory of personal identity is that the self is social from its inception. In Mead's view, "minds and selves are essentially social products" (1956: 116). That is, the individual self, or soul, does not preexist society but is constituted out of it. Thus, rather than following a traditional liberal approach, which begins with individuals to explain how society develops, Mead begins, like communitarian theory, with society—what he calls "the social process"—to understand how individual selves develop. In his view, without the social process, there would be no individual selves (169–70).

A summary of this process by which moral identity is formed will enable us to see how Mead's theory of the moral self surpasses those on which both liberal and communitarian approaches to religious lawmaking are premised. The characteristics of Mead's social self can be summarized as socially produced yet independent, socially dependent yet autonomous, multiple yet unitary, and role-based yet spontaneous and unpredictable. The following discussion takes up each of these characteristics in turn.

In Mead's account, the self is built up by taking and responding to the attitudes or roles that others express toward it (1964: 288). In fact, Mead describes the self as initially an object that is merely "the reflection of the attitudes of others toward it" (369). The ability to organize these attitudes and roles gives rise to the "generalized other," an internalization of the organized community or social group. It is itself composed of the internalized attitudes and roles of particular others. The generalized other is the basis for determining the appropriateness of one's own conduct and constitutes a necessary condition for the development of a full or complete self, what Mead calls a "unity of self" (1956: 218–19, see 169–70; Hanson 1986: 17). The generalized other functions as the social and rational aspect of the self, the self-consciousness that is invoked in decision making.[1]

In several respects, then, the conception of the self that Mead develops is essentially social. Nonetheless, it does not lack the characteristics necessary for the self to be an independent and autonomous moral agent. The generalized other enables individuals to obtain a certain distance from—in effect to transcend—the attitudes of particular others and to develop individual and unique personalities (Mead 1956: 214–17). Internalizing the generalized other enables the individual to control his or her responses and conduct, that is, to "think" (169). Thinking permits the ability to engage in both abstract and objective thinking and, thereby, gives the self agency to control her own conduct (Mead 1964: 288; see 1956: 159). By acquiring a generalized other and, with it, the ability to think, the self emerges out of the social field and develops a unique personality capable of independent agency and the ability to act on, and not merely react to, its environment.

The self in Mead's conception is thus neither completely determined and constrained by the social situation nor completely free or autonomous. Rather, it is composed of both a socially determined aspect (the *me*) and an individual spontaneous, novel, or indeterminate aspect (the *I*). Mead describes the *me* as the aspect of the self composed basically of the internalized attitudes and roles of others. Because these others include a multiplicity of individual others as well as a single generalized other, the self is itself multiple or plural. Thus, the more comprehensive and inclusive of individual others the generalized other is, the more complete and full the moral self will be (see Hanson 1986: 24).

In contrast to the *me*, the *I* is the subjective part of the self that acts in accordance with impulse or habit. According to Mead, we identify "ourselves" with the *I* and its individualized responses or expressions which raise the self "above the institutionalized individual" (1956: 230, 237, 239). The *I*, then, is that aspect of our selves that is relatively more autonomous and less determined by the social situation, consistent with liberal theory. Paradoxically, however, because the *I* is spontaneous, we can never completely know or predict ourselves in advance of actually acting or making a decision, and thus, we can never be completely certain of who we are until after we have acted (Mead 1964: 142–43; 1956: 236). In this analysis, then, selves can never completely know themselves.

Selves may act or make decisions on the basis of their membership in a social group, such as a religion, in accordance with the roles appropriate for members of that group. In this regard, Mead claims that the socially constituted *me* "acts as a censor for the impulsive conduct of the 'I'" (1956: 239). However, the spontaneity and unpredictability of the *I* means that it is also always possible that selves will act contrary to the roles appropriate to or expected of persons in their social position. Moral selves will not, therefore, always make decisions on the basis of their established convictions, group affiliations, or institutional roles. This analysis suggests that even persons with deeply held religious convictions cannot be completely certain that they always will act on the basis of those convictions.

Thus, although the self in Mead's conception is produced and limited by its social environment, it is not completely fixed and determined thereby. Selves are also unique individuals because each reflects the social process "as a whole from its own particular and unique standpoint within that process" (Mead 1964: 386). Thus, "the common social origin and constitution of individual selves and their structures does not preclude wide individual differences and variations among them or contradict the peculiar and more or less distinctive individuality which each of them in fact possesses" (Mead 1956: 234–35). This implies that even selves who identify primarily as members of a religious community nonetheless are capable of acting independently.

In addition, selves are not fixed or static: a healthy, socially adjusted self is fluid, adapting to new circumstances, and continues to change and grow over the person's life. Mead explains that the ability to internalize the attitudes of others enables the self to "undertake and effect intelligent reconstructions of that self or personality in terms of its relations to the given social order, whenever the exigencies of adaptation to his social environment demand such reconstructions" (1956: 269 n. 7; see Joas 1985: 192; Miller 1973: 239–40). Such changes may be prompted by changes within and among those others with whom the self comes into contact. These alter the social field and, thus, the attitudes and roles that the individual has available to take on, as well as the particular character of the generalized other.

The self is, therefore, a process and not a fixed entity, one that changes in response to changes in its social environment. Reciprocally, the self is not totally determined by the social process but can also influence its own development. Mead does not clearly specify the limits of the self's control over its development, however, especially with respect to the boundaries or parameters of the community or social group that forms the generalized other and consequently shapes self identity.

Mead's description of this community as limited to those who share "a social environment or context of experience and behavior" with the individual leaves unspecified what constitutes a "shared environment" or common "context" (see 1956: 202–3). In particular, it is not clear from his account whether individuals can choose to limit the generalized other, for example, to the attitudes and roles of those with whom they most closely identify or associate and exclude others. This issue is significant with respect to the claim by communitarian theorists that religious lawmakers are constrained to make decisions based on their religious convictions because their religious affiliation is constitutive of who they are.

Certain of Mead's statements suggest the possibility of imposing such limitations. For example, he claims that "we all belong to small cliques, and we may remain simply inside of them" (1956: 353). The "organized other" present in ourselves is then a "community of a narrow diameter" (253). In addition, he suggests that an individual "is restricted to the group whose roles it assumes, and it will never abandon this self until it finds itself entering into the larger society and maintaining itself there" (1964: 292).

These statements imply that persons who identify primarily with a specific community, such as a religious group, could develop selves on the basis of a generalized other composed only of members of that community. This interpretation is supported by Mead's view that a caste society impedes the development of a complete self by severely restricting the extent to which common attitudes can develop (1956: 272). On this understanding, if caste differences are significant enough to inhibit the development of common attitudes, then so are other sorts of differences, including those based on religion. The implication of this interpretation is that members of a tightly knit community within a socially stratified society will develop selves limited to a generalized other composed of that community's members rather than a more inclusive generalized other encompassing members of the larger society. Although Mead states that such a self would be not be "a whole self" (272), it would, nonetheless, be a self.

Several other features of Mead's account counter such an interpretation, however. First, as a descriptive matter, Mead specifically observes that the self tends "to organize *all* experience into that of a self" (1956: 200; emphasis added). This would necessarily include observations of and interactions with the attitudes of others with whom the self does not specifically identify. In addition, Mead specifies that self-reflexiveness brings "the *whole* social process" into the experience of the individuals involved in it (196; emphasis added).

Here, Mead explains that "selves can only exist in definite relationships to other selves. No hard-and-fast line can be drawn between our own selves and the selves of others, since our own selves exist and enter as such into our experience only insofar as the selves of others exist and enter as such into our experience also" (1956: 227). Thus, we must be able to identify with others—at least to the extent of being able to take on their role in our imagination—to recognize both them and ourselves as selves. He emphasizes that "the unity and structure of the complete self reflects the unity and structure of the social process as a whole. . . . In other words, the various elementary selves which constitute, or are organized into, a complete self are the various aspects of the structure of that complete self answering to the various aspects of the structure of the social process as a whole; the structure of the complete self is thus a reflection of the complete social process" (208). This description posits an overarching unity for which selves strive, a unity symbolized by the social process as a whole.

On this alternative understanding, in which the full self is a kind of microcosm of the entire social process, not merely one aspect of it (Mead 1956: 208), religious selves, like others, are formed and influenced by the entire social process, not only that part of it which represents or is consistent with their religious commitments. Thus, the more pluralistic the social environment is, the greater will be the diversity of others who form the generalized other that enters the individual's experience. The result will be a more diversified and full generalized other, and, consequently, a more complete—or what Mead refers to as "whole"—self. An important implication of this perspective for our purposes is its implication that religious communities are not completely constitutive of an individual's self-identity.

On either the limited or inclusive interpretation, however, the ability to identify with the attitudes and roles of others is both descriptive and normative for Mead. In his view, there is no relevant distinction between socially appropriate conduct and moral conduct. Rather, "as human nature is essentially social in character, moral ends must be also social in their nature" (1964: 385). Ethical obligations are a function of what is required for society to function cooperatively. They emerge naturally out of the social situation rather than being imposed on it.

In addition to its simultaneous sociality and individuality, a third key feature of Mead's conception of the self is its character as at once multiple and unitary. We have already seen that the self is plural in Mead's theory by virtue of having both subjective and objective aspects (the *I* and the *me*) and having the latter composed of a multiplicity of individual others as well as a generalized other. Indeed, taking the attitudes of individual others may result in the formation of a number of different *me*'s (see Mead 1964: 146; Cook 1993: 65; Joas 1985: 118). Mead describes selves as having "a number of different social facets or aspects, a number of different sets of social attitudes" (1956: 268). And since persons are never completely certain how their spontaneous, novel, and unpredictable *I* will act in a given situation, their selves can never be completely unified but will always bear an element of contingency and unpredictability.

Mead's view in this regard is substantiated by recent work by feminist theorists, who challenge the communitarian notion that selves are completely determined by their community and tradition. As Marilyn Friedman argues

> The potential for deviating from relationship norms must lie predominantly, it seems to me, in the complexity of selves and the diversity of ways in which we are constituted by our social contexts. A complex self can depart from this or that particular social influence, even those which (partially) constitute her identity, because of the combined effect of her various and varied identity constituents. Selves do not simply replicate a small cohesive set of social norms. . . . We can move back and forth among a plurality of partial identities, now interrogating this or that relational norm from the standpoint of other commitments. (76–77)

In addition, as Young notes, members of culturally dominated groups, such as women; racial, ethnic, and religious minorities; and the economically impoverished, both "internalize the subject position of the dominant culture and also live a subjectivity derived from their positive identification and social networks with others in their group" (1990: 148). This results in a dialectic of "double consciousness" that precludes a completely unified self.

The self is also multiple or plural because it is mediated through roles. Mead states, "We carry on a whole series of different relationships to different people. We are one thing to one man and another thing to another. There are parts of the self which exist only for the self in relationship to itself. We divide ourselves up in all sorts of different selves with reference to our acquaintances. *We discuss politics with one and religion with another*. There are all sorts of different selves answering to all sorts of different social reactions. . . . A multiple personality is in a certain sense normal" (1956: 207; emphasis added). The quoted statement suggests that Mead considers a multiple or polyvalent identity to be a natural consequence of self development. Mead's view that in a highly developed and organized society, "conflicts arise between different aspects or phases of the same individual self . . . as well as between different individual selves" (268) also supports his understanding of the self as plural or multiple.

This depiction of the self as multiple, however, is in tension with Mead's claims that unity is required for the self to be full or complete. In fact, he says that having different selves can be a result of "pathological personalities," which result from a failure to internalize a generalized other and lead to the breakdown of a unitary self into its component selves (1956: 207–9). Mead's use of the term *pathological* here indicates his presupposition that the plural or multiple self is unhealthy. This is because of his view, as noted previously, that nonunified selves are only able to express part of the social process in which they are embedded and so are themselves incomplete.

Here, Mead appears to overlook the irreducible plurality of selves that are produced in a social process involving a diversified generalized other. If, as Mead claims, the generalized other literally represents the attitude of "the whole community" (1956: 218), then in a pluralistic society the generalized other will also be plural rather than unified. It will embrace tensions and points of conflict rather than a homogeneity of attitudes and roles. If the generalized other is irreducibly multiple, then so will be the selves that develop on the basis of it.

Mead does recognize, however, that the unified self is never fully realized. It is achieved only as a result of struggle and never completely successfully or with any assurance of permanency. Similarly, because the unity of the social process is a contingent, shifting, and unstable accomplishment, so is the unity of any individual self.

Despite these ambiguities, overall Mead provides a persuasive account of how the self becomes an individual agent with an individual identity and the capacity for agency and autonomy. So long as there are options available in the social situation, there is no fixed, predestined, or prescribed course the self must take. Rather, because selves emerging from the same general social process have different personalities, or "minds," there can be wide variations in personality and beliefs even among members of the same social group or community. Mead's approach can thus account for social pluralism, even within the same social group.

In sum, Mead's theoretical understanding of moral identity improves on liberal and communitarian approaches by positing a self that is both socially constructed and an independent individual agent with a separate and unique identity. Mead's conception of moral identity avoids the undue emphasis on the individuality of the self found in liberal theory as well as the total and un-relenting sociality of selfhood found in communitarianism. His description of how self-consciousness depends on the social process in order for individual identity to arise (1956: 245) calls into question the accuracy of liberal concep-tions of the self as atomistic, autonomous, and independent of others. These aspects of Mead's description align it more closely with communitarian no-tions of moral identity.

However, Mead's focus on the objectivity and distancing of the self from its environment is closer to liberal notions of the autonomous, independent indi-vidual than to communitarian understandings of the socially constituted self. His account of how unique and individual identities are formed out of the en-tire social process weakens the credibility of the communitarian tendency to view selves as established or fixed completely by their particular community and tradition.

These features of Mead's conception of the social self make it a more ap-propriate model for considering the moral obligations of religious lawmakers. Before turning to that inquiry, however, Mead's more general views about morality and religion provide an important context for understanding the applicability of his ideas about religious and moral identity to religious lawmakers.

Relation of the Social Self to Moral and Religious Identity

Unfortunately, Mead did not write extensively on the topic of religion, and what he did write is fairly simplistic and undeveloped (e.g., Mead 1934: 475–78; 1964: 250–58, 292–96; see Miller 1973: 44–50). For example, he claims that religions express certain universal forms because they are all founded on "such fundamental attitudes of human beings toward each other as kindliness, helpfulness, and assistance," attitudes that are natural aspects of social life and are not unique to religion (1964: 258, 292–93; see Mead 1956: 256). He also asserts that from a religious standpoint, "there is a uni-versal society that includes the whole human race, and into which all can enter into relationship with others through the medium of communication" (1956: 257; see 263).

In these respects, like Perry, Mead reduces the diversity and complexity of religious traditions to an overly simplistic description based on universalistic assumptions that ignore racial, ethnic, religious, and other cultural differences. His description ignores those religious traditions that are more centrally concerned with soteriology or eschatology than with morality. His assumptions about a commonality among religions obscures the fundamental differences that divide religions and lead to intractable conflicts of understanding among (and even sometimes within) religious groups (as well as between religious and secular ones) over moral issues such as abortion.

In addition to making universal assumptions about the common foundations of all religions, Mead does not recognize the importance of a specifically religious morality in many people's lives. He understands morality as social and practical rather than religious, in keeping with the pragmatist orientation of his general approach. He does not draw a sharp distinction between moral action and other forms of rationally directed action but, instead, assumes that morality universally conforms to his secular understanding.

In fact, Mead describes religious morality as "committed to an unquestioned and unquestionable" view of rights and wrongs (1964: 92–93), a posture that is opposed to logic and the scientific method, which require an openness to considering all relevant values, not only those that have been dogmatically prescribed (see 252, 256–57). Mead's assumption that religious morality is not true morality obscures the reality that for many people, especially religious believers, moral action is premised on principles such as faith, revelation, or the authority of tradition, and community rather than or in addition to those principles Mead himself adopts, those of social relatedness, interdependence, and rationality.[2]

Despite these inadequacies with Mead's view of religion and religious morality, however, he is correct in his understanding that religion lacks public accessibility. He contends that the religious "cult" reflects an extreme degree of specialization, which makes it difficult for outsiders to understand its members, in contrast to the "commercial attitudes" of secular groups, which are "readily understandable" (1964: 296). He also asserts that religion posits an unachievable degree of identification among members of a social group, a level of cohesiveness that cannot be realized in actual society (1956: 281).

From a Meadian perspective, then, individuals who understand their identity completely in terms of their religion would be, in a pluralistic society, less than whole or complete. This understanding of the character of moral selves is consistent with those of other scholars who consider religion to be an important aspect of the moral identity of many persons but not the exclusive determinant, as discussed in chapter 1. Mead's view of morality thereby casts doubt on views like Perry's that morality can or should be determined exclusively or even primarily by one's religion or religious community, without reference to secular considerations.

Before turning to look specifically at the implications of Mead's theory of moral identity for religious lawmaking, let us consider in some further detail the elements of Mead's account of morality as role based.

Mead's Theory of Role-Based Morality

As already noted, Mead understands moral selves as constituted by a number of different roles. The self learns its social and moral obligations through knowing what is required to perform its roles satisfactorily. The capacity for morality develops out of the childhood experience of distinguishing good and bad by reacting to one's own acts with the attitudes of one's parents (Mead 1964: 146). In this sense, having others establish guidelines for what constitutes acceptable and unacceptable behavior as a child is a necessary precondition for the moral self's development.

Moral identity is later expressed through care for the neighbor (which Mead understands as the universal basis of religion). The full or complete moral self performs its roles in accordance with and only with reference to the roles of others (see Miller 1973: 242). Indeed, it is the mark of a moral self to be able to recognize the interests of others, even when they conflict with one's own. Mead admits there are difficulties involved in this enterprise because it runs contrary to our temptation to ignore interests that are opposed to our own and recognize only those we identify with (Mead 1964: 387–88).

Mead defines the mature moral person's principles as "the acknowledged attitudes of all members of the community toward what are the values of that community" (1964: 162). He insists that "to be interested in the public good we must be disinterested, that is, not [only] interested in goods in which our personal selves are wrapped up" (355). Here, Mead describes the "narrow self" as acting impulsively, concerned only with its own interests, in contrast with the "larger self," which identifies with the interests of others and acts only in accordance with what is in the interests of the common good (see Miller 1973: 231–32).

Although moral actions are conducted in terms of social roles, they do not merely involve acting in accordance with preestablished or conventional roles. Mead himself argues that it is inappropriate to resolve moral problems only by reference to the values represented by the "old self," values that are often incommensurable with the current self's situation (1964: 83, 257–62; see Cook 1993: 118–20). Rather, the "growth of the self arises out of a partial disintegration—the appearance of the different interests in the forum of reflection, the reconstruction of the social world, and the consequent appearance of the new self that answers to the new object" (Mead 1964: 147–49; see Cook 1993: 121–22).

Thus, the social roles of the moral self are continually changing and being reconstructed, providing a dynamic and shifting basis for identity rather than a fixed and rigidly determined one. This view represents a sharp contrast with communitarian views of the self as fixed by its social location in a particular set of roles which are defined by community and tradition.

Mead's own conception of morality as fundamentally social and role-based suggests that the decision making of morally conscious selves, including those moral selves whose fundamental moral orientation is religious, must take into consideration the roles and interests of *all* relevant others in their social environment when they make decisions. It might be argued that since Mead describes the individual as selecting her environment and potentially choosing a narrowly defined community, that she can choose to limit the others she identifies as relevant to her decision making (e.g., Mead 1956: 191, 253; 1964: 292). This would suggest that moral selves, including religious lawmakers, can screen out consideration of persons they do not wish to identify themselves with and restrict their consideration to the roles and interests of members of a narrower community they most closely identify with, such as a religious group.

However, as discussed earlier, this interpretation is less persuasive than one suggesting that Mead intended to conceptualize moral selves as products of their entire social field, not only a discrete segment of it. As such, selves cannot insulate themselves from aspects of the social environment with which they would prefer not to identify. To live morally in a society requires some attitude toward all of its members, regardless of how proximate or far removed those others are to one's own life.[3]

This interpretation is supported by Mead's suggestion that moral selves become more complete as they are better able to incorporate a more all-encompassing social situation into their generalized other (1956: 258–59). In addition, he specifies that inadequate moral judgments arise from incomplete consideration of different social interests. An adequate solution to a moral problem will reconstruct the social situation so as to do justice to all of the relevant interests (Mead 1964: 387; Miller 1973: 229). Thus, the moral self is obligated to take on the attitudes and consider the roles of all others in the social field, not merely those it identifies with. Nevertheless, as Mead recognizes, the pluralisms of self and of community limit the capacity of moral selves to take the roles of all others.

Mead emphasizes the need for common attitudes and unity at the social as well as the individual level. He claims that there must be a common goal or purpose to bind individuals in a society together (1964: 370). Only if a unity can be established out of the diversity of individual persons, Mead argues, can society exist and full or complete selves emerge (see 1964: 366–67, 364–65; 1956: 276–77). Social unity requires individuals to abandon their narrow social group for the larger society (1964: 292). As I will demonstrate shortly, this suggests that in cases of conflict between the "small group" of a religious lawmaker's religious community and the common good of the larger society, the moral lawmaker, in his or her role as leader, will act in accordance with the latter.

Taking on the roles or attitudes of others is not only pragmatically necessary for social cooperation in Mead's framework; it also becomes a moral obligation for leaders by virtue of their particular social roles. Mead describes leaders as persons who are able to take in more than others of an act in process and who can put themselves into relation with groups in the community whose attitudes have not entered into the lives of other community members (1964: 256). As public officials whose decisions directly impact the lives of others, lawmakers are leaders in Mead's sense of the word. This brings us to the next part of the chapter, which directly considers how Mead's theory of the social self applies to the specific problems of religious lawmaking.

Implications of a Meadian Account for Religious Lawmaking

Although Mead does not address the specific issue of religious lawmaking, his general conception of the social self and role-based morality provide the basis for resolving the dilemma more satisfactorily than either liberal or communitarian theoretical approaches have done. In this part of the chapter, I first develop the implications of a role-based morality for the moral obligations of lawmakers and then illustrate the applicability of a Meadian approach to religious lawmakers and their public decision making more generally.

The Implications of Role-Based Morality for Lawmakers Generally

As we have seen, Mead argues that moral selves are responsible for taking into account all values and interests relevant to a particular issue or problem and for formulating resolutions that more satisfactorily address all of these values and interests (1964: 148, 387). He admits that the extent to which individuals can take the attitudes of all involved is limited by their capacity but that everyone is "able sufficiently to take the roles of those involved in the activity to make our own action intelligent" (256). Taking the attitude of the other includes an effort to try to see the world from another's point of view, which requires a certain open mindedness and tolerance for difference, as well as a capacity for empathy and imaginative identification.

Of particular relevance to thinking about the moral obligations of lawmakers is Mead's explanation that "the sort of capacity we speak of is in politics the attitude of the statesman who is able to enter into the attitudes of the group and to mediate between them by making his own experience universal, so that others can enter into this form of communication through him" (1964: 256). This capacity of leaders to mediate between disparate groups in the community takes on normative significance in the context of religious lawmaking.

Leaders are morally obligated to take on the attitudes of others by virtue of their ability to do so, as well as by their social roles as representatives of the people. Thus, in Mead's framework, lawmakers, as leaders, are responsible for taking on the attitudes of those beyond their narrow social group to include all of their constituents, especially those who are on the margins of the community. This understanding of moral obligations as role-based is reflected in the views of Cuomo and Hatfield as discussed in chapter 3. Although each lawmaker identified himself as a deeply religious person, he also expressed himself as occupying sometimes conflicting roles that required him to make policy decisions consistent with his responsibilities as a public official representing a religiously pluralistic constituency.

In contrast to those liberal and communitarian theorists I have discussed who tend to discount or ignore the distinction between lawmakers and others, a number of other theorists concur with Mead's view that lawmakers, as public officials, have a heightened responsibility to take the attitudes of others into consideration in their decision making (see Schauer 1986; cf. Tushnet 1991: 199; Held 1984). As an example, Virginia Held argues that "Professionals and public officials should at least be as moral as everybody else. . . . They ought to be, if anything, *more* moral because their power and influence are greater. They have a greater capacity to see the moral flaws in the special domains in which they now hold their positions and a greater ability to move the society closer to what could be morally acceptable" (1984: 76). It also must be noted that the Meadian notion of role-based morality differs significantly from the dominant conception of professional ethics. According to that conception, the professionals' roles give them an "institutional excuse" for ignoring or failing to comply with ordinary moral norms (see Luban 1988: 7; Wasserstrom 1984: 28–29; Postema 1980: 73, 78; Wasserstrom 1975: 5–6). For example, David Luban claims that role morality "establishes a monolithic point of view" within which the role agent is not responsible for the whole of morality because responsibility has been parceled out "in such a way that no single role is sensitive to all situations or has available to it a full range of responses" (1988: 127).

In the prevailing view, then, lawmakers typically inhabit a narrower moral universe than others (e.g., Wasserstrom 1975: 1). In Mead's theory, by contrast, the social roles of public officials give them additional or broader moral responsibilities. In addition, whereas the standard conception of professional ethics opposes role morality to common morality (e.g., Luban 1988; Wasserstrom 1984: 28), in Mead's approach role morality is derived from and thus is largely consistent with common morality. Mead's understanding of role-based morality is also far more contextual than that of the standard conception. For Mead, the self acts in accordance with the characteristics of the roles that are appropriate to the particular situation rather than through consistent, habitual presentation of the same role. These elements of a role-based morality provide the framework for assessing the moral obligations of religious lawmakers.

The Implications of Role-Based Morality for Religious Lawmakers in Particular

In order to be full or complete selves, lawmakers must take on or consider the attitudes or interests of all relevant others in the social situation. In a pluralistic society, this will include all of the constituents to whom the lawmaker is accountable, either directly as representatives or indirectly as holders of the public trust, not merely those who happen to share their religious (or other primary) commitments. Taking on the attitudes of constituents requires lawmakers to cultivate an openness to different moral perspectives and points of view, even if they are in tension or conflict with their own.

In order to act morally within a Meadian framework, then, lawmakers, as leaders in a morally pluralistic society, must set aside those religious convictions that interfere with their ability fully to consider the interests of their constituents by taking on their attitudes and roles. This includes religious convictions that lack public accessibility. In a socially and religiously pluralistic society such as the United States, religion is an especially inappropriate basis for lawmaking from a Meadian perspective because it requires a degree of identification and social cohesiveness that is lacking in a religiously pluralistic society.

When the lawmaker's only grounds for decision are religious, the likelihood for Establishment Concerns to be present is enhanced because of the lack of publicly accessible reasons to support many religious beliefs. Religious rationales for legal decisions are inappropriate if they are unable to provide common attitudes (which they frequently will not be able to do when controversial moral issues are involved).

Mead's conception of a role-based morality indicates that lawmakers generally should make public policy decisions on controversial moral issues such as abortion on secular grounds because making decisions on sectarian religious grounds is inconsistent with taking on the attitudes of all relevant others. However, lawmakers are not precluded in this analysis from using religious grounds to attempt to persuade their constituents of the merits of their position in discussion and debate in the public arena. Advocacy on religious grounds does not necessarily violate Mead's requirement of taking the attitudes of all relevant others.

However, when shared understandings or common attitudes do not (yet) exist, lawmakers should not impose their particularistic religious convictions on their constituents, especially where publicly accessible reasons do not exist and especially not through coercive laws and sanctions. To do so promotes a breakdown in the social communication that is so essential for cooperation, especially in a pluralistic society. As a pragmatic strategy, lawmakers are likely to be more successful using secular, rationally coherent arguments than expressly theological ones.

Mario Cuomo's approach to religious lawmaking, discussed in chapter 3, illustrates the model of a moral leader from a Meadian perspective. Although deeply religious, Cuomo claims to base his political decisions on what is realistically possible in a religiously pluralistic polity that maintains respect and tolerance for diversity. Jesse Jackson and Mark Hatfield also exhibit aspects of a Meadian model to the extent that they are willing to base their public decision making on a set of considerations wider than their personal religious views alone.

However, the ability to be self-reflective about the actual grounds for one's decision making (especially accurately) may be impossible for some lawmakers and unduly burdensome for others, as already discussed. Several of the lawmakers discussed in chapter 3 would certainly fail to measure up to the Meadian model of the moral leader, in view of their unwillingness or inability to consider perspectives outside of their own religious beliefs and, consequently, failure to meet the secular reliance requirement. An approach to religious lawmaking based on Mead's role-based morality need not require such secular reliance, however. It is able to accommodate lawmakers whose self understandings obligate them to make political decisions on the basis of religious grounds as long as they are willing and able to justify their decisions on the basis of secular reasons.

Adhering to a requirement of a secular rationale for lawmaking does not unduly burden religious lawmakers because it does not require them to abandon or bracket their personal religious convictions, as liberal proposals like Audi's do. Although requiring a secular justification for their decisions does burden religious lawmakers slightly more than secular lawmakers who would justify their decisions in secular terms in any event, this requirement is justified by virtue of lawmakers' special roles as public officials and representatives.

In addition, lawmakers better accord respect to their constituents by making arguments in terms that are publicly accessible to them and that are less likely to raise Establishment Concerns than religious ones. From this perspective, government or official impositions of religious values for which a widespread agreement or consensus does not exist is an illegitimate imposition of power over the citizenry that violates principles of tolerance and respect for difference.

Requiring that lawmakers justify their political decisions with secular rationales is also required by the oath of office that most lawmakers are required to take to uphold the Constitution, as specified in Article VI of that document (see Tribe 1990: 77; 1988: 116). As we have seen, the Constitution protects the rights of all citizens, among them the rights to the free exercise and nonestablishment of religion, which religiously justified laws may offend. The obligation to protect Citizenship Rights thus provides an additional reason for lawmakers to justify their publicly binding decisions on secular grounds.

With respect to Mead's views in the context of abortion lawmaking specifically, an ideal Meadian lawmaker is obligated to consider the attitudes and roles of all relevant parties. This will include those of pregnant women and may even include medical personnel who are involved in performing abortions, the family members of women who wish to terminate unwanted pregnancies, and the fetus, depending on the beliefs of the lawmaker and his or her constituents about when human life begins, and so on.

The breadth and depth of the obligation to take the attitudes of others is necessarily defined in part by the lawmakers' particular context, however, such as whether constituents hold radically different views, either among themselves or in relation to the lawmakers'. In a religiously pluralistic polity, it simply may not be possible for the lawmaker to even know what all of these views are, never mind "take on" all of them. Thus, the standard for taking the attitudes of others must be a realistic one.

In addition, according to Mead's criteria for the moral obligations of leaders, lawmakers are required to make a decision that takes all of these interests into account and to represent them fairly in the process of reconciling or harmonizing them. To do this properly requires lawmakers to be aware of the coercive effects of restrictive abortion laws on women, especially those lacking in the social and political power to participate in the formulation of the legal and moral values that regulate their lives.

Lawmakers, by definition, have some degree of political and social power, and those who are male, white, and from elite socioeconomic backgrounds have even more. In the context of abortion lawmaking, such power disparities enable lawmakers to exercise regulatory authority over the reproductive lives of women. Because pregnant women are frequently of races, ethnicities, religions, and economic statuses that lack social power, the inequality of power is exacerbated. Thus, abortion lawmaking involves power inequalities not only of gender but also of race, class, ethnicity, and religion.

These inequalities are exacerbated when lawmakers base their official decisions on their religious convictions. As discussed previously, the traditional male gender bias of most dominant religious traditions contributes to the lack of consideration of women in religious views of abortion. This bias is more likely to emerge in abortion lawmaking when (predominantly male) lawmakers base their decisions primarily or exclusively on their religious convictions. In addition, as noted previously, the religious affiliations of lawmakers in the United States are predominantly Christian, in contrast with the greater diversity of religious affiliations of their constituents. The result of these considerations, in conjunction with the unequal power relations that frequently exist between lawmakers and constituents, is that mainstream and dominant religious traditions have a disproportionately greater influence on public legislation than those of non-mainstream or minority traditions.

Thus, lawmakers also need to be aware that their decision making involves an exercise of power, one which is somewhat obscured under the guise of neutral decision making "in the public interest" or "for the common good." They need to consider their own power within the social context, both that resulting from their roles as well as other aspects of their social location and the implications of their public decision making for the Citizenship Rights of their constituents, especially those at the margins of society and particularly those disadvantaged on the basis of gender and religion.

Laws passed in conformity with the constraints of this Meadian model will have at least the potential for garnering widespread public support, thereby reducing the possibilities of raising Establishment Concerns and/or infringing on Citizenship Rights. In addition, this framework functions to diminish to some extent the inequalities of gender and religious power that we have seen operating in religious lawmaking, especially with respect to the issue of abortion.

Summary and Conclusions

As we have seen, Mead's pragmatist philosophy provides a better basis for conceptualizing the moral self than the models provided by liberal and communitarian theorists. Although Mead's conception of moral identity shares significant elements with both liberal and communitarian views, it avoids many of their deficiencies. By offering an empirically based account rather than a theoretical one, Mead's approach better demonstrates how moral identity is formed in interaction with individual others in the social situation rather than assumed to be independent and autonomous, as in the liberal view, or as rigidly determined by one's community and tradition, as in the communitarian one. Mead's understanding of moral identity is thereby better able to account for how the self is both a socially produced community member and a self-determining individual, contrary to the communitarian fixation with relationality or the liberal one with independence.

Mead's understanding of the social self also points up the flaw in communitarian notions that coercing individuals for the sake of the common good is justified because individuals are socially constructed anyway by showing that the collectivity produces individual selves with independent agency and distinct points of view that may not cohere with those of the majority or dominant group. His description of how self-identity is composed of a multiplicity of elements, both objective and subjective, in a fashion that precludes complete self knowledge, calls into question both liberal and communitarian assumptions that the moral self is a self-transparent, coherent, unitary entity.

Mead's approach to moral identity indicates that religious convictions, while comprising one dimension of the self's identity for some persons, are not the only determinant of that identity nor, consequently, of the decisions that are made pursuant to it. Mead shows how complete moral selves reflect the full diversity of the social situation in which they are implicated, not only one aspect of it, as communitarian theories tend to posit. In a pluralistic society like the United States, the social environment for any individual self will extend across multiple communities, some of which may be religious and which may be in tension or outright conflict with one another.

Consequently, a Meadian approach to public decision making advocates an inclusive model, one that includes one's own religious convictions as only one element among the many attitudes of others that the moral self is obligated to consider. This contrasts starkly with the exclusive approaches of both liberal and communitarian theory (the liberal approach is exclusive in dictating strict secularity, to the exclusion of religious convictions, whereas the communitarian approach is exclusive in arguing that sectarianism is fine, without engaging with other perspectives outside of that of one's community).

The agency of the moral selves of Mead's theory reinforces the liberal view that moral selves in fact do choose how they will respond to situations of moral conflict. An individual's religious convictions need not be determinative of who they are or how they will decide particular matters, regardless of their self-understandings. The novelty and unpredictability of the *I* implies that the self's reliance on its religious convictions will always be contingent, never certain or secure.

Mead's account thus suggests that despite being produced by the social process, including the religious community that is a constituent of that process, moral selves are not inextricably or inherently bound by the moral teachings of their religious communities. Rather, they are able to develop capacities for independent moral judgment and decision making. These capacities include the ability to decide whether or not to rely on one's religious convictions, even if doing so runs counter to the norms of their entire community.

In addition to offering a model of the moral self that better recognizes both moral identity and social or religious pluralism than either liberal or communitarian approaches, Mead's theory of role-based morality provides a helpful method for considering the appropriate moral conduct of religious lawmakers in a pluralistic democracy, also circumventing many of the problems left unresolved in liberal and communitarian proposals. In contrast to liberalism, Mead's views of the moral obligations of leaders are not premised on the liberal assumption that selves are morally capable of separating themselves from their religious convictions.

Rather, Mead's pragmatist approach suggests that lawmakers are morally obligated to take on the attitudes of all relevant others in making legally binding enactments and to promote the interests of society as a whole, not only their own personal interests. In addition, it suggests that, at a minimum, lawmakers should justify their decisions on publicly accessible grounds (which more often will be secular than religious).

At the same time, Mead's role-based morality need not unduly restrict lawmakers' reliance on their religious convictions because its only necessary requirement is directed to the lawmakers' roles as public decision makers and to the justifications or rationales they provide for their political decision making. Mead's focus on taking all relevant interests into account holds more promise for decision making in a morally and religiously pluralistic society than prevailing liberal approaches that undervalue community or communitarian ones that overvalue it.

The preceding discussion suggests that religious lawmakers are both constitutionally able and normatively obligated to rely on considerations beyond their personal religious convictions when acting in roles as public policy makers. Notwithstanding these conclusions, such a theoretical or ideal solution to the dilemma of religious lawmaking is of limited practical usefulness. As noted in chapter 1, the vast majority of the American polity, including lawmakers, identify themselves as religious persons. Religion provides many people with a sense of meaning and a framework for organizing and making sense of their lives. Even if religious identity does not actually provide a unity and coherence to moral selves, it may nonetheless provide the psychological or emotional sense of doing so.

As chapter 3 suggests, many religious lawmakers are unlikely to be convinced by theoretical arguments that their self-understandings as intrinsically or primarily religious are mistaken and that, consequently, they generally should not rely on their religious convictions in their public policy making. In view of these circumstances, a practical legal strategy is needed to supplement the Meadian theoretical approach described here. In the following, and final, chapter, I propose a constitutionally based strategy for resolving the dilemma of religious lawmaking.

SEVEN

A Legal Strategy for Addressing Religious Lawmaking

In the preceding chapter, I suggested that Meadian conceptions of the social self and role-based morality provide a useful theoretical framework for addressing the dilemma of religious lawmaking. According to this theoretical or pragmatist approach, potential conflicts between the religious identity of lawmakers and their constituents in a culturally pluralistic society can be significantly mitigated, if not eliminated, if lawmakers based their decisions on publicly accessible reasons, in accordance with their role-based obligations as public officials. This approach is unlikely to provide a fully effective resolution of the dilemma as a practical matter, however, because it is dependent on the voluntary willingness of religious lawmakers to adhere to the requirements of such a role-based morality. In other words, as a practical matter, voluntary self regulation by the nation's lawmakers is inadequate to ensure protection against the potential harms that religious lawmaking may cause to Establishment Concerns and Citizenship Rights.

Thus, a practical strategy is also needed to supplement the Meadian-based theoretical approach. Even though lawmakers' special social roles as leaders justifies imposing some restrictions on their public decision making in the interests of securing social justice for all citizens, lawmakers are also citizens entitled to the protections of the Free Exercise Clause. Thus, a proposal for resolving the dilemma should not constrain their free exercise rights and interests more than necessary to accomplish the goal of protecting Citizenship Rights.

In this chapter, I propose a legal strategy able to accommodate both the rights of religious lawmakers to the free exercise of their religious convictions and the free exercise and Citizenship Rights of other citizens, including women and religious minorities. In the first part, I outline a proposed legal model for addressing religious lawmaking and describe each of its elements. I then describe how each element of the proposed model applies in the context of religious lawmaking on abortion and consider how the proposed model remedies several problems with the Supreme Court's decisions in this area.

In the third part of the chapter, I describe how the proposed model applies to several other issues involving religious lawmaking, in particular, to the regulation of homosexual conduct and environmental protection. Because these two issues differ significantly from each another as well as from abortion, they present a sound basis for testing the extent of the proposal's usefulness. The chapter ends with some concluding reflections about how the proposed legal model is preferable to other approaches for resolving the dilemma of religious lawmaking.

An Alternative Legal Approach

As the discussion in chapter 2 illustrated, the Supreme Court's jurisprudence on religious lawmaking has failed to protect adequately either the free exercise rights of religious lawmakers or the Citizenship Rights of others, especially pregnant women and religious minorities. The inadequacies we have seen in the Supreme Court's jurisprudence on religious lawmaking stem in large part from the Court's failure to recognize the harms of such lawmaking. Specifically, the Court's decisions have largely ignored how religious lawmaking infringes on Citizenship Rights other than those directly covered by the First Amendment religion clauses. They have also failed to recognize or redress the way that religious lawmaking raises Establishment Concerns that may exacerbate infringements on Citizenship Rights. The Court's voluntarist assumptions about the character of religious adherence have contributed to its lack of concern about the ways that religious lawmaking may interfere with constitutional rights of citizens, especially those of women and religious minorities. At the same time, the Court has largely overlooked the significance of religious convictions in the lives of religious lawmakers.

Although it is not reasonable to expect that all judges are either willing or capable of taking a Meadian perspective requiring them to "take the attitude of the other" in the cases that come before them, some judges certainly are. For others, the criteria set out later for determining whether constitutional rights or interests have been harmed by religious lawmaking can be incorporated into the regular procedures for judicial review.

The following outlines a proposed modified Establishment Clause test for assessing the constitutional validity of religious lawmaking. This test supplements the Court's conventional Establishment Clause jurisprudence with additional (and sometimes modified) criteria. Because the strategy proposed here is a legal one, it is framed primarily in terms of individual rights, consistent with traditional judicial approaches to religious freedom. As noted earlier, it is not intended to be an endorsement of the liberal model but, rather, reflects an acknowledgment that the American legal system is currently structured predominantly in liberal terms, including the language of rights.

The elements of the proposed model are as follows:

A. Petitioner's Case: The petitioner bears the burden of establishing that the challenged enactment:
   1. Has been based on or influenced by religious considerations.
   2. Has effects that are alienating, exclusionary, coercive, and/or politically divisive (raises Establishment Concerns).
   3. Infringes on a constitutionally protected right of citizenship.

If the petitioner is successful in satisfying all three requirements of this part, the enactment is presumptively invalid.

These steps of the petitioner's case are successive. That is, the petitioner must be able to satisfy the requirements of 1 before the case progresses to 2 and 2 before it proceeds to 3. If the petitioner is successful in satisfying the requirements of at least 1 and 2 (the basic test), the burden of persuasion shifts to the government to attempt to justify the challenged legislation. The requirements of the government's case are as follows:

B. Government's Case:
   1. To sustain an enactment demonstrated to be invalid under requirements A1 and A2 , the burden of persuasion shifts to the government to show that it has a substantial secular justification or rationale for the proposed law.
   2. To sustain an enactment demonstrated to be invalid under all sections of Part A (the comprehensive test), the government's burden is to show that it has a compelling secular State interest in effectuating the subject of the enactment that cannot be achieved through the use of less restrictive means.

A guiding assumption behind the model is that when religious lawmaking abridges Citizenship Rights, Establishment Concerns will usually be present in some form, whether in the form of alienation, exclusion, coercion, or political divisiveness. The opposite presumption, that the existence of Establishment Concerns means that Citizenship Rights have been violated, does not hold, however. Even though the presence of Establishment Concerns is sufficient to create an inference or suspicion that Citizenship Rights have been infringed on, it is not sufficient to create an irrebuttable presumption because not all forms of alienation, exclusion, coercion, and political divisiveness rise to the level of full-scale violations of the Constitution.

The first two requirements of the petitioner's case remain the same in the test for violation of Citizenship Rights as for Establishment Concerns. The only difference is whether there is evidence that Citizenship Rights have been abridged, triggering the third requirement (the comprehensive test). The government's case differs between the two tests only in the level of justification it must be able to provide. Where only Establishment Concerns are at issue, the government has a lower burden of persuasion. It need only show that it has a "substantial secular interest" for its law, in accordance with the Court's middle-tier standard of review of suspect classes, as discussed in chapter 2. Where Citizenship Rights are shown to have been abridged, however, the State is required to show a compelling secular interest for its law, corresponding to the "strict scrutiny" level of analysis applied in cases involving fundamental rights and invidious classifications such as race.

If the petitioner is unable to show a religious influence on the challenged law, then the case should be analyzed in accordance with traditional standards of interpretation for alleged violations of constitutional rights, without applying the proposed test. There is no justification for using the proposed test in this circumstance because any harm to petitioner's rights is not the proximate result of religious influences on the law at issue.

Imposing a higher burden of proof on the government in cases of religious lawmaking is warranted because of the distinctive harms that may result when the State becomes so closely aligned with religion. Restricting the role of religion in lawmaking that disadvantages Citizenship Rights is justified in part under the proposed model by allowing an expanded role for religion in other types of lawmaking, as well as in the public sphere more generally.

One of the merits of this two-tiered approach is to make it easier to validate religious lawmaking that does not involve Establishment Concerns or infringements on Citizenship Rights. This can be effected under the proposed model without needing to engage in contorted or disingenuous interpretations that the law does not have a religious basis or influence, as we have seen the Court sometimes resort to in the cases discussed in chapter 2. Where the danger of coercion is limited, the rationale for excluding religion from public policy making weakens.

Elements of the Petitioner's Case

In the following sections, I describe the rationale for each element of the petitioner's case and then illustrate how it would apply to the abortion cases discussed in chapter 2.

Religious Influence

The first step of a successful challenge to religious lawmaking under the proposed test requires petitioners to show that the challenged enactment is, in fact, based on or influenced by religious considerations. The model is intended to apply primarily to the first and second types of religious influence described earlier: those of Motivation and Justification because these are the types of religious influences most likely to raise Establishment Concerns and run afoul of Citizenship Rights.

Some objective evidence of religious influence on the challenged enactment must be available to satisfy this requirement. This may be demonstrated to satisfy this first requirement in several ways. A religious influence may be evident on the face of a particular law, as in the presence of an explicitly theological rationale or language. It may be apparent in the absence of an adequate secular rationale or purpose for an enactment. In this situation, the evidence of religious influence is more circumstantial than direct.

The lack of a plausible nonreligious rationale, in combination with some similarity to or continuity with religious rationales, will also satisfy the requirement by suggesting that religious influence on a legal decision was more likely than not. In addition, religious influence may also be suggested if a facially neutral law has disparate consequences for religious believers and nonbelievers or was introduced by primarily or predominantly religious organizations and interests rather than by some combination of religious and secular individuals or groups.

Satisfaction of this first requirement permits petitioners to move to the second step of their case, where the harmful effects of the prima facie religious influence must be shown. The purpose of requiring that laws bear a specifically religious influence is to justify the proposed model's use of liberalized standing requirements and lower burdens of persuasion. These loosened burdens on petitioners are only justifiable in those limited cases that warrant heightened scrutiny because of their religious character.

Most of the abortion regulations described in chapter 2 plainly qualify under this requirement. These include the influence of religious groups on the legislature's passage of the Hyde Amendment in *Harris v. McRae*, as detailed in the legislative history to the Hyde Amendment (see *McRae v. Califano*, 491 F. Supp. 630 [E.D.N.Y. 1980]) and as evidenced by the district court's conclusion that organized religious efforts may have been decisive in the vote in favor of the amendment (491 F. Supp. at 724).

Similarly, in *Webster v. Reproductive Health Services* (492 U.S. 490 [1989]), there was independent evidence that religious groups influenced members of the Missouri legislature. In addition, the abortion restrictions in this case reflect a view of when human life begins that is more consistent with dominant religious beliefs than with secular views. In addition, because such views are almost always—and were in fact in these cases—promoted by religious organizations rather than secular ones, the presumption that both statutes are religiously influenced is warranted for purposes of the proposed assessment. This is especially justified as here, where there is no evidence to suggest that they were not so influenced.

It is less clear that the *Adolescent Family Life Act* (*AFLA*) statute at risk in *Bowen v. Kendrick* (487 U.S. 589, 597 [1988]) was religiously influenced. In this case, the "mischief" that religion causes does not result primarily from religious influences supporting the passage of the act but instead from statutory funding being awarded to both religiously affiliated and secular institutions. It is the (alleged) teaching of explicitly religious doctrines by some of the grantees that raises religion clause concerns, not religious influences in the statute itself. It is possible that Congress's motivation for passing *AFLA* was to promote alternatives to abortion based on religious convictions about its morality, but there is no explicit evidence on the face of the statute or in the legislative history to suggest that this was the case (although, as we saw earlier, Congress did anticipate Establishment Clause objections as witnessed by its defensive statement in the Senate Report that accompanied the bill for *AFLA*). Thus, in the absence of additional evidence, a challenge in *AFLA* would be disqualified under the first step of the proposed assessment test, regardless of its possible effects in promoting Establishment Concerns or violating Citizenship Rights.

In sum, although many abortion regulations that have been legally challenged as violating the First Amendment religion clauses would be able to satisfy the first step of the proposed assessment model, application of the proposed model to the *Bowen v. Kendrick* case demonstrates its inability to address all infringements on Citizenship Rights that arise from lawmaking that relates in some way to religion.

Presence of Establishment Concerns

The second step of the proposed legal model requires petitioners to show that the law at issue raises Establishment Concerns, that is, has religious effects that are alienating, exclusionary, coercive, or politically divisive. Because many secular laws also raise Establishment Concerns, petitioners must show not only the presence of an Establishment Concern but also that it is related to religious influence.

Although restrictive abortion regulations that are not based on religious considerations, such as the *AFLA* at issue in *Bowen v. Kendrick*, may also be alienating, coercive, and politically divisive, if they are based on secular reasons, they are amenable to being debated and contested on the basis of publicly accessible reasons. It is the combination of religion with restrictive regulations, not either religious influence or restrictiveness alone, that creates significant risks of raising Establishment Concerns. A showing of more likely than not is an appropriate burden of proof to impose on petitioners here because it requires a significant showing of harmful religious influence without being overly burdensome.

Although the presence of Establishment Concerns, considered alone, may not be sufficient to establish an Establishment Clause violation under the Court's traditional interpretations of that Clause, the presence of any one of these concerns is sufficient under the proposed test to warrant heightened scrutiny of the challenged enactment. Reviewing religious lawmaking to determine whether it raises Establishment Concerns provides a way of scrutinizing laws that are influenced by religion but do not violate the Court's established tests for Establishment Clause cases.

This would include, for example, laws that involve multiple or mixed purposes and effects, not merely religious or secular ones. For example, an abortion law passed both to protect fetal life and do the will of God or to protect traditional family values and prevent government from condoning the sin of nonmarital sexuality would show the presence of Establishment Concerns under the proposed test, despite the presence of a secular purpose, even a primary one. Thus, the proposed test considers Establishment Concerns to be problematic, regardless of whether they constitute a violation of the core Establishment Clause or other constitutional rights.

At the same time, the fact that a law has a religious purpose or motivation does not necessitate that it cannot be fully supported by secular reasons or that its effects necessarily will raise Establishment Concerns or disadvantage Citizenship Rights. If petitioners cannot demonstrate that Establishment Concerns actually exist, the case should be analyzed in accordance with traditional constitutional law because there is no warrant for applying the higher burdens of proof standards and heightened scrutiny of the proposed test.

The presence of Establishment Concerns functions as supplemental evidence that constitutional rights have been violated. In the context of the proposed test, they serve to lower the burden of proof petitioners are required to put forward to show that their Citizenship Rights have been abridged. However, the proposed assessment model does not invalidate every religiously influenced law that has alienating, exclusionary, coercive, or politically divisive effects. Such laws are valid, notwithstanding their religious character, if they can be justified by a substantial secular interest.

The challenged abortion regulations in the cases considered in chapter 2 would each satisfy the second requirement of the proposed test in being alienating to nonbelievers, especially those with different religious convictions than the Catholic and other religious doctrines that influenced their enactment The laws in *Harris v. McRae* and *Webster v. Reproductive Health Services* are also exclusionary and coercive to indigent pregnant women who desire to exercise their constitutional right to terminate an unwanted pregnancy but who are denied the public funding necessary to enable them to do so. Although such language in these statutes may not be directly coercive, in the sense of prohibiting women from obtaining abortions, it may contribute to the restriction of women's constitutional rights because of a strong symbolic message that is sent regarding the morality of abortion.

Because petitioners in most of the abortion cases considered here would be able to satisfy the two steps of their required showing under the proposed test, the burden would shift to the government to offer a substantial secular interest to sustain the validity of its enactments. However, since most of these regulations also meet the conditions of the third step of petitioner's case, which is required to make a prima facie case of violation of Citizenship Rights, I defer discussion of the government's requirements until the following section.

Infringement on Citizenship Rights

The infringement standard requires petitioners to show that the challenged law results in some burden on, interference with, or disadvantage to their Citizenship Rights. This showing does not require plaintiffs to demonstrate that the law makes their exercise of Citizenship Rights impossible. The standard of infringement here is intended to be lower than the violation or compulsion standards traditionally applied by the Supreme Court.

Thus, when Establishment Concerns are present, petitioners should only be obligated to demonstrate that their Citizenship Rights have been abridged rather than completely denied or violated. In effect, the presence of Establishment Concerns reduces the burden of evidence that plaintiffs must present in order to successfully challenge the constitutional validity of religious lawmaking. The lower standard is justified because the petitioner's demonstration of Establishment Concerns already provides some grounds for invalidating a religiously influenced enactment.

In particular, the lower standard provides protections for women and subordinate religious groups from coercive treatment by politically and socially dominant religious influences on lawmaking. For example, showing that a religiously influenced abortion restriction limits a plaintiff's ability to exercise her right to choose to have an abortion would satisfy this requirement. However, the mere fact that a humanitarian aid authorization to a disaster-stricken region was motivated in part by religious concerns would not be adequate to invalidate the authorization without evidence of harmful consequences to plaintiffs.

Petitioners need not prove that there is a causal relationship between the presence of religious influence and the abridgement of their Citizenship Rights. The test is religious influence plus violation of Citizenship Rights, not violation of Citizenship Rights caused by religious influences. To require such strict causation would be unduly burdensome, especially since there has already been some causal connection established by the second step's requirement that Establishment Concerns be demonstrably related to religious influence. Because religious influences on law have a demonstrated history of being problematic, an inference is warranted that where a law has a religious character and infringes on Citizenship Rights, that the religious influence contributed to the violation.

In the following sections of this chapter, I explore how this requirement applies to Citizenship Rights in the context of legal regulations of abortion, homosexual conduct, and environmental pollution. I discuss some of the more significant considerations for evaluating whether religious lawmaking infringes on Citizenship Rights that are relevant in the context of abortion regulation.

Establishment Clause

Demonstrating that religious lawmaking violates core Establishment Clause rights requires petitioners to satisfy the standards of the Supreme Court's tests for Establishment Clause violations. Given the ambiguities of the Court's current test for Establishment Clause violations, the constitutionality of religious lawmaking for purposes of the proposed assessment model is determined basically by applying the neutrality and endorsement standards established in the Supreme Court's decision in *Lee v. Weisman*, as discussed in chapter 2.

As we have seen, restrictive abortion laws based on or influenced by religious considerations risk violating Establishment Clause rights when they enact into law a particular religious view of when human life begins. This is not only because they cannot be fully supported on the basis of nonreligious considerations, but partly as a consequence because they inevitably will conflict with other religious (as well as secular) views about the status and intrinsic value of fetal life, thereby violating government's obligation of neutrality toward religion.

The preamble in the *Webster v. Reproductive Health Services* case, like the Hyde Amendment in *Harris v. McRae*, fails the neutrality test by endorsing tenets of particular religious groups regarding when personal human life begins and the value of that life. In addition, the government prohibition on funding for abortions in *Harris v. McRae* and on allowing public facilities and employees to be used for abortions in *Webster v. Reproductive Health Services* sends a message that the government endorses religious anti-abortion views. This message would also arguably violate the Establishment Clause under the proposed test.

Free Exercise Clause Violations. As noted previously, for religious lawmaking to be invalidated as an infringement on free exercise rights according to the Court's traditional test, a petitioner generally is required to show: (1) a sincerely held religious belief (2) that is burdened by a governmental requirement that is not generally applicable to all citizens. Whereas the Court traditionally has refused to find a free exercise violation unless the petitioner's ability to exercise his or her religion is directly burdened, it is sufficient under the proposed test that petitioners demonstrate that the law have a demonstrable influence on their ability to exercise their religious beliefs. Given that religious beliefs may be central to moral identity, a standard that only requires petitioners to show that free exercise rights have been infringed, burdened, obstructed, or otherwise abridged is more appropriate than one requiring them to demonstrate that their religious beliefs compel them to violate a law.

The standard for evaluating free exercise violations proposed here is also broader than the Court's because it covers conflicts with or burdens on religious practices and not simply religious beliefs. Although, as mentioned previously, the Court has stated that the Free Exercise Clause protects conduct as well as belief (e.g., *McDaniel v. Paty*, 435 U.S. at 631 [Brennan, J., concurring]), its rulings have favored protections for religious belief over practice (see *Employment Division v. Smith*, 494 U.S. 872 [1990]; *Lyng v. Indian Cemetery Protective Association*, 485 U.S. 439 [1988]).

However, the test does not expand protections for free exercise claims to encompass all deeply held beliefs of conscience, regardless of whether they are religious. The primary reason is, again, the text of the First Amendment, which applies, literally and by interpretation, to religion, not secular beliefs generally. To maintain respect for this constitutional distinction but without undermining or completely denying protection to nonreligious beliefs of conscience, I propose that nonreligious beliefs should be protected by the

Free Exercise Clause only if they hold a place in the life of the believer analogous to those of religious faith. This moderately expanded interpretation of religion is based on the family resemblances standard for defining religion discussed in chapter 1 and is consistent with the Court's interpretation of religion in *United States v. Seeger* (380 U.S. 163, 176 [1965]) regarding conscientious objectors.

As noted previously, insofar as restrictive abortion laws are based on or influenced by religious beliefs contrary to those held by a pregnant woman, they may burden her ability to freely exercise her religious beliefs, in violation of the Free Exercise Clause. As Dworkin argues, "a state has no business prescribing what people should think about the ultimate point and value of human life, about why life has intrinsic importance, and about how that value is respected" in circumstances involving prenatal life (1993: 164–65). I would add that it particularly has no business doing so when the basis for its prescription is religious. The restrictive abortion laws considered here infringe on the free exercise rights of pregnant women whose ability to exercise their religious beliefs is hampered by their inability to obtain an abortion. Such restrictions most conspicuously violate the free exercise rights of those women whose religious traditions make abortion a matter of conscience or even duty in certain circumstances.

In addition, under the relaxed standard of the proposed test, which requires plaintiffs to show only that their free exercise rights have been burdened, not that they are completely made impossible, in combination with the presence of Establishment Concerns, courts applying the proposed test legitimately could find a free exercise violation in several of the cases discussed here. The liberalized burden of proof requirements in the proposed test would thereby enable plaintiffs in *Harris v. McRae* and *Webster v. Reproductive Health Services* to go forward to establish their claim of Free Exercise Clause violations by showing that the abortion restrictions at issue precluded them from acting in accordance with their religious beliefs.[1]

Due Process Clause Violations.   A showing that religious lawmaking infringes on substantive due process rights will trigger a presumption of invalidity under the proposed test. This presumption applies to situations in which religious lawmaking obstructs citizens' ability to act in accordance with their own personal convictions, whether religiously informed or not, on matters protected by the constitutional guarantees of liberty and privacy.

In the abortion context, such infringements would include restrictions on the liberty and privacy rights found in *Roe v. Wade* and reaffirmed in *Planned Parenthood v. Casey*. In both *Harris v. McRae* and *Webster v. Reproductive Health Services*, the Court failed to take the religious infringements on the plaintiffs' privacy and liberty rights seriously in its assessments. Even if the regulations at issue do not burden women's exercise of specifically religious convictions, they certainly do restrict women's liberty rights. Under the proposed test, the denial of Medicaid funding in *Harris v. McRae* and of publicly funded abortion facilities or personnel in *Webster v. Reproductive*

Health Services deny indigent women the right to exercise their privacy rights to abortion.

Equal Protection Rights.   Because the effect of restrictive abortion laws is to reinforce the subordination of women in society by treating them differently than men and leaving them involuntarily pregnant and unable to act as freely in the world as men do (Olsen 1989: 120), women should be recognized as a suspect class in relation to restrictive abortion regulations. All of the abortion laws considered here have the effect of disadvantaging women in relation to men by restricting women's ability to control their reproduction. They also have the effect of disadvantaging pregnant females over nonpregnant females and pregnant females with unwanted pregnancies over those with wanted ones. Thus, the abortion laws in the cases considered here all satisfy the third requirement of the petitioner's case by infringing on women's Citizenship Rights.

Indeed, most religiously influenced restrictive abortion laws would fail the third requirement of the proposed test. Less restrictive abortion regulations, such as regulations of the time, place, and circumstances under which the abortion is performed; notification requirements; informed consent provisions; and so on could survive invalidation at this stage, however. For example, parental notification or consent statutes may be motivated by religious concerns about family values, (patriarchal) notions of parental control over the family, the immorality of teen sexual activity, the sin of abortion, and so on. These religious concerns would certainly raise Establishment Concerns, especially with respect to families not subscribing to such views. However, given the limited constitutional rights that judicial interpretations have accorded to minors, it is unlikely that such restrictions would be interpreted as infringing on Citizenship Rights as long as certain procedural mechanisms, such as a judicial bypass procedure, were in place (see, e.g., *Planned Parenthood of Central Missouri v. Danforth*, 425 U.S. 52 [1976]; *Planned Parenthood v. Casey*, 505 U.S. 833 [1992]; *Bellotti v. Baird*, II, 443 U.S. 622 [1979]; *H. L. v. Matheson*, 450 U.S. 398 [1981]). Because such regulations do not significantly interfere with Citizenship Rights (under the Court's interpretations), they would be assessed under the basic test, even if they were the outcome of religious lawmaking.

Elements of the Government's Case

If petitioners satisfy the requirements for showing that religious lawmaking infringes on either Establishment Concerns or Citizenship Rights, the burden shifts to the government to attempt to justify the law, despite its presumptive invalidity. To rebut a showing of Establishment Concerns, the government has the burden of demonstrating that it has a substantial interest in pursuing the challenged policy. To rebut a demonstration that Citizenship Rights have been violated, the government must demonstrate that it has a compelling State interest for maintaining the religiously influenced provision. Regardless of which level of interest the State is seeking to establish, it must also demonstrate that its interest is a secular one. Otherwise, a lawmaking body could theoretically claim that it had a compelling religious interest for passing a religiously based law, such as to prevent the apocalypse or to avoid the wrath of God.

In addition, although as noted previously, the existence of a religious purpose alone is not enough to invalidate a law, so also the existence of a secular purpose (whether substantial or compelling) should not be enough to validate a religiously based law (especially where Citizenship Rights are at stake) unless the effects can be shown to not harm Citizenship Rights. On one hand, for example, the effect of religiously motivated legislation to increase aid to the poor or reduce taxes may be completely secular (Tribe 1988: 1277), whereas on the other, "public decision making may manifest entirely secular legislative intent, yet consistently understate the concerns of minority religions" (Teitel 1993: 776). Thus, it is important to attend to the religious consequences of lawmaking and not simply the intentions underlying it.

Where the law can be justified by a substantial (or compelling) secular interest, its character as having religious origins or influences does not warrant its invalidation under the proposed test because Citizenship Rights are not in danger. Although under a Meadian model, the ideal lawmaker would avoid using discourse that either raised Establishment Concerns or threatened Citizenship Rights, the strategy outlined here is designed as a reasonable middle ground between imposing no restrictions on political discourse, as communitarian theories have proposed, and prohibiting religious discourse completely, as some liberal theorists have advocated. This middle-ground standard is thus more fair than either Greenawalt's proposal to require only "plausible" secular arguments or Perry's requirement of a "persuasive secular argument" (1997: 76).

The use of the secular rationale or justification standard is deliberately designed to avoid the problems discussed earlier that are entailed in using public accessibility as the standard. Requiring a secular rationale is not intended to privilege secular reasons as somehow epistemologically more valid or true or even neutral in some ultimate sense than religious reasons (cf. Alexander 1993) but instead to signal that there are fewer pragmatic difficulties with using a secular standard than a religious one. Using the secular standard avoids the possible Establishment Concerns of alienation, political divisiveness, and so on that arise when reasons are publicly accessible (at least in some respects) but also religious in character.

Responding to the Presence of Establishment Concerns

The appropriate focus of the first requirement of the government's case is on whether the law can be justified by a substantial secular State interest, not whether the lawmaker's actual purpose or motivation or particular structure was religious. The term *interest* in the "substantial secular interest" standard should be interpreted to mean "rationale" or "justification." The justification or rationale for the law is the most important aspect because it determines whether the influence of religion has been dispositive in the law's enactment. That is, could the law have been enacted without reference to religion? (Whether it would have been so enacted is a separate question beyond the scope of objective analysis.) If so, the religious influence has not been the proximate cause of any harms to Citizenship Rights.

Even though the effects of a law motivated by religious considerations (but sustainable on a secular rationale) may infringe on Citizenship Rights, that infringement should be addressed on the basis of the Court's traditional tests rather than on one designed to address the distinctive harms of religious lawmaking. Again, as in the case where petitioners are unable to show a religious influence on a challenged law, if the religious dimension cannot be shown to have influenced the outcome of lawmaking, the justification for applying an interpretive model that diverges from the Court's traditional interpretations disappears.

The requirement that the government be able to show a substantial interest is designed to require the government to do more than simply forward some plausible secular interest, as in the Court's interpretation of some Establishment Clause cases. Rather, the interest must be one that is both within the appropriate jurisdiction of the lawmaking body and designed to forward the legitimate central business of the State. The government need not prove that the law is without any religious purpose, as long as it can demonstrate that it has substantial secular reasons for enacting the law. This standard avoids the problem of legislation that may have a religious purpose but nonetheless can be sustained on the basis of secular reasons. This proposed standard is consistent with Supreme Court decisions that have invalidated laws on the basis that they were not justified in terms of a nonreligious purpose (see *Wallace v. Jaffree*, 472 U.S. 38 [1985]; *Epperson v. Arkansas*, 393 U.S. 97 [1968]).

Further, the availability of a substantial government interest for a law will be sufficient to satisfy the government's burden, regardless of whether individual lawmakers actually raised or relied on such grounds (see Tushnet 1991: 195; cf. Audi 1990, 1989). This avoids problems of proof associated with having to ascertain legislative intent and also better protects the moral identity and free exercise rights of religious lawmakers than does the Court's traditional test.

Courts and others applying the test can make an independent assessment of whether there is a substantial secular rationale that can sustain the enactment, regardless of whether it actually was raised or relied on in the enactment process. By meeting this standard, the State can demonstrate that it has substantial reasons not having to do with religion that make its decision a sound one. This standard allows religion to play a role in the lawmaking process but not one that raises Establishment Concerns. Again, although in accordance with an ideal Median conception of lawmakers' moral obligations, it would be preferable if lawmakers would take the attitudes of their constituents into account in the process of enacting and justifying laws, their failure to do so does not constitute grounds under the proposed test to invalidate those laws where a substantial secular interest can be forwarded in support.

In the context of abortion regulation, some religiously influenced abortion restrictions, such as the parental notification or consent requirements just discussed, could satisfy the substantial secular interest standard. Whereas such regulations actually might be motivated by, for example, legislators' religious concerns about the sanctity of the family as the basis for Christian life, they could be justified under the State's secular interest in promoting strong families as the basis for a strong society, facilitating parental involvement in the lives of their offspring, ensuring responsible adult involvement in such momentous decisions by minors, and so on. Such laws, then, would be upheld under the standards for assessing religious lawmaking proposed here.

Responding to Infringements of Citizenship Rights

Once a violation of Citizenship Rights has been shown under the proposed test, government must demonstrate that it has a compelling interest in the contested law, that is, that the law is designed to respond to some public exigency or necessity that warrants infringement of citizens' constitutional rights. Further, the government must show that its compelling purpose cannot be achieved by methods that are less restrictive of citizens' rights, the so-called less restrictive means test (see *Larson v. Valente*, 456 U.S. 229 [1982]).

Government would fail the compelling interest test in several of the abortion cases we have been considering. As the Court found in *Roe*, the State's interest in protecting fetal life only becomes compelling in the third trimester of pregnancy, when the fetus becomes viable. Although the Court in *Planned Parenthood v. Casey* and *Webster v. Reproductive Health Services* suggests that the State has an interest in potential life throughout the pregnancy and not only in the third trimester, it does not specify that this interest is compelling throughout.

Nor could it. From a constitutional perspective, the State's interest in protecting potential life is not sufficiently compelling to override fundamental rights of citizenship that would be abridged by the State's pursuit of its interest prior to viability. As Dworkin observes, once one accepts that the fetus is not a "person" under the Constitution, it is difficult to imagine what could constitute a compelling secular State interest for restrictive abortion laws (1993: 21–24). This is especially the case given the government's failure to protect other forms of nonpersonal life, such as human embryos used for scientific research and infertility treatment and nonhuman animals.

In addition, the State cannot plausibly claim a compelling State interest in imposing stringent restrictions on abortion rights to enhance respect for life because, as Dworkin notes, "there is no evidence beyond the barest speculation that allowing the abortion of nonviable fetuses generates a culture in which people take a more callous attitude toward the slaughter of children or adults. Abortion is, in effect, freely permitted in many European countries in the first trimester of pregnancy, and these are much less violent societies than many American communities are now or were when abortion was still mostly forbidden" (1993: 115). There is also no evidence that restrictive abortion laws will succeed in protecting potential life by deterring women from seeking illegal means to terminate unwanted pregnancies. As Olsen suggests, "generally, laws against abortion do not save fetal life, but merely make abortions less safe and make women criminals" (1989: 132). Thus, such laws undermine rather than promote respect for human life by ignoring the disrespect and devaluation of women's lives that are involved in coercing women to continue unwanted pregnancies (see Olsen 1989: 132).

None of the laws in the cases discussed here can be justified in accordance with the compelling State interest standard. First, the basis for the government's interest in none of these cases can be demonstrated to be a compelling secular interest. Given the conflicting interests that are at stake, the State's interest in protecting potential life should not be deemed to be "compelling" because it cannot outweigh the interests of actual pregnant women in their health, well-being, liberty, and privacy rights. In particular, this rationale cannot support the abortion restrictions in *Webster v. Reproductive Health Services* and *Harris v. McRae* because government has no compelling interest in protecting the potential life gestating in pregnant indigent women but not in middle- and upper-class women, who are able to secure abortions without public funding.

Even if, for the sake of argument, the government's interest in protecting potential life is deemed to be compelling, the means selected to promote that interest cannot be justified as the least restrictive (as required by the second step of the government's case). Coercing indigent women to become mothers against their wills cannot be the least restrictive means the State has available at its disposal for promoting the protection of prenatal life. Less restrictive alternatives at a minimum include providing ready access to the abortifacient RU-486 to prevent the necessity of abortion (at least where personhood is defined to involve at least the implantation of the fetus on the uterine wall), enabling women to give birth prematurely as soon as possible following viability, and providing better services for adoption following normal birth for women who are unable or unwilling to raise their newborns. In addition, less restrictive alternatives prior to conception include providing better sexual education to adolescents and access to safe, effective, and convenient methods of contraception for all who want it to prevent unwanted pregnancies, as well as eliminating the conditions that lead to rape, incest, and other forms of sexual coercion that result in unwanted pregnancies.

In addition, establishing feasible alternatives for pregnant women contemplating abortion, such as adequate social and financial support, especially child support, prenatal care, reasonable adoption arrangements, job training and employment opportunities for working mothers, child care leaves, affordable child care, and so on, would also facilitate a decrease in abortion without infringing on women's Citizenship Rights. These considerations should be factored into any public policy genuinely concerned with the protection of human life. In sum, most of the abortion cases we have discussed here could not be sustained under the proposed test.

Additional Considerations

In addition to the specific requirements of the proposed legal test, a few general considerations should be mentioned, especially the applicability of the test to and beyond the judiciary, the requirements for who should have standing to challenge the constitutionality of religious lawmaking, and the effectiveness of the proposed test for remedying the harms of religious lawmaking. I discuss each of these considerations in turn.

Scope of Application of the Proposed Test

The proposed legal test calls for a certain degree of discretion by courts in determining whether religion has influenced the passage of a challenged law, whether Establishment Concerns are present, whether Citizenship Rights have been infringed upon, and whether the government has a substantial or compelling secular rationale for religious lawmaking. The discretion required to make these determinations is no different in kind from that required in many well-established principles of legal interpretation. It does not require any unusual or extraordinary expertise from or burden on judges.

In addition, courts need not be the only bodies to apply this proposed test. Even though the judiciary is the final arbiter of the constitutionality of lawmaking and even though the model is designed as a supplement to the Supreme Court's interpretations of the Constitution, legislators and other lawmakers can also apply the model. They need not wait for an enactment to be challenged before assessing for themselves its likely constitutionality and making any necessary or appropriate modifications prior to enactment. Such self-assessment would be likely to reduce the need for litigation. However, to avoid bracketing lawmakers' free exercise rights, the test does not require such a priori self-assessment but is designed to apply primarily following a legal challenge to the enactment of a law.

Standing Requirements for Invoking the Proposed Test

Who should be able to challenge the validity of religious lawmaking? The proposed assessment model requires only minimal satisfaction of standing criteria when religious lawmaking is alleged to infringe on Establishment Concerns and/or other Citizenship Rights. Because religious lawmaking bears special risks of harming Citizenship Rights and because these rights are so fundamental to individual liberty and dignity, minimal standing requirements are appropriate. In addition, because the test imposes no prior restraints or "chilling effect" on lawmakers that would inhibit their reliance on religious convictions in making law, it is appropriate to loosen the traditional standing requirements to facilitate aggrieved citizens who bring challenges to religious lawmaking. A plausible showing that a law was influenced by or based on religious considerations and that the law has the effect of raising Establishment Concerns or infringing on Citizenship Rights is sufficient to sustain a plaintiff's standing under the proposed test.

Under this modified standard for standing, the plaintiff's argument in *Harris v. McRae* that religious influences on the passage of the Hyde Amendment violated the free exercise rights of pregnant women should have been enough to sustain the plaintiff's cause of action without also showing that the law directly burdened the plaintiff's exercise of religion, as the Court required. In *Bowen v. Kendrick*, the plaintiffs' claims that *AFLA*'s funding of religiously affiliated groups violated the Establishment Clause by supporting the teaching of religious doctrine similarly should have been sustained to allow the plaintiffs to proceed in offering evidence to demonstrate their allegations.

The proposed assessment model also loosens the traditional limitations on standing for institutional plaintiffs, taxpayers, and citizens. Because social inequalities frequently deter those who are most likely to be harmed by religious lawmaking, especially women, religious minorities and other traditionally marginalized citizens, from stepping forward to challenge laws influenced by dominant religious traditions (see Tribe 1988: 1297), organizations and individuals who are willing and able to challenge such lawmaking should be given standing, even if they are not themselves immediately or directly aggrieved.

However, a grant of standing to institutional, taxpayer, or citizen plaintiffs in such instances should be contingent on their ability to join, as named plaintiffs, citizens whose rights have been directly infringed by the challenged lawmaking. This requirement will ensure that traditional standing concerns are satisfied, while not unduly limiting the ability of citizens to challenge religious lawmaking.

Effectiveness of the Proposed Test for Remedying the Harms of Religious Lawmaking

Although more effective in ensuring the protection of Citizenship Rights, the legal assessment model proposed here is not an ideal solution to the dilemma of religious lawmaking. Relying on individual litigants to bring judicial proceedings to challenge religious lawmaking is subject to the criticism of being too heavily focused on the individuals who are harmed by religious lawmaking and not enough on the social consequences of such lawmaking. In other words, the proposed test only addresses the outcomes or consequences of religious lawmaking, without addressing the root of the problem that enables such lawmaking to be enacted in the first place.

The proposed model is also subject to the criticism that it only addresses a specific set of problems that results from the interaction of religion and government and is unable to address others. One example discussed earlier is the failure of the proposed model to provide a remedy for the potential harms debated in the *Bowen v. Kendrick* case in connection with *AFLA*. Nevertheless, the proposed model represents a significant improvement over both the Supreme Court's jurisprudence in this area and the prominent liberal and communitarian proposals to date. It draws a fair balance between protecting the constitutional rights and interests of religious lawmakers and protecting those of other citizens. The discussion in the following section demonstrates the usefulness of the model by applying it to other contemporary public policy issues where religious lawmaking either has been or may be a significant influence: religious lawmaking on homosexual conduct and environmental protection.

Evaluating Other Kinds of Religious Lawmaking

Applying the proposed legal test to even a limited sample of issues other than abortion will demonstrate how well it addresses religious lawmaking generally. Among the range of religiously based or influenced laws that might be considered, I have chosen those relating to homosexual conduct and environmental protection. These two issues provide interesting comparative cases, the former actual and the latter hypothetical, that involve sufficiently different considerations to provide a useful basis for assessing the effectiveness of the proposed model. These issues all have involved (or might involve) the use of religious standards to regulate secular conduct.

Regulation of Homosexual Conduct

Despite an overall trend of increasing toleration toward homosexuality in our society, a number of states continue to regulate homosexual conduct through antisodomy statutes (see Clark, Brown, and Hochstein 1989: 269). In addition, until recently, the armed services excluded all acknowledged homosexuals and made a declaration of nonhomosexuality a condition for admission. Even today, controversy rages over the extent to which discrimination against homosexuals in the armed services, as well as in other social institutions, should be tolerated.

The most vehement and vocal objections to according basic civil rights to homosexuals have come from religious voices, both institutional and individual (see Clark, Brown, and Hochstein 1989: 266–68). These voices have undertaken a number of efforts to influence public and church policy to restrict rights and opportunities for gays and lesbians, as well as to deny enforcement of basic civil rights to protect homosexuals (at least those who openly acknowledge their homosexuality; see Jacobs and Moberly 1993: 5).

The origins of antisodomy laws are based in biblical standards of morality, which condemn nonheterosexual sex as unnatural, deviant, and sinful (see Clark, Brown, and Hochstein 1989: 267–78). These views of homosexuality continue to be promoted by many religious and legal institutions, especially the Catholic Church and prominent Christian Protestant and evangelical denominations (see Clark, Brown, and Hochstein 1989; Thumma 1991: 333). For example, the Catholic Church's statement *On the Pastoral Care of Homosexual Persons* (Ratzinger 1986) considers that homosexual behavior is not "morally acceptable," and even that the inclination toward homosexual behavior is "more or less a strong tendency toward an intrinsic moral evil" (see O'Brien 1991: 30; Clark, Brown, and Hochstein 1989: 277–78).

Despite the seemingly clear influence of religion on laws restricting or failing to protect the Citizenship Rights of gays and lesbians, in 1986 the Supreme Court upheld the constitutionality of Georgia's antisodomy law in *Bowers v. Hardwick* (478 U.S. 186 [1986]). The high Court ruled that there was no fundamental right to engage in homosexual activity that would protect the practice from legislative restrictions. The Constitution, it stated, only protects rights that are "deeply rooted" in history and tradition. Marriage, procreation, and family relations meet this standard, according to the Court, but consensual homosexual activity does not. Because the majority concluded that there was no basis for an independent review of the law, it deferred to the legislature's judgment regarding the appropriateness of making this type of sexual activity illegal to protect the public welfare and morality of citizens.

Chief Justice Burger's concurring opinion called antisodomy laws "firmly rooted in Judeo-Christian moral and ethical standards" and as having the weight of "millennia of moral teaching" (*Bowers v. Hardwick*, 196, 197). Justice White's majority opinion likewise found that proscriptions against sodomy "have ancient roots" (*Bowers v. Hardwick*, 192). Justice Blackmun's dissent objected to the majority's endorsement of religious lawmaking, clearly recognizing that "the assertion that 'traditional Judeo-Christian values' proscribe the conduct involved cannot provide an adequate justification for [the Georgia statute]. That certain, but by no means all, religious groups condemn the behavior at issue gives the state no license to impose their judgments on the entire citizenry. The legitimacy of secular legislation depends instead on whether the state can advance some justification for its law beyond its conformity to religious doctrine" (*Bowers v. Hardwick*, 211). The *Bowers* decision represents a miscarriage of justice in a number of respects, most of which are not relevant to the immediate issue at hand. The key point is that the Georgia antisodomy statute is invalid as unconstitutional religious lawmaking under the proposed assessment model. Beginning with the requirements for the petitioner's case, the evidence suggests that the basis for—as well as the continuing interest in perpetuating—antisodomy statutes is religious. There is objective evidence that religious beliefs played a substantial role in Georgia's antisodomy law, satisfying requirement 1.

In addition, the "ancient roots" of antisodomy statutes have not been accepted by a public consensus nor do they enjoy widespread support, as required under the definition of secular described earlier. No common agreement or public consensus exists about the immorality of homosexual conduct. Although many traditional religions condemn homosexuality, a growing number of religious groups accept homosexual expressions of love and intimacy as just as worthy of validation and support as heterosexual ones. In addition, many nonreligious voices in society are tolerant, if not positively affirming, of homosexual conduct. Thus, there is no shared social value regarding homosexual conduct that could sustain such laws as secular. Instead, the interest underlying the law is both religious and highly contested; it is one on which both religious and nonreligious views are in conflict.

With respect to requirement 2 of the petitioner's case, religiously influenced laws regulating homosexual conduct raise Establishment Concerns. They send a symbolic message that homosexual citizens are legitimately subject to greater infringements on their privacy and liberty than are heterosexual citizens. In prohibiting certain forms of consensual sexual conduct, such laws are certainly likely to be alienating to homosexuals, as well as exclusionary and coercive. By contributing to the political controversy surrounding the rights of homosexuals in American society, such statutes are also politically divisive.

Religiously motivated antisodomy laws are also invalid under requirement 3 of the petitioner's case, as abridging Citizenship Rights. The most obvious violation is the one rejected by the Supreme Court, that is, the substantive due process rights of privacy and liberty of conscience to conduct one's most intimate sexual activities in accordance with one's sexual identity, free from unwarranted State interference. The Court's refusal to extend the right of privacy to the facts at issue in *Bowers* is clearly inconsistent with the rationales of the Court's other privacy cases (see Conkle 1987).

Antisodomy statutes also implicate core Establishment Clause concerns by legislating a particular and controversial religious view of the morality of homosexual conduct. They also violate the principle of neutrality applied by the Court in some Establishment Clause cases by endorsing a religious view as the government's official position on a contested issue. This reflects an illegitimate bias in favor of a particular religious view of homosexuality and against other views, both religious and secular.

Although not reflected on the face of the law at issue in *Bowers*, the result of the statute as applied also violates equal protection guarantees by restricting a significant form of sexual expression engaged in by homosexuals without an analogous restriction on the range of legal sexual activities of heterosexuals. Although the law at issue in *Bowers* does not, some antisodomy statutes even violate the Equal Protection Clause on their face by making an invidious classification among persons on the basis of their sexual orientation. Nevertheless, there was evidence produced in the court hearings in the *Bowers* case that the antisodomy statute was enforced in a biased manner, thereby violating the requirement that laws accord equal treatment to citizens, both on their face and as applied. Finally, such statutes may also conflict with the petitioner's personal religious beliefs regarding the acceptability of homosexual conduct, thereby infringing on free exercise rights.

Consequently, antisodomy statutes easily qualify for invalidation under the requirements of the petitioner's case. They also fail to meet the conditions for being sustained under the terms of the government's case. Because Citizenship Rights are implicated, the compelling secular State interest standard is applicable. The only justification for the antisodomy law in *Bowers* was the moral judgment of the majority of the Georgia electorate that homosexual sodomy is "immoral" and "unacceptable" (196). This hardly rises to the level of a compelling interest, especially not one which is supported by a secular rationale.

Further, the State does not have a significant enough interest to accommodate those religious lawmakers and citizens who believe that homosexuality is morally wrong. Given the widespread disagreement about the issue and the trend toward according equal rights to all citizens, there is no warrant for protecting the religious views of certain lawmakers, especially when their views are based on non-publicly accessible beliefs. Finally, there is no indication that the State could satisfy its burden of proving that it has no less restrictive means for promoting its interest in heterosexual sexual norms. Thus, the religiously influenced antisodomy statute at issue in *Bowers* is invalid under the proposed test. Similar types of regulations of homosexual conduct would be similarly suspect.

Regulation of Environmental Pollution

To consider religious lawmaking in relation to environmental protection, let us imagine a hypothetical case in which the Texas state legislature has recently passed an environmental protection law. The statute imposes severe penalties on manufacturing plants if their emissions result in even a slight deterioration in current levels of air and water quality in the surrounding locale. The penalties are exacted on the basis of "strict liability," that is, regardless of the polluting manufacturers' knowledge or intent to violate the law. Most manufacturers have made the necessary expenditures to equip their plants with emission controls that meet the new regulatory standards. A few, however, have been financially unable to do so. These manufacturers, as it happens, are primarily owned and operated by Mexican Americans along the U.S.–Mexico border.

The impetus for the environmental regulation originated with a religious group that believes that any harm to the natural environment unnecessary to sustain human life is a sin against God's creation. A number of lawmakers sharing the religious group's faith were instrumental to the statute's enactment. A Mexican American manufacturer convicted of violating the statute has brought a lawsuit to challenge the law as violating his Citizenship Rights to free exercise, substantive due process, and equal protection. He alleges that his Christian beliefs dictate that he "exercise dominion" over God's creation in the manner he best sees fit and that the statute prevents him from doing so.

Under requirement 1 of the petitioner's case, evidence of a religious influence on the statute is apparent. The purpose of the law is avowedly religious, and one of the major motivations behind its passage is the beliefs of a religious group. Under step 2, Establishment Concerns are evident. The law may be alienating to those who do not share the religious convictions underlying the environmental regulations. The regulations are also exclusionary and coercive to those who are compelled thereby to conduct themselves in a manner contrary to their religious or personal convictions of conscience. The manufacturer might also show that the statute is coercive as applied to his company because it results in obstructing his ability to carry on his business. Although the law may also foster political divisiveness, it is difficult to surmise that it would be on the basis of religious differences.

Regarding the third requirement of the petitioner's case, the potential for abridgement of several different Citizenship Rights must be considered. Because the law potentially infringes on plaintiff's liberty and property interests, the Fourteenth Amendment's guarantee that persons will not be deprived of "life, liberty, or property, without due process of law" must be considered here, in addition to the manufacturer's First Amendment and equal protection claims.

The law infringes on the manufacturer's free exercise rights by interfering with his ability to act in accordance with his religious beliefs. It also potentially infringes on Establishment Clause rights. The regulation also might be invalid as an endorsement of religion because it enacts particular religious beliefs about God's relationship to the environment into a legal restriction on pollution.

A third constitutional basis for challenging the environmental regulation is that it infringes on the manufacturer's right to equal protection. Because the statute does not infringe on fundamental rights or discriminate among persons on its face, however, the manufacturer would have to show that the statute was discriminatory as applied to sustain this claim. He might satisfy this requirement by, for example, showing that the law was only enforced against Mexican American manufacturers and not others. There is no evidence in the hypothetical to suggest such discrimination, however. He might also claim that the law violates his equal protection rights by making an invidious classification between persons holding the religious beliefs undergirding the statute, and those with different beliefs. This claim is also unlikely to succeed, however, given the Supreme Court's precedents in cases involving religious beliefs, as discussed in chapter 2.

Substantive due process provides another possible basis for invalidating the pollution regulations. This ground would be difficult to prove, however, because the constitutional validity of economic and public welfare regulations is assessed using a rational basis standard of review rather than the strict scrutiny test, and the government undoubtedly has a rational purpose for the challenged requirements.

However, the petitioner might also challenge the statute on the grounds that the economic burdens of compliance are so onerous that they constitute a "taking" of his property without due process, in violation of the Fifth Amendment. Such claims have been recognized by the Supreme Court when regulations deny owners the economically viable use of their land or impose "unconstitutional conditions" on the exercise of constitutional rights (see *Dolman v. City of Tigard*, 114 S. Ct. 2309 [1994]; *Lucas v. South Carolina Coastal Council*, 112 S. Ct. 2886 [1992]). It is unlikely that the manufacturer in our hypothetical could sustain such a claim, however, because the environmental protection statute does not deprive manufacturers of all economically viable use of their land, and it does bear an "essential nexus" to a legitimate State interest (see *Dolman*, 2317; *Lucas*, 2892–93).

Despite the tenuousness of several of these alleged violations of Citizenship Rights, the petitioner can demonstrate that the environmental regulation infringes on his establishment and free exercise rights. Thus, the government is obligated to show a compelling secular State interest for the statute. This the State can do easily. The State's interest in providing a clean environment falls squarely under the valid governmental authority to provide for the safety and public welfare of its citizens. Improving pollution controls in the interests of environmental protection is also a compelling interest related to protecting the public welfare. Further, the statutory penalties are carefully drawn to directly correspond to the statutory purpose of environmental protection. These are compelling secular interests that legitimate the statute, despite its underlying religious motivations.

This essential nexus should sustain the legislation against even artful efforts by the petitioner to demonstrate that the State could accomplish its purpose using less restrictive means. The history of environmental pollution by corporate interests in the United States and elsewhere provides ample evidence to sustain the conclusion that the State is warranted in providing strict liability and harsh sanctions for violations of environmental regulations. Thus, application of the proposed test to the issue of religious lawmaking on the environment would be likely to result in validating the legislation, despite its religious character and interference with Citizenship Rights.

General Applicability of the Model

The varied results from applying the proposed assessment model to different types of religious lawmaking demonstrate that it does not invalidate any and all laws that have been influenced by religious considerations. Instead, these results suggest that the test is a fair and reasonable method for assessing the validity of religious lawmaking generally, one which balances the interests of religious lawmakers against those of citizens impacted by religiously influenced laws. The environmental protection case suggests that the concept of Citizenship Rights needs to be flexibly defined in accordance with the type of subject matter with which religious lawmaking may be concerned. Whereas property rights are not a relevant consideration in regulations of abortion or homosexual conduct, for example, they are an important element in analyzing environmental regulations.

Summary of the Proposed Model over Alternative Strategies

We have seen how the proposed assessment model better protects the constitutional rights and interests of all citizens who may be harmed by religious lawmaking than either the Supreme Court's approach or those proposed by liberal and communitarian theorists. Applying the test to the difficult issues of abortion, homosexual conduct, and environmental protection shows how the test enables lawmakers to rely on their religious convictions without thereby unduly infringing on the constitutional rights and interests of their constituents, especially religious minorities and pregnant women. Examining how the proposed test would apply to the latter two issues shows that its usefulness is not limited to assessing the constitutionality of abortion regulations but that it is suited to apply to religious lawmaking on a wide range of other moral issues.

This practical, legal strategy for resolving issues of religious lawmaking improves on the Court's traditional test for Establishment Clause violations in several respects. First, it recognizes the specific Establishment Concerns of alienation, exclusion, coercion, and political divisiveness in which religious lawmaking may result and provides a distinct remedy for such violations, even if core Establishment Clause violations are absent. Second, it shifts the emphasis of the Court's traditional concern with a law's purpose to that of its effects and justification by invalidating only those religiously influenced laws that cannot be fully supported on the basis of a secular rationale. The hypothetical environmental regulation case discussed in the previous section demonstrates that a law may be expressly motivated by religious concerns yet be justified by a secular governmental rationale.

Not automatically invalidating all laws that have a religious purpose or motivation also promotes the goal of protecting the free exercise rights of all citizens. Invalidating religiously influenced laws only after they are shown to have the effect of raising Establishment Concerns or, alternatively, infringing on Citizenship Rights is less intrusive on the moral identity and free exercise rights of religious legislators than invalidating laws because they are religiously based or influenced or attempting to persuade or coerce lawmakers not to rely on their religious convictions in their public decision making in the first place. The proposed model is thus fairer to religious lawmakers than liberal proposals.

At the same time, this modified Establishment Clause test better protects against the risks of Establishment Concerns and infringements on Citizenship Rights than communitarian approaches by invalidating religiously influenced laws that create these harms that the State cannot justify as necessary to effect its interests. It thereby accords better protection to those citizens who may be the most adversely affected by religious lawmaking: women and members of politically subordinate religious groups.

Given the likelihood of conflicts between the free exercise rights of religious lawmakers and the Citizenship Rights of other citizens, as well as the distinctive harms that religious lawmaking may cause in a religiously pluralistic and gender stratified society, it is important that assessments of the validity of religious lawmaking relax the stringency of the Court's traditional standing and burden of proof requirements. Easing these traditional limitations on judicial access facilitates the ability of citizens to protect their Citizenship Rights from undue infringement by religiously influenced laws, without unduly restricting the free exercise rights of lawmakers.

The legal model proposed here thus provides an effective strategy for accommodating the conflicts engendered by religious identity in lawmaking for a pluralistic society, one that surpasses liberal and communitarian alternatives in fairness and effectiveness. At the same time, it does not prevent all of the harms that religious lawmaking may engender. Rather than obligating religious lawmakers to refrain from relying on their religious convictions in their political decision making, it depends on individual litigators stepping forward to challenge specific instances of religious lawmaking through the judicial process. This aspect of the test might be viewed as a weakness because it makes citizens dependent on the legal process for redress of harms caused by religious lawmaking.

However, this very weakness in the legal approach is also one of its greatest virtues: by not imposing special obligations on lawmakers to monitor their religious discourse in the political sphere, it accords due respect to their self-conceptions as religious persons for whom bracketing their religious convictions may be repugnant, if not impossible. It also accords them equal rights as citizens entitled to the full protections of the Constitution, including the rights to free speech and free exercise. It thereby avoids the communitarian criticism that restricting religious lawmaking is unfair because of the constitutive nature of religion to the identity of all lawmakers as well as other citizens.

At the same time that it meets communitarian concerns with religious identity, the proposed legal strategy also satisfies liberal interests by providing respect for religious pluralism. By providing a method for evaluating whether laws that were allegedly made, interpreted, or implemented on the basis of religious convictions in fact harm constitutionally protected rights and interests, the proposed model ensures that every citizen can live in accordance with the dictates of his or her own conscience, to the fullest extent that is consistent with the rights of all citizens to do likewise.

Conclusion

As we have seen, lawmakers' reliance on their religious convictions in political decision making can be problematic in a religiously and morally pluralistic society such as the United States. Practical problems arise from the distinctive character of religion and its symbolic role in public life. In the context of the radical pluralism of religion in America, common agreement or even understanding about difficult moral issues on the bases of sectarian principles is seemingly impossible. Religious convictions are often held unyieldingly, without room for negotiation or compromise or sometimes even intelligibility to nonbelievers, while lacking public accessibility. The distinctive potential of religious lawmaking to foster exclusion, alienation, coercion, or political divisiveness makes religious influences on public policy making more problematic than secular ones and also makes religious influences on law more problematic than religious influences in other areas of public life.

In addition to these Establishment Concerns, legal problems result from the distinctive status given to religion in the Constitution and from the potential of religiously based or influenced laws to run afoul of Citizenship Rights and interests protected by that document. Moral problems arise from social inequalities of power and authority that enable only majoritarian religions to influence lawmaking, especially in ways that disadvantage those who have been excluded from participation in those religions on the basis of gender and minority status.

As we have seen, these problems can be vividly illustrated in cases of religious lawmaking on abortion. Abortion regulations that are based on religious convictions frequently raise Establishment Concerns and infringe on the Citizenship Rights of pregnant women. The Supreme Court's traditional approach to religious lawmaking fails to fully or successfully address these problems. The Court neither fully acknowledges nor provides sufficient protection for either the free speech and free exercise rights of religious lawmakers or the Establishment Concerns and Citizenship Rights of their constituents, especially religious minorities and women. In addition, the Court's decisions on religious lawmaking have imposed restrictive standing and burden of proof requirements, which have served to unduly limit the ability of aggrieved citizens to protect their Citizenship Rights.

Scholarly proposals have also failed to develop a satisfactory alternative to the Court's jurisprudence in this area. Both liberal and communitarian approaches are problematic in part because they are premised on inaccurate conceptions of moral identity. Liberal theories tend to undervalue how fundamental religion may be to moral identity. Their proposed limitations on the role of religion in politics and lawmaking protect respect for religious pluralism but tend to do so at the expense of respect for the religious identity and the free speech and free exercise rights of lawmakers. This unduly restricts the interests of religious lawmakers to rely on their religious convictions and undermines their constitutionally protected free exercise rights.

In contrast, communitarian theories tend to ignore the capacity of moral selves for agency and judgment independent of community (including religious) norms and values. Communitarian approaches tend to protect the religious identity of lawmakers as essential, while doing so at the expense of respect for religious pluralism. Such disregard results in proposals that accord religion an inappropriately expansive role in public policy making, one that endangers the Establishment Concerns and Citizenship Rights of other citizens, especially those from the nondominant community, often religious minorities and women.

The analysis of the self-understandings of several religious lawmakers in chapter 3 highlighted the flaws in both of these conceptions. The assessments of these political leaders about the role religion plays in their public decision making suggest that lawmakers sometimes (but not always) understand themselves to be unable to separate their policy making from their religious convictions. They also indicate, however, that at least some lawmakers are able (and so perceive themselves) to make public policy determinations on moral issues independently of even strongly held personal religious convictions.

These problems are highlighted in liberal and communitarian proposals for addressing religious lawmaking on abortion. Both liberal and communitarian theorists fail to recognize that religious views of abortion often reflect sexist and patriarchal influences that are in tension or conflict with the Establishment Concerns and Citizenship Rights of pregnant women. Like many religious lawmakers, both Greenawalt and Perry in particular fixate their analysis of the abortion issue so one-pointedly on the moral status of the fetus that they largely ignore the moral or constitutional rights and interests of pregnant women. In addition, both liberals and communitarians tend to overlook the range of constitutional rights and interests that are potentially harmed by religious lawmaking. They also tend to overlook the special role-based obligations of lawmakers that make it acceptable to hold them to different standards with respect to reliance on their religious reasons than ordinary citizens.

Having explored a number of alternative approaches for resolving the dilemma of religious lawmaking, both legal and philosophical, liberal and communitarian, established and novel, let us return to the questions with which this thesis began: what role, if any, should religious influences have on public lawmaking? How should the significance that religion may have to the moral identity of lawmakers be weighed against the constitutional rights and interests of their constituents? Can respect for religious pluralism, moral identity, and gender justice be simultaneously recognized and accommodated?

Searching for a more adequate model of moral identity on which to develop a satisfactory approach to religious lawmaking, I have argued that the pragmatist philosophy of George Herbert Mead offers a basic framework. Mead's theories of the social self and role-based morality share significant elements with both liberal and communitarian conceptions yet avoid many of their deficiencies. Similar to communitarian theory, Mead describes how moral identity is formed in interaction with individual others in the social situation rather than in isolation, as in the liberal view. Yet Mead's description of the agency of selves also reinforces the liberal view that moral selves in fact can choose, at least within some parameters, to make decisions on the basis of a wider set of considerations than their personal religious convictions.

Mead's conception of the self as plural offers a way of thinking about the relationship of religion to moral identity that recognizes both the socially constructed character of the self as well as its agency to make moral decisions that are not necessarily synonymous with its religious beliefs. Mead's approach shows how moral identity in a pluralistic society is itself plural or multiple, fluid and shifting, rather than singular and fixed, unified, and stable. His theory thus suggests that lawmakers' religious convictions are not fully determinative of who they are or how they will decide particular matters. By conceptualizing moral responsibility in terms of social roles, Mead's model demonstrates how even deeply religious selves are capable of taking the attitudes of others, that is, considering the views of persons holding views at variance from their own.

Indeed, Mead's approach suggests that lawmakers, as leaders, are both constitutionally able and morally obligated to take on the attitudes of all relevant others and to formulate decisions that best accommodate all of those interests. Mead's approach persuasively suggests that lawmakers can take on interests widely divergent from their own and incorporate consideration of these attitudes into their decision making. Mead's framework also suggests that in the absence of a public consensus on or widespread public support for a religious issue, lawmakers better represent their constituents by justifying their decisions with secular reasons. A Meadian approach to religious lawmaking thus suggests that lawmakers have a moral obligation to justify their political decisions on a secular rationale when relying on religious ones would harm the Citizenship Rights and interests of their constituents.

Although a Meadian approach to the dilemma of religious lawmaking provides an ideal theoretical account, it is unable to provide effective protections against the potential harms of lawmaking at a practical level, given that some lawmakers understand themselves to be fundamentally religious persons unwilling or unable to consider the interests of all of their constituents or use only secular rationales in their public policy making.

Consequently, the legal assessment model proposed in chapter 7 presents a more practical approach to resolving issues arising out of religious lawmaking. Although it does not provide an ideal resolution to all of the problems that religious lawmaking potentially engenders, the proposed legal model better protects against the most serious harms to Citizenship Rights and interests than either liberal or communitarian approaches.

The proposed legal model succeeds in recognizing both the values of respect for religious identity and for religious pluralism where alternative approaches, including the Supreme Court's, have failed. This is evident when the proposed assessment test is applied to religiously influenced abortion laws, which the Supreme Court has validated. Applying the legal test to the regulation of homosexual conduct and environmental protection reveals its effectiveness as a framework for resolving a wide range of issues besides abortion where religious lawmaking may be at play.

To return to the hypothetical cases that opened this text, both the Meadian, theoretical approach as well as the proposed practical, legal strategy suggest resolutions that satisfactorily address the main problems involved in the dilemma of religious lawmaking. First, under the Meadian proposal developed in chapter 6, none of the lawmakers in these hypothetical situations would rely on religious convictions because to do so would be inconsistent with taking the attitudes of all relevant others into consideration in a morally and religiously pluralistic society.

Following his moral obligation as a leader, the senator in case A should vote against the parental consent requirement, consistent with the expressed wishes of a majority of his constituents. Applying the legal assessment model proposed in chapter 7 to case A, if we assume the senator votes in favor of the bill based on his religiously grounded opposition to abortion, the issue is whether the law can be fully justified on the basis of a secular rationale. If we consider that the State's interest is in promoting parental authority, not in avoiding religious justifications for its political decisions, and that the State has greater jurisdiction to regulate the lives of minors than adults, then the law can be sustained.

Case B is more difficult under the Meadian model because the expressed interests of a majority of the legislature are inconsistent with what the governor views as the best interests of pregnant women, especially those who are indigent. If she takes the attitude of her constituents, she would support the law. However, given her obligation also to take the attitude of indigent, pregnant women, her role-based obligation to uphold the Constitution under her oath of office, as well as her interpretation of the forty-eight-hour waiting period as presenting an undue burden, she should veto the bill as infringing on the Citizenship Rights of pregnant women.

Under the legal assessment test, if the governor chooses to sign the forty-eight-hour waiting period bill in reliance on her religious convictions, whether there are secular reasons to fully justify the result is a difficult question to answer. If there is evidence to show that hardships would result to some pregnant women if the waiting period is imposed, the law should be invalidated as presenting an undue burden on women's constitutionally protected right to choose to have an abortion. If the state cannot provide evidence that it has a compelling interest in violating women's Citizenship Rights or that there is no less restrictive means of forwarding that compelling interest, the law also should be invalidated.

In case C, the judge is also obligated to uphold the Constitution under Meadian role-based obligations. The ban on abortions at overseas military facilities creates an undue burden on enlisted women's liberty rights to terminate unwanted pregnancies and also infringes on their equal protection rights by disadvantaging them in ways that enlisted men are not. Thus, the judge should strike down the law even aside from the religious influence on its passage.

Under the proposed legal test, if the judge overcomes his doubts and votes against the law on the basis of his religious opposition to the religiously conservative views that motivated it, his decision would be upheld. As already noted, there are substantial reasons to invalidate the ban as an unconstitutional infringement on pregnant military personnel's Citizenship Rights.

Analysis of these hypothetical cases indicates that the two approaches to religious lawmaking developed here are consistent with each other, as well as with according broad protections for Citizenship Rights that do not unduly restrict or burden the religious identities of lawmakers.

Having explored these alternative approaches, we can now appreciate that the appropriate place of religious influences in politics generally is dependent on several factors. These include (1) whether the influence is related to public discussion and debate about moral issues or to the establishment of laws backed by the coerciveness of state sanctions, (2) whether the influence is enacted by an average citizen or by a public official or lawmaker with special role-based obligations, (3) whether the influence takes the form of Guidance on the one side or Justification and/or Motivation on the other, (4) whether the influence raises Establishment Concerns or infringes on Citizenship Rights, and finally, (5) whether the influence results in a law that can be fully justified on the basis of a secular rationale.

Despite the usefulness of both the ideal Meadian and practical legal approaches, however, there are no completely acceptable solutions to the conflicts that arise between incompatible religious perspectives in a constitutional democracy. It is simply not possible to accord complete recognition and respect to the religiously informed consciences of lawmakers without infringing to some extent on the recognition and respect due to Citizenship Rights and

Establishment Concerns of the constituents bound by their decisions. Conversely, there is no way to completely protect constitutional rights and interests in a religiously diverse society without imposing some limitation on the expression of religious convictions by the nation's lawmakers.

Such conflicts are especially likely to result in the context of religious lawmaking on abortion. Allowing lawmakers to rely on their religious convictions to any extent in making abortion policy will undoubtedly infringe on the Establishment Concerns and Citizenship Rights of some pregnant women. The philosophical and legal strategies proposed here cannot eliminate gender bias or the other obstacles encountered by women with unwanted pregnancies. Attempting to restrict those religious influences that result in laws antithetical to the rights and interests of pregnant women is likely to somewhat abridge the free speech and free exercise rights of lawmakers for whom religion is fundamental.

Despite these insurmountable obstacles to a completely satisfactory solution, the Meadian and legal approaches to religious lawmaking proposed here respect women and religious minorities as well as religious lawmakers. They thereby offer a more just resolution of the dilemma that religious lawmaking presents in a pluralistic polity than the strategies evidenced in Supreme Court decisions or proposed by liberal and communitarian theories. They suggest ways that lawmakers should think about the influence of religion on the legal enactments they are responsible for implementing, interpreting, and obeying, regardless of whether they themselves are religious.

Notes

Chapter One

1. As Rosiland Petchesky has noted, from this perspective, abortion is a sin because it violates women's natures, true desires, and interests as mothers (1990: 342–43).

2. For example, a Hawaii state court explained the difference between the sexes as divinely ordained, "as we are told in Holy Writ, when God created man, 'male and female created he them'" (*Territory v. Armstrong*, 28 Haw. 88, 96 [1924]).

3. This type of power over women is manifest in restrictions on access to contraception as well as abortion. Karst reminds us that it is not only abortion but also contraception that has been opposed on the basis of religious beliefs. This complete opposition to "interference" with natural reproductive processes results in a double bind for women: no birth control to prevent conception and no abortion to counter the likely results of the failure to use birth control (see Karst 1993: 181).

4. The first version of the amendment Hyde introduced included no exceptions to the prohibition on funding abortions (see *Congressional Record*, Vol. 122 [June 24, 1977], pp. H. 6646–47).

5. This is consistent with polls taken over this country's history, which consistently reveal that most Americans think of themselves as religious persons. A survey conducted in 1993, for example, found that 90 percent of Americans assert a belief in God and more than half claim to pray at least once a day (see, e.g. Woodward 1993: 80; Kosmin and Lachman 1993: 2; Gallup and Castelli 1989: 3–4; see Conkle 1 993: 4).

Chapter Two

1. For example, Perry argues that "Neither citizens nor legislators or other governmental policy makers would violate the constitutional requirement that government not 'establish' religion were they to present religiously-based moral arguments in public political debate" (1998: 4). Michael McConnell notes, "It is strange, to say the least, that in a book about the relation between what Perry calls 'morality/religion'

and 'politics/law' he does not attempt to relate his constitutional vision to the establishment or free exercise principles of the First Amendment" (1989: 1517). McConnell's assessment is no longer entirely accurate because in a later work, *Love and Power*, Perry considers whether his proposed approach to religious lawmaking violates the religion clauses (see 1991).

2. For example, Catholic bishop James Malone argues: "As a nation we are constitutionally committed to the separation of Church and State, but not to the separation of religious and moral values from public life" (quoted in Hofman 1986: 226).

3. In *Board of Education of Kiryas Joel v. Grumet* (114 S. Ct. 2481 [1994]), the Court held that children's entitlement to handicapped services in their public-school educations did not justify the state of New York passing legislation to make the village a separate school district. The Court's rationale was that the legislation violated the Establishment Clause by empowering a religious group to make legislative decisions as the Board of Education.

In *Larkin v. Grendel's Den, Inc.* (459 U.S. 116, 126 [1982]), the Court found that a municipality's authorization for churches to decide whether establishments selling liquor could be located in proximity to them constituted a united civic and religious authority "in violation of the core rationale underlying the Establishment Clause." The Court also declared that a state preference for certain religions constitutes an excessive entanglement (see, e.g., *Larson v. Valente* [456 U.S. 228 {1982}]). In *Larson*, the Court struck down a state statute regulating the solicitation of donations by charitable organizations only if the organization solicited more than 50 percent of its funds from nonmembers, ruling that the law created a "denominational preference." The Court has also sometimes considered political divisiveness to be a factor in determining whether a law constitutes "excessive entanglement" (see *Aguilar v. Felton*, 473 U.S. 402 [1985]; *Meek v. Pittinger*, 421 U.S. 349, 365 n. 15, 372 [1975]; *Committee for Public Education v. Nyquist*, 413 U.S. 756, 795–97 [1973]).

4. See, for example, *Marsh v. Chambers* (463 U.S. 783 [1983]), *Zobrest v. Catalina Foothills School District* (113 S. Ct. 2462 [1993]), and *Lee v. Weisman* (507 U.S. 557 [1992]).

5. Scholarly evidence suggests that there are multiple traditions represented in the Constitution rather than a single one, with widely differing interpretations of what the Framers' aspirations were for the religion clauses of the First Amendment (see Feldman 1980: 951–55; Smith 1991: 156–66, 1986: 959–74; McConnell 1992: 154–55, 1986).

6. See *Jimmy Swaggart Ministries v. Board of Equalization* (498 U.S. 378, 391–92 [1990]), *Bowen v. Roy* (476 U.S. 693, 709 [1986]), *Tony and Susan Alamo Foundation v. Secretary of Labor* (471 U.S. 290, 303–5 [1985]), and McConnell (1992: 165).

7. See, for example, *Hobbie v. Unemployment Appeals Commission* (480 U.S. 136, 141 [1987]), *Thomas v. Review Board* (450 U.S. 707, 717–18 [1981]), and *Sherbert v. Verner* (374 U.S. 398, 403–4 [1963]).

8. *Griswold v. Connecticut* (381 U.S. 479 [1965]), *Eisenstadt v. Baird* (405 U.S. 438 [1972]).

9. *Roe v. Wade* (410 U.S. 113, 168 [1973; Stevens, J., concurring]), *Planned Parenthood v. Casey* (505 U.S. 833 [1992]).

10. See *Frontiero v. Richardson* (411 U.S. 677 [1973]) and *Craig v. Boren* (429 U.S. 190 [1976]).

11. *Mississippi University for Women v. Hogan* (458 U.S. 718, 725–26 [1982]). See also *Califano v. Webster* (430 U.S. 313, 317 [1977]), *Craig v. Boren* (429 U.S. 190, 198 [1976]), and *Stanton v. Stanton* (421 U.S. 7, 14 [1975]).

Chapter Three

1. He raises this argument to reject other views about when human life becomes legally protectable, including viability, the ability of the fetus to feel or experience, and social recognition of the fetus as human by related others (Noonan 1970: 51–55).

2. Likewise, Noonan's (1979) contrast between the story of Jesus' nativity as one that "every human being in our culture can grasp its joyful meaning" (175) and abortion, which he characterizes as always having been evaluated negatively, is meaningless to those who are ignorant of the theological reference and to those who reject it.

3. He continues, "The issue was acute in ancient embryology . . . [and] is no less acute in contemporary America where over 12,000 rapes are reported annually, and emotions aroused by racial consciousness sometimes have added to the natural repugnance to be physically reminded of the ugly origin of a pregnancy in violence" (Noonan 1970: xi).

4. Reagan's stated rationale for prayer in school—that it will lead children to understand what they have in common and bring them closer together (1984: 9)—completely overlooks the potential of mandatory school prayer to coerce and alienate children who are raised without religion or in religious traditions that do not involve formal prayer. In *Lee v. Weisman* (112 S. Ct 2649 [1992]) the Supreme Court ruled that such infringements on the religious freedom of nonbelievers invalidated a state-sponsored school prayer, even in the relatively optional context of a high school graduation ceremony. The letter also misinterprets the import of Supreme Court decisions by characterizing them as prohibiting prayer in school (see Reagan 1982, 1984: 9). In fact, the Court only held that *state-mandated* or *sponsored* prayers are unconstitutional (see *Lee v. Weisman*; *Abington School District v. Schempp*, 374 U.S. 203 [1963]; and *Engel v. Vitale*, 370 U.S. 421 [1962]). It has never outlawed *voluntary* prayer in schools.

In addition, during the first 100 days of the Reagan administration, an office in the Department of Health and Human Services sent suggested sermons that promoted adoption to 500 child-welfare agencies, stating, "How blessed we are to have been chosen before the world was made to become adopted children through Jesus Christ. . . . Let us open our minds and our hearts to our Christian and community responsibility and restore these children to their rightful place within the family" (quoted in Castelli 1985: 526–27).

Chapter Four

1. Moreover, "where a state establishes or prefers a given religion, we may expect (though it is perhaps not inevitable) that certain laws will significantly reflect the world view associated with that religion" (Audi 1997: 40).

2. In fact, Greenawalt argues that Audi's approach to religious lawmaking, which requires moral agents to scrutinize the basis for their decisions and determine whether they would reach the same conclusion if they were to excise the religious reasons from consideration, is unrealistic (Greenawalt 1988: 150).

3. This includes prohibitions based exclusively on perceived religious harms, such as the sin of out-of-wedlock sexual activity; those designed to promote illiberal outcomes or outlaw behavior just because it is believed to be wrong, such as homosexuality; and those that support programs because they promote separable religious objectives rather than secular ones, such as the preparation of society for Armageddon (Greenawalt 1988: 94, 203).

4. He insists, however, that this exclusion of religion from the political does not deny that such values may apply, say, to the personal, the familial, and the associational; nor does he say that political values are separate from, or discontinuous with, other values (Rawls 1993: 180).

5. This phrasing represents a slightly more restrictive tone than a formulation published only a year or so earlier, which specifies that even though "legislators should feel that giving some weight to their comprehensive views is often appropriate," they "should give greater weight to grounds rooted in public reasons" than to their comprehensive views (Greenawalt 1995: 162).

6. From a liberal perspective, moral selves understand themselves as independent of their views and ideas, considering them to be fallible and subject to being proven incorrect and corrected (see Kymlicka 1989, 1990).

7. It is thus unclear whether Greenawalt holds to his earlier view that it is legitimate for legislators to rely on their constituents' religious convictions in their political decision making. The reasons he gives to support this stance are largely pragmatic. First, if legislators fail to do so, they risk being voted out of office (Greenawalt 1995: 151). Second, it is even more difficult for legislators to assess the extent to which religious convictions influence the convictions of their constituents than to make that determination about their own decisions (1988: 235). For a contrary view, see Tushnet (1991: 200–201).

Chapter Five

1. Perhaps not coincidentally, both Perry's and Greenawalt's first major works on the place of religion in political decision making were published in 1988 by the same publisher (Oxford University Press).

2. In fact, Perry contends that such a politics is already partly realized and embodied "in the practices of the American political-constitutional community" (1988: 77).

3. Perry's optimistic view that historically religions "have probably done more to moderate the worst human impulses than to call them forth" (1991: 143, quoting Glendon 1990: 9) fails to appreciate the depth and extent of controversy that religions are capable of provoking. These claims are opposed by numerous examples of internecine religious strife around the world.

4. In response to criticisms, Perry speculates that perhaps ecumenical political dialogue is possible, even without fallibilism (1991: 140).

5. Similar to Greenawalt, Perry at one point proposes to limit this reliance to situations "when no other basis is available" (1993: 708, 17; italics added). In so limiting religious justifications for decisions, Perry's inclusivist proposal suffers from the same problem as Greenawalt's in failing to explain why the *presence* of other bases *should* preclude reliance on one's religious convictions. It also appears to be inconsistent with Perry's views about the centrality of religious beliefs to moral identity.

6. This erroneous conclusion is based on an unfounded conflation of basic secular principles of human dignity and respect for persons with the religious value of sacredness. Allowing religious convictions to support arguments that regard human worth, as Perry wants to do, also opens the door to the permission of religious convictions that run contrary to constitutional principles of equal protection, as many religious fundamentalists and other conservative religious believers would like to do. This double-edged nature of religious rationales illustrates a fundamental problem with reliance on religious arguments in lawmaking.

7. In addition, Sandel argues that the Court inappropriately applied the right of privacy in the abortion context (1989b: 536–37).

8. Such tensions among communities also undercut Perry's claims in *Love and Power* about the possibility of shared understandings, as well as the possibility of agreement among moral communities about what constitutes flourishing.

9. Perry (1991) also overemphasizes the purported similarities among Western religions and with other world religions, sometimes defined vaguely as only "Indic," as opposed to "Semitic" (e.g., 1991: 77–78).

Chapter Six

1. Mead insists that self consciousness is the "core and primary structure" of the self (1956: 228), its "essential form." Without consciousness of self, there is no self (see Hanson 1986: 16).

2. In addition to taking the attitudes and roles of all relevant persons in the particular social situation (see, e.g., Mead 1964: 256–57, 260, 387–88; see Cook 1993: 128; Miller 1973: 239), moral action for Mead also requires *rationality*. This he describes as "a type of conduct in which the individual puts himself in the attitude of the whole group to which he belongs" and uses the generalized other to engage in self-criticism and to guide his actions (1934: 334; see Cook 1993: 133–36).

3. Moreover, even alien or rejected aspects of the social environment are constitutive of the self, albeit in a negative rather than a positive sense. For example, certain religious groups like the Amish define their identity in opposition to the larger secular society. In particular, they have prohibited the use of many products of modern technology, such as televisions, motorized equipment, and sometimes even automobiles and electricity. But even those prohibited activities are relevant to Amish identity because it is precisely such activities—television viewing, for example—that enables them to define their own identity as people who do not engage in such diversions. Even members of dominant or mainstream religious traditions define themselves against aspects of their social environment that are less familiar and well known to them. Christians define themselves in opposition to Jews and Muslims, for example, Catholics in opposition to Protestants; and so on.

Chapter Seven

1. This argument was made by plaintiffs in *Harris v. McRae* (448 U.S. 297 [1980]), and by the amicus curaie brief of the American Jewish Congress et al. in *Webster v. Reproductive Health Services* (492 U.S. 490 [1989]). (See RFRA Hearings 1992: 7–11.)

Bibliography

Aboulafia, Mitchell, "Was George Herbert Mead a Feminist?," *Hypatia*, Vol. 8 (1993), pp. 145–58.

Ackerman, Bruce, *Social Justice in the Liberal State* (New Haven, Conn.: Yale University Press, 1980).

Adler, Margot, *Drawing down the Moon: Witches, Druids, Goddess-Worshippers, and Other Pagans in America Today* (Boston: Beacon, 1986).

Alan Gutmacher Institute, *Facts in Brief: Abortion in the United States* (New York: Alan Gutmacher Institute, 1991).

Alexander, Larry, "Liberalism, Religion, and the Unity of Epistemology," *San Diego Law Review*, Vol. 30 (1993), pp. 763–97.

Alvare, Helen, "Testimony before the U.S. Senate," in *Hearings on Freedom of Choice Act of 1991*, Committee on Labor and Human Resources y 4.L 11/4: S.hrg. 102–813 (May 13, 1992), 102nd Congress, 2nd Session, S. 25 (Washington, D.C.: U.S. Government Printing Office, 1992), pp. 65–73.

Audi, Robert, "The Separation of Church and State and the Obligations of Citizenship," *Philosophy and Public Affairs*, Vol. 18 (1989), pp. 259–308.

———, "Religion and the Ethics of Political Participation," *Ethics*, Vol. 100 (1990), pp. 386–97.

———, "The Place of Religious Argument in a Free and Democratic Society," *San Diego Law Review*, Vol. 30 (1993), pp. 677–702.

———, "The Church, the State, and the Citizen," in Paul Weithman, ed., *Religion and Contemporary Liberalism* (South Bend, Ind.: University of Notre Dame Press, 1997), pp. 38–75.

Badawi, Leila, "Islam," in Jean Holm and John Bowher, eds., *Women in Religion* (London: Printer Publishers, 1994), pp. 102–19.

Baier, Annette, *Postures of the Mind: Essays on Mind and Morals* (Minneapolis: University of Minnesota Press, 1985).

Becker, Mary, "The Politics of Women's Wrongs and the Bill of 'Rights': A Bicentennial Perspective," *University of Chicago Law Review*, Vol. 59 (1992), pp. 453–518.

Behuniak-Lonn, Susan, "Friendly Fire: Amici Curiae and *Webster v. Reproductive Health Services*," *Judicature*, Vol. 74 (1991), pp. 261–71.

Beiner, Ronald, *Political Judgment* (Chicago: University of Chicago Press, 1983).

Benshoof, Janet, "*Planned Parenthood v. Casey*: The Impact of the New Undue Burden Standard on Reproductive Health Care," *Journal of the American Medical Association*, Vol. 269, (1993), pp. 2249–57.

Benson, Peter, and Dorothy Williams, *Religion on Capital Hill: Myths and Realities* (San Francisco: Harper and Row, 1982).

Berman, Harold, "Religion and Law: The First Amendment in Historical Perspective," *Emory Law Journal*, Vol. 35 (1986), pp. 777–93.

Bernadin, Joseph, "Consistent Ethic of Life after *Webster*," *Origins*, Vol. 19 (1990), p. 747.

Biale, Rachel, *Women and Jewish Law: An Exploration of Women's Issues in Halakhic Sources* (New York: Schocken, 1984).

————, "Abortion in Jewish Law," *Tikkun*, Vol. 4 (July-Aug. 1989), pp. 26–28.

Biskupic, Joan, "Abortion Dispute Entangles Religious Freedom Bill," *Congressional Quarterly Weekly Report*, Vol. 49 (April 13, 1991), pp. 913–18.

Blanchard, Dallas, *The Anti-Abortion Movement and the Rise of the Religious Right: From Polite to Fiery Protest* (New York: Twayne, 1994).

Block, Sharon, "Congressional Action on Abortion: 1984–1991," in J. Douglas Butler and David Walbert, eds., *Abortion, Medicine, and the Law*, 4th ed. (New York: Facts on File, 1992), pp. 648–66.

Bopp, James, *Restoring the Right to Life: The Human Life Amendment* (Provo, Utah: Brigham Young University Press, 1984).

————, "An Examination of Proposals for a Human Life Amendment," *Capital University Law Review*, Vol. 15 (1986), pp. 417–74.

————, "Why the Religious Freedom Restoration Act Must Expressly Exclude a Right to Abortion," in *Hearing before the Committee on the Judiciary, United States Senate, 102d Congress, 2d Session on S. 2969, A Bill to Protect the Free Exercise of Religion on September 18, 1992* (Washington, D.C.: U.S. Government Printing Office, 1993), pp. 209–38.

Bopp, James, and Richard Coleson, "The Right to Abortion: Anomalous, Absolute, and Ripe for Reversal," *Brigham Young University Journal of Public Law*, Vol. 3 (1989), pp. 181–209.

Bruce, Steve, *The Rise and Fall of the New Christian Right: Conservative Protestant Politics in America, 1978–1988* (New York: Clarendon, 1988).

Buddhist Churches of America Social Issues Committee, "A Shin Buddhist Stance on Abortion," *Buddhist Peace Fellowship Newsletter*, Vol. 6, No. 3 (1984), p. 6.

Butler, Judith, *Gender Trouble: Feminism and the Subversion of Identity* (New York: Routledge, 1990).

————, "Contingent Foundations: Feminism and the Question of 'Postmodernism,'" in Judith Butler and Joan Scott, eds., *Feminists Theorize the Political* (New York: Routledge, 1992), pp. 3–21.

Byrnes, Timothy, ed., *The Catholic Bishops in American Politics* (Princeton, N.J.: Princeton University Press, 1991).

Byrnes, Timothy, and Mary Segers, eds., *The Catholic Church and the Politics of Abortion: A View from the States* (Boulder, Colo.: Westview, 1992).

Calabresi, Guido, *Ideals, Beliefs, Attitudes, and the Law: Private Law Perspectives on a Public Law Problem* (Syracuse, N.Y.: Syracuse University Press, 1985).

Carter, Stephen, *The American Catholic People: Their Beliefs, Practices, and Values* (Garden City, N.Y.: Doubleday, 1987).

————, "Evolutionism, Creationism, and Treating Religion as a Hobby," *1987 Duke Law Journal* (1987), pp. 977–96.

————, "The Religiously Devout Judge," *Notre Dame Law Review*, Vol. 64 (1989), pp. 932–44.

————, *The Culture of Disbelief: How American Law and Politics Trivialize Religious Devotion* (New York: Basic Books, 1993).

Chodorow, Nancy, *The Reproduction of Mothering: Psychoanalysis and the Sociology of Gender* (Berkeley: University of California Press, 1978).

Chopko, Mark, "Testimony on behalf of the United States Catholic Conference," in *Hearing Before the Committee on the Judiciary, United States Senate, 102d Congress, 2d Session on S. 2969, A Bill to Protect the Free Exercise of Religion on September 18, 1992* (Washington, D.C.: U.S. Government Printing Office, 1993), pp. 101–11.

Chressanthis, George, Kathie Gilbert, and Paul Grimes, "Ideology, Constituent Interests, and Senatorial Voting: The Case of Abortion," *Social Science Quarterly*, Vol. 72 (1991), pp. 588–600.

Church and State Editorial Staff, "America Must Become Christian Nation under 'God's Law,' Says OR's Terry," *Church and State*, Vol. 46 (1993), p. 19.

Clark, J. Michael, Joanne Brown, and Lorna Hochstein, "Institutional Religion and Gay/Lesbian Oppression," *Marriage and Family Review*, Vol. 14 (1989), pp. 265–84.

Clemente, Frank, with Frank Watkins, eds., *Keep Hope Alive: Jesse Jackson's 1988 Presidential Campaign* (Boston: South End, 1989).

Code, Lorraine, *What Can She Know? Feminist Theory and the Construction of Knowledge* (Ithaca, N.Y.: Cornell University Press, 1991).

Coleman, John, *An American Strategic Theology* (New York: Paulist, 1982).

Colker, Ruth, "Abortion and Dialogue," review of *Morality, Politics and the Law*, by Michael J. Perry, *Tulane Law Review*, Vol. 63 (1989), pp. 1363–403.

————, *Abortion & Dialogue: Pro-Choice, Pro-Life, & American Law* (Bloomington: Indiana University Press, 1992).

————, *Pregnant Men: Practice, Theory, and the Law* (Bloomington: Indiana University Press, 1994).

Colton, Elizabeth, *The Jackson Phenomenon: The Man, the Power, the Message* (New York: Doubleday, 1989).

Conkle, Dan, "The Second Death of Substantive Due Process," *Indiana Law Journal*, Vol. 62 (1987), pp. 215–42.

————, "Toward a General Theory of the Establishment Clause," *Northwestern Law Review*, Vol. 82 (1988), pp. 1113–97.

————, "Religious Purpose, Inerrance, and the Establishment Clause," *Indiana Law Journal*, Vol. 67 (1991), pp. 1–59.

————, "God Loveth Adverbs," *DePaul Law Review*, Vol. 42 (1992), pp. 339–47.

————, "Different Religions, Different Politics: Evaluating the Role of Competing Religious Traditions in American Politics and Law," *Journal of Law and Religion*, Vol. 10 (1993), pp. 1–32.

Cook, Elizabeth Adell, Ted Jelen, and Clyde Wilcox, *Between Two Absolutes: Public Opinion and the Politics of Abortion* (Boulder, Colo.: Westview, 1992).

Cook, Gary, *George Herbert Mead: The Making of a Social Pragmatist* (Urbana: University of Illinois Press, 1993).

Cord, Robert, *Separation of Church and State* (New York: Lambeth, 1982).

Cornell, Drucilla, "Gender, Sex, and Equivalent Rights," in Judith Butler and Joan Scott, eds., *Feminists Theorize the Political* (New York: Routledge, 1992), pp. 280–96.

Cox, Barbara, "Refocusing Abortion Jurisprudence to Include the Woman: A Response to Bopp and Coleson and *Webster v. Reproductive Health Services*," *Utah Law Review* (1990), pp. 543–611.

Coyle, Marcia, and Marianne Lavelle, "High Court Has 78 'Friends' in Abortion Case," *National Law Journal*, Vol. 11, No. 32 (1989), p. 5.

Craig, Barbara, and David O'Brien, *Abortion and American Politics* (Chatham, N.J.: Chatham House, 1993).

Cuomo, Mario, *Diaries of Mario Cuomo: The Campaign for Governor* (New York: Random House, 1984a).

———, "Religious Belief and Public Morality: A Catholic Governor's Perspective," *Notre Dame Journal of Law, Ethics, and Public Policy*, Vol. 1 (1984b), pp. 13–31.

———, "A Governor Responds," *America*, Vol. 161 (1989), p. 265.

———, "By Way of Reply (Mario Cuomo and Abortion)," *Commonweal*, Vol. 117, No. 7 (1990a), pp. 203–4.

———, "Governor Replies," *America*, Vol. 162 (1990b), p. 70.

———, "Joining the Debate," *Commonweal*, Vol. 117 (1990c), pp. 170–75.

———, *More than Words: The Speeches of Mario Cuomo* (New York: St. Martin's, 1993).

Curran, Charles E., "Abortion: Its Moral Aspects," in Edward Batchelor, ed., *Abortion: The Moral Issues* (New York: Pilgrim, 1982), pp. 115–28.

Day, Christine, "Abortion and Religious Coalitions: The Case of Louisiana," in Timothy Byrnes and Mary Segers, eds., *The Catholic Church and the Politics of Abortion: A View from the States* (Boulder, Colo.: Westview, 1992), pp. 105–17.

Delaney, C. F., ed., *The Liberal-Communitarian Debate* (Lanham, Md.: Rowman & Littlefield, 1994).

Destro, Robert, "Abortion and the Constitution: The Need for a Life Protective Amendment," *California Law Review*, Vol. 63 (1975), pp. 1250–351.

———, "Religion, Establishment, Free Exercise, and Abortion," in Thomas Hilgers, Dennis Moran, and David Mall, eds., *New Perspectives on Human Abortion* (Frederick, Md.: University Publications of America, 1981), pp. 236–56.

Dow, David, "The Establishment Clause Argument for Choice," *Golden Gate University Law Review*, Vol. 20 (1990), pp. 479–500.

Duke, James, and Barry Johnson, "Religious Affiliation and Congressional Representation," *Journal for the Scientific Study of Religion*, Vol. 31 (1992), pp. 324–29.

Dworkin, Ronald, *A Matter of Principle* (New York: Oxford University Press, 1986).

———, "Liberal Community," *California Law Review*, Vol. 77 (1989), pp. 479–504.

———, "Unenumerated Rights: Whether and How *Roe* Should Be Overruled," *University of Chicago Law Review*, Vol. 59 (1992), pp. 381–432.

———, *Life's Dominion: An Argument about Abortion, Euthanasia, and Individual Freedom* (New York: Knopf, 1993).

Edel, Wilbur, *Defenders of the Faith: Religion and Politics from the Pilgrim Fathers to Ronald Reagan* (New York: Praeger, 1987).

Eells, Robert, and Bartell Nyberg, *Lonely Walk: The Life of Senator Mark Hatfield* (Chappaqua, N.Y.: Christian Herald, 1979).

Eller, Cynthia, *In the Lap of the Goddess: The Feminist Spirituality Movement in America* (New York: Crossroads, 1993).

Enquist, Roy, "The Churches' Response to Abortion," *Word and World*, Vol. 5 (1985), pp. 414–25.

Feldman, Jan, "The Establishment Clause and Religious Influences on Legislation," *Northwestern University School of Law*, Vol. 75 (1980), pp. 944–76.

Ferguson, Kathy, *The Man Question: Visions of Subjectivity in Feminist Theory* (Berkeley: University of California Press, 1993).

Finnis, John, *Natural Law and Natural Rights* (New York: Clarendon, 1980).

Flax, Jane, "Postmodernism and Gender Relations in Feminist Theory," in Linda Nicholson, ed., *Feminism/Postmodernism* (New York: Routledge, 1989), pp. 39–62.

Foley, Edward, "Book Review Essay: Tillich and Camus, Talking Politics," review of *Love and Power* by Michael Perry, *Columbia Law Review*, Vol. 92 (1992), pp. 954–83.

Fowler, Robert Booth, and Allen Hertzke, eds., *Religion and Politics in America* (Metuchen, N.J.: Scarecrow, 1995).

Fox, William, "Jesse Jackson's Kingdom Theology," *Christian Century*, Vol. 105, No. 15 (1988), pp. 446–47.

Frankel, Marvin, "Religion in Public Life: Reasons for Minimal Access," in James Swanson, ed., *First Amendment Handbook, 1993–1994* (Deerfield, Ill.: Clark Boardman, Callaghan, 1993).

Fraser, Nancy, "The Uses and Abuses of French Discourse Theories for Feminist Politics," in Nancy Fraser and Sandra Bartky, eds., *Revaluing French Feminism: Critical Essays on Difference, Agency, and Culture* (Bloomington: Indiana University Press, 1992), pp. 177–94.

Frazer, Elizabeth, and Nicola Lacey, *The Politics of Community: A Feminist Critique of the Liberal-Communitarian Debate* (Toronto, Canada: University of Toronto Press, 1993).

Friedman, Marilyn, "Feminism and Modern Friendship: Dislocating the Community," *Ethics*, Vol. 99 (1989), pp. 275–90.

———, *What Are Friends For? Feminist Perspectives on Personal Relationships and Moral Theory* (Ithaca, N.Y.: Cornell University Press, 1993).

Gaffney, Edward, "Politics without Brackets on Religious Convictions: Michael Perry and Bruce Ackerman on Neutrality," *Tulane Law Review*, Vol. 64 (1990), pp. 1143–94.

Gallup, George, Jr., and Jim Castelli, *The People's Religion: American Faith in the 90's* (New York: Macmillan, 1989).

Galston, William, *Liberal Purposes: Goods, Virtues, and Diversity in the Liberal State* (Cambridge: Cambridge University Press, 1991).

Garvey, John, "A Comment on Religious Convictions and Lawmaking," *Michigan Law Review*, Vol. 84 (1986), pp. 1288–94.

———, "The Pope's Submarine," *San Diego Law Review*, Vol. 30 (1993), pp. 949–76.

Gaustad, Edwin, ed., *A Documentary History of Religion in America* (Grand Rapids, Mich.: Eerdmans, 1982).

Gest, Ted, "The Abortion Furor," *U.S. News & World Report*, Vol. 107, No. 3 (1989), p. 18(5).

Gibson, Todd, and David Stott, "Discussion: Buddhadharma and Contemporary Ethics," *Religion*, Vol. 23 (1993), pp. 183–87.

Gilligan, Carol, *In a Different Voice: Psychological Theory and Women's Development* (Cambridge: Harvard University Press, 1982).

Ginsburg, Faye, *Contested Lives: The Abortion Debate in an American Community* (Berkeley: University of California Press, 1989).

Ginsburg, Ruth Bader, "Some Thoughts on Autonomy and Equality in Relation to *Roe v. Wade*," *North Carolina Law Review*, Vol. 63 (1985), pp. 375–95.

Glendon, Mary Anne, *Abortion and Divorce in Western Law: American Failures, European Challenges* (Cambridge: Harvard University Press, 1987).

————, "Notes on the Cultural Struggle: Dr. King in the Law Schools," *First Things* 7 (Nov. 1990), pp. 9–12.

————, *Rights Talk: The Impoverishment of Political Discourse* (New York: Free Press, 1991).

Goggin, Malcolm, ed., *Understanding the New Politics of Abortion* (Newbury Park, Calif.: Sage, 1993).

Gray, Karen, "Case Comments: An Establishment Clause Analysis of *Webster v. Reproductive Health Services,*" *Georgia Law Review*, Vol. 24 (1990), pp. 399–421.

Greenawalt, Kent, "Religious Convictions and Lawmaking," *Michigan Law Review*, Vol. 84 (1985), pp. 352–404.

————, *Religious Convictions and Political Choice* (New York: Oxford University Press, 1988).

————, "Religious Convictions and Political Choice: Some Further Thoughts," *DePaul Law Review*, Vol. 39 (1990), pp. 1019–99.

————, "Grounds for Political Judgment: The Status of Personal Experience and the Autonomy and Generality of Principles of Restraint," *San Diego Law Review*, Vol. 30 (1993a), pp. 647–76.

————, "The Role of Religion in a Liberal Democracy: Dilemmas and Possible Resolutions," *Journal of Church and State*, Vol. 35 (1993b), pp. 503–19.

————, *Private Consciences and Public Reasons* (New York: Oxford University Press, 1995).

————, "1996 Siebenthaler Lecture: Religious Liberty and Democratic Politics," *Northern Kentucky Law Review*, Vol. 23 (1996a), pp. 629–45.

————, "Religious Expression in the Public Square—The Building Blocks for an Intermediate Position," *Loyola of Los Angeles Law Review*, Vol. 29 (1996b), pp. 1411–19.

Greene, Abner, "The Political Balance of the Religion Clauses," *Yale Law Journal*, Vol. 102 (1993), pp. 1611–44.

————, "Is Religion Special? A Rejoinder to Scott Idleman," *1994 University of Illinois Law Review* (1994), pp. 535–44.

Griffin, Leslie, "Good Catholics Should be Rawlsian Liberals," *Southern California Interdisciplinary Law Journal*, Vol. 5 (1997), pp. 297–373.

Gross, Rita, *Buddhism after Patriarchy* (Albany: State University of New York Press, 1992).

Guth, James, and John Green, "God and the GOP: Religion among Republican Activists," in Ted Jelen, ed., *Religion and Political Behavior in the United States* (New York: Praeger, 1989), pp. 223–42.

Guth, James, Lyman Kellstedt, Corwin Smidt, and John C. Green, "Cut from the Whole Cloth: Antiabortion Mobilization among Religious Activists," in Ted Jelen and Marthe Chandler, eds., *Abortion Politics in the United States and Canada: Studies in Public Opinion* (Westport, Conn.: Praeger, 1994), pp. 107–30.

Haddad, Yvonne Yazbeck, ed., *The Muslims of America* (New York: Oxford University Press, 1991).

Haddad, Yvonne Yazbeck, and Adair Lummis, eds., *Islamic Values in the United States: A Comparative Study* (New York: Oxford University Press, 1987).

Haddad, Yvonne Yazbeck, and Jane Idleman Smith, eds., *Muslim Communities in North America* (Albany: State University of New York Press, 1994).

Hall, Mimi, "Abortions in USA Fall to 13-Year Low," *U.S.A. Today* (June 16, 1994), p. A1.

Handy, Robert, *Undermined Establishment: Church-State Relations in America* (Princeton, N.J.: Princeton University Press, 1991).

Hanna, Mary, *Catholics and American Politics* (Cambridge: Harvard University Press, 1979).

Hanson, Karen, *The Self Imagined: Philosophical Reflections on the Social Character of Psyche* (New York: Routledge & Kegan Paul, 1986).

Harris, Angela, "Race and Essentialism in Feminist Legal Theory," in Katherine Bartlett and Roseanne Kennedy, eds., *Feminist Legal Theory: Readings in Law and Gender* (Boulder, Colo.: Westview, 1991), pp. 235–62.

Hatch, Roger, "Jesse Jackson's Presidential Campaign: A Religious Assessment," *Soundings*, Vol. 70 (1987), pp. 379–405.

———, *Beyond Opportunity: Jesse Jackson's Vision for America* (Philadelphia: Fortress, 1988).

———, "Jesse Jackson in Two Worlds," in Charles Dunn, ed., *Religion in American Politics* (Washington, D.C.: Congressional Quarterly Press, 1989), pp. 87–101.

Hatfield, Mark, *Conflict and Conscience* (Waco, Tex.: Word, 1971).

———, "Testimony before United States Senate," in *Hearings on S.J. Res. 199 and S.J. Res. 130 (Abortion)*, Subcommittee on Constitutional Amendments of the Committee on the Judiciary, 93rd Congress, 2nd Session (Washington, D.C.: U.S. Government Printing Office, 1974), pp. 4–19.

———, *Between a Rock and a Hard Place* (Waco, Tex.: Word, 1976).

———, "Christ's Call to Service," in James Skillen, ed., *Confessing Christ and Doing Politics* (Washington, D.C.: Association for Public Justice Education Fund, 1982), pp. 11–18.

———, [Testimony], *Congressional Record, Senate,* 98th Congress, 1st Session (Washington, D.C., U.S. Government Printing Office, June 27, 1983), pp. S9089-92.

Hauerwas, Stanley, *A Community of Character: Toward a Constructive Christian Social Ethic* (Notre Dame, Ind.: University of Notre Dame Press, 1981).

Hekman, Susan, *Gender and Knowledge: Elements of a Postmodern Feminism* (Cambridge: Polity, 1990).

———, "The Embodiment of the Subject: Feminism and the Communitarian Critique of Liberalism," *Journal of Politics*, Vol. 54 (1992), pp. 1098–119.

Held, Virginia, "The Division of Moral Labor and the Role of the Lawyer," in David Luban, ed., *The Good Lawyer: Lawyers' Roles and Lawyers' Ethics* (Totowa, N.J.: Rowman & Allanheld, 1984), pp. 60–82.

Hertzke, Allen, *Representing God in Washington: The Role of Religious Lobbies in the American Polity* (Knoxville: University of Tennessee Press, 1988).

Hilgers, Thomas, Dennis Moran, and David Mall, eds., *New Perspectives on Human Abortion* (Frederick, Md.: University Publications of America, 1981).

Himmelstein, Jerome, "The Social Basis of Antifeminism: Religious Networks and Culture," *Journal for the Scientific Study of Religion*, Vol. 25 (1986), pp. 1–39.

Hofman, Brenda, "Political Theology: The Role of Organized Religion in the Anti-Abortion Movement," *Journal of Church and State*, Vol. 28 (1986), pp. 25–47.

Hudson, Winthrop, *Religion in America*, 4th ed. (New York: Macmillan, 1987).

Hutcheson, Richard, *God in the White House* (New York: Macmillan, 1988).

Hyde, Henry, "The Human Life Bill: Some Issues and Answers," *New York Law School Law Review*, Vol. 27 (1982), pp. 1077–100.

———, "Keeping God in the Closet: Some Thoughts on the Exorcism of Religious Values from Public Life," *Notre Dame Journal of Law, Ethics, and Public Policy*, Vol. 1 (1984), pp. 33–51.

Hyde, Henry, "Overturn Roe v. Wade: The Value of Human Life," *ABA Journal*, Vol. 74 (1988), p. 32.

———, "Transcript" [of opening remarks on House Hearings on Don Edward's proposed Freedom of Choice Act], reprint, *Human Life Review*, Vol. 18 (1992), pp. 112–15.

———, "A Mom and Pop Manifesto: What the Pro-Family Movement Wants from Congress," *Policy Review*, No. 68 (1994), pp. 29–33.

Idelson, Holly, "Panel Approves Bill to Limit State Curbs on Religion," *Congressional Quarterly Weekly Report*, Vol. 51 (May 27, 1993), p. 760.

Idleman, Scott, "A Reply to Professor Greene's Theory of the Religion Clauses," *1994 University of Illinois Law Review* (1994), pp. 337–59.

Jackson, Jesse, *Straight from the Heart*, ed. Roger Hatch and Frank Watkins (Philadelphia: Fortress, 1987).

Jackson, Kathryn, "And Justice for All? Human Nature and the Feminist Critique of Liberalism," in J. O. Barr, ed., *Women and a New Academy* (Madison: University of Wisconsin, 1989), pp. 122–39.

Jacobs, Bradley, and Elizabeth Moberly, "Knowing Rights from Wrong," *Christian Legal Society Quarterly*, Vol. 14 (Summer 1993), pp. 4–6.

Jacobson, Jodi, "Global Dimensions of Forced Motherhood," *U.S.A. Today*, Vol. 121, No. 2576 (1993), pp. 34–35.

Jaffee, Frederick, "Enacting Religious Beliefs in a Pluralistic Context," *Hastings Center Report* (August 1978), pp. 14–15.

James, William, *The Principles of Psychology*, Vol. 1 (New York: Dover, 1950).

Joas, Hans, *G. H. Mead: A Contemporary Re-Examination of His Thought*, trans. Raymond Meyer (Cambridge: MIT Press, 1985).

Johnsen, Dawn, and March Wilder, "*Webster* and Women's Equality," *American Journal of Law and Medicine*, Vol. 15 (1989), pp. 178–84.

Johnston, Michael, "The 'New Christian Right' in American Politics," in Stephen D. Johnson and Joseph Tamney, eds., *The Political Role of Religion in the United States* (Boulder, Colo.: Westview, 1986), pp. 125–46.

Jones, Gordon, "Abortion's Muddy Feet," in Dave Andrusko, ed., *To Rescue the Future: The Pro-Life Movement in the 1980's* (Harrison, N.Y.: Life Cycle, 1983), pp. 235–46.

Karst, Kenneth, *Belonging to America: Equal Citizenship and the Constitution* (New Haven, Conn.: Yale University Press, 1989).

———, "Religion, Sex, and Politics: Cultural Counterrevolution in Constitutional Perspective," *University of California at Davis Law Review*, Vol. 24 (1991), pp. 677–734.

———, *Law's Promise, Law's Expression: Visions of Power in the Politics of Race, Gender, and Religion* (New Haven, Conn.: Yale University Press, 1993).

Kelley, Dean, "The Rationale for the Involvement of Religion in the Body Politic," in James Wood, (ed.), *The Role of Religion in the Making of Public Policy* (Waco, Tex.: Baylor University Press, 1991), pp. 159–90.

Kolbert, Kathryn, "Introduction: Did the Amici Effort Make a Difference?," *American Journal of Law and Medicine*, Vol. 15 (1989), pp. 178–84.

Konvitz, Milton, "The Problem of a Constitutional Definition of Religion," in James Wood, ed., *Religion and the State: Essays in Honor of Leo Pfeffer* (Waco, Tex.: Baylor University Press, 1985), pp. 147–66.

Kosmin, Barry, and Seymour Lachman, *One Nation under God* (New York: Harmony, 1993).

Krason, Stephen, *Abortion, Politics, Morality and the Constitution* (Lanham, Md.: University Press of America, 1984).

Krauthammer, Charles, "The Church-State Debate," *New Republic* (Sept. 17, 1984), pp. 15–19.

Kymlicka, Will, *Liberalism, Community, and Culture* (Oxford: Clarendon, 1989).

———, *Contemporary Political Philosophy: An Introduction* (Oxford: Clarendon, 1990).

———, ed., *Justice in Political Philosophy* (Oxford: Clarendon, 1992).

Lang, Karen, "Lord Death's Share: Gender-Related Imagery in the Theragatha and Therigatha," *Journal of Feminist Studies in Religion*, Vol. 2 (1986), pp. 63–79.

Lawler, Peter, "The Bishops Versus Cuomo," in Mary Segers, ed., *Church Polity and American Politics: Issues in Contemporary Catholicism* (New York: Garland, 1990), pp. 175–93.

Lawrence, Bruce B., *Defenders of God: The Fundamentalist Revolt against the Modern Age* (New York: Harper & Row, 1989).

Laycock, Douglas, "Formal, Substantive, and Disaggregated Neutrality toward Religion," *DePaul Law Review*, Vol. 39 (1990), pp. 993–1018.

Lear, Norman, and Ronald Reagan, "Readings: A Debate on Religious Freedom," *Harpers*, Vol. 269 (Oct. 1984), pp. 15–19.

Levinson, Sanford, "The Confrontation of Religious Faith and Civil Religion: Catholics Becoming Justices," *DePaul Law Review*, Vol. 39 (1990), pp. 1047–82.

———, "Religious Language and the Public Square," review of *Love and Power*, by Michael Perry, *Harvard Law Review*, Vol. 105 (1991), pp. 2061–79.

Levy, Leonard, "The Original Meaning of the Establishment Clause of the First Amendment," in James Wood, ed., *Religion and the State* (Waco, Tex.: Baylor University Press, 1985), pp. 43–84.

Liebman, Charles, *Deceptive Images* (New Brunswick, N.J.: Transaction, 1988).

Luban, David, *Lawyers and Justice: An Ethical Study* (Princeton, N.J.: Princeton University Press, 1988).

Luker, Kristin, "Abortion and Conscience," in Daniel Callahan and Sidney Callahan, eds., *Abortion: Understanding Differences* (New York: Plenum, 1984a), pp. 25–46.

———, *Abortion and the Politics of Motherhood* (Berkeley: University of California Press, 1984b).

Lupu, Ira, "Models of Church-State Interaction and the Strategy of the Religion Clauses," *DePaul Law Review*, Vol. 42 (1992), pp. 223–33.

MacIntyre, Alisdair, *After Virtue* (Notre Dame, Ind.: University of Notre Dame Press, 1981).

Madison, James, "Memorial and Remonstrance against Religious Assessments" (1785), reprinted in John Patrick and Gerald Lang, eds., *Constitutional Debates on Freedom of Religion: A Documentary History* (Westport, Conn.: Greenwood, 1999), document 22.

Mansbridge, Jane, *Why We Lost the ERA* (Chicago: University of Chicago Press, 1986).

Marshall, William, "The Other Side of Religion," *Hastings Law Journal*, Vol. 44 (1993), pp. 843–63.

Marty, Martin, *Religion and Republic: The American Circumstance* (Boston: Beacon, 1987).

Masci, David, "Religious Freedom Bill Wins Subcommittee Approval," *Congressional Quarterly Weekly Report*, Vol. 51 (March 20, 1993), p. 676.

McConnell, Michael, "Political and Religious Disestablishment," *1986 Brigham Young University Law Review* (1986), pp. 405–63.

———, "The Role of Democratic Politics in Transforming Moral Convictions into Law: Morality, Politics and Law," *Yale Law Journal*, Vol. 98 (1989), pp. 1501–43.

McConnell, Michael, "Religious Freedom at a Crossroads," *University of Chicago Law Review*, Vol. 59 (1992), pp. 115–94.

McDonald, Kathleen, "Battered Wives, Religion, & Law: An Interdisciplinary Approach," *Yale Journal of Law and Feminism*, Vol. 2 (1989), pp. 251–98.

McElvaine, Robert, *Mario Cuomo: A Biography* (New York: Scribner's, 1988).

McKeegan, Michele, *Abortion Politics: Mutiny in the Ranks of the Right* (New York: Free Press, 1992).

McNay, Lois, *Foucault and Feminism: Power, Gender and the Self* (Boston: Northeastern University Press, 1992).

McTighe, Michael, "Jesse Jackson and the Dilemmas of a Prophet in Politics," *Journal of Church and State*, Vol. 32 (1990), pp. 585–607.

Mead, George Herbert, *Mind, Self, & Society from the Standpoint of a Social Behaviorist*, ed. Charles Morris (Chicago: University of Chicago Press, 1934).

———, *On Social Psychology*, ed. Anselm Strauss (Chicago: University of Chicago Press, 1956).

———, *Selected Writings*, ed. Andrew Reck (Chicago: University of Chicago Press, 1964).

Melton, J. Gordon, ed., *The Churches Speak On: Abortion* (Detroit, Mich.: Gale Research, 1989).

Merel, Gail, "The Protection of Individual Choice: A Consistent Understanding of Religion under the First Amendment," *University of Chicago Law Review*, Vol. 45 (1978), pp. 805–99.

Meyers, Diana, "The Socialized Individual and Individual Autonomy: An Intersection between Philosophy and Psychology," in Eva Kittay and Diana Meyers, eds., *Women and Moral Theory* (Stonybrook, N.Y.: Rowman & Littlefield, 1987), pp. 139–53.

Meyers, Marvin, ed., *The Mind of the Founder: Sources of the Political Thought of James Madison* (Hanover, N.H.: University Press of New England, 1981).

Michelman, Frank, Norman Redlich, Stephen Neuwirth, and Denise Carty-Bennia, "Brief for 995 Law Professors in Support of Maintaining Adherence to the *Roe* Decision," *American Journal of Law and Medicine*, Vol. 15 (1989), pp. 195–203.

Miller, Barbara, *The Law Giveth: Legal Aspects of the Abortion Controversy* (New York: Atheneum, 1983).

Miller, David, *George Herbert Mead: Self, Language, and the World* (Austin: University of Texas Press, 1973).

Miller, William Lee, *The First Liberty: Religion and the American Republic* (New York: Knopf, 1986).

Mills, Samuel, "Abortion and Religious Freedom: The Religious Coalition for Abortion Rights (RCAR) and the Pro-Choice Movement, 1973–1989," *Journal of Church and State*, Vol. 32 (1991), pp. 569–94.

Moen, Matthew, *The Christian Right and Congress* (Tuscaloosa: University of Alabama Press, 1989).

Mohr, James, *Abortion in America: The Origins and Evolution of National Policy, 1800–1900* (New York: Oxford University Press, 1978).

Moore, Margaret, *Foundations of Liberalism* (Oxford: Clarendon, 1993).

Mouffe, Chantal, "Feminism, Citizenship, and Radical Democratic Politics," in Judith Butler and Joan Scott, eds., *Feminists Theorize the Political* (New York: Routledge, 1992), pp. 369–84.

Nahmod, Sheldon, "The Public Square and the Jew as Religious Other," *Hastings Law Journal*, Vol. 44 (1993), pp. 865–70.

National Abortion Federation, "Women Who Have Abortions," *Fact Sheet* (Washington, D.C.: National Abortion Federation, 1991).

Neuhaus, Richard John, *The Naked Public Square* (Grand Rapids, Mich.: Eerdmans, 1984).

New Republic Editorial Staff, "Reverend Reagan," *New Republic,* Vol. 188, No. 13 (1983), pp. 7–9.

Nicholson, Linda, "Feminism and the Politics of Postmodernism," *boundary 2,* Vol. 19 (1992), pp. 53–69.

Noam, Gil, and Thomas Wren, *The Moral Self* (Cambridge: MIT Press, 1993).

Noddings, Nel, *Caring: A Feminine Approach to Ethics & Moral Education* (Berkeley: University of California Press, 1984).

Noonan, John T., Jr., "An Almost Absolute Value in History," in John T. Noonan, Jr., ed., *The Morality of Abortion: Legal and Historical Perspectives* (Cambridge: Harvard University Press, 1970), pp. 1–59.

———, *A Private Choice: Abortion in America in the Seventies* (New York: Free Press, 1979).

———, "Commentary: The Root and Branch of *Roe v. Wade,*" *Nebraska Law Review,* Vol. 63 (1984), pp. 668–79.

———, "The Experience of Pain by the Unborn," in J. Douglas Butler and David Walbert, eds., *Abortion, Medicine, and the Law,* 3rd ed. (New York: Facts on File, 1986), pp. 360–69.

———, *The Believer and the Powers that Are: Cases, History, and Other Data Bearing on the Relation of Religion and Government* (New York: Macmillan, 1987a).

———, "The John Dewy Memorial Lecture: Education, Intelligence, and Character in Judges," *Minnesota Law Review,* Vol. 71 (1987b), pp. 1119–33.

———, "The Constitution's Protection of Individual Rights: The Real Role of the Religion Clauses," *University of Pittsburgh Law Review,* Vol. 49 (1988), pp. 717–22.

Noonan, John T., Jr., and David Louisell, "Constitutional Balance," in John T. Noonan, Jr., ed., *The Morality of Abortion: Legal and Historical Perspectives* (Cambridge: Harvard University Press, 1970), pp. 200–260.

O'Brien, Thomas, "A Survey of Gay/Lesbian Catholics Concerning Attitudes towards Sexual Orientation and Religious Beliefs," *Journal of Homosexuality,* Vol. 21 (1991), pp. 29–44.

O'Failain, Julia, and Lauro Martines, eds., *Not in God's Image: Women in History from the Greeks to the Victorians* (New York: Harper Colophon, 1973).

O'Hara, Thomas, "The Abortion Control Act of 1989: The Pennsylvania Catholics," in Timothy Byrnes and Mary Segers, eds., *The Catholic Church and the Politics of Abortion: A View from the States* (Boulder, Colo.: Westview, 1992), pp. 87–104.

Okin, Susan Moller, *Justice, Gender and the Family* (New York: Basic Books, 1989).

Olsen, Fran, "Unravelling Compromise," *Harvard Law Review,* Vol. 103 (1989), pp. 105–35.

Page, Benjamin, Robert Shapiro, Paul Gronke, and Robert Rosenberg, "Constituency, Party, and Representation in Congress," *Public Opinion Quarterly,* Vol. 48 (1984), pp. 741–56.

Paige, Connie, *The Right to Lifers: Who They Are, How They Operate, Where They Get Their Money* (New York: Summit, 1983).

Paul, Diana, "Buddhist Attitudes toward Women's Bodies," *Buddhist Christian Studies,* Vol. 2 (1982), pp. 63–71.

Peach, Lucinda, "From Spiritual Descriptions to Legal Prescriptions: Religious Imagery of Women as 'Fetal Containers' in the Law," *Journal of Law and Religion*, Vol. 10 (1993–1994), pp. 73–93.

Peek, Charles, George Lowe, and L. Susan Williams, "Gender and God's Word: Another Look at Religious Fundamentalism and Sexism," *Social Forces*, Vol. 69 (1991), pp. 1205–21.

Perry, Michael, "Abortion, Public Morals, and the Police Power: The Ethical Function of Substantive Due Process," *UCLA Law Review*, Vol. 23 (1976), pp. 689–736.

———, "Promises in Morality and Law," *Harvard Law Review*, Vol. 95 (1985), pp. 916–38.

———, "Comment on 'The Limits of Rationality and the Place of Religious Conviction: Protecting Animals and the Environment,'" *William and Mary Law Review*, Vol. 27 (1986), pp. 1067–73.

———, *Morality, Politics, and Law: A Bicentennial Essay* (New York: Oxford University Press, 1988).

———, *Love and Power: The Role of Religion and Morality in American Politics* (New York: Oxford University Press, 1991).

———, "Religious Morality and Political Choice: Further Thoughts—and Second Thoughts—on *Love and Power*," *San Diego Law Review*, Vol. 30 (1993), pp. 703–28.

———, *Religion in Politics: Constitutional and Moral Perspectives* (New York: Oxford University Press, 1997).

———, "Liberal Democracy and Religious Morality," *DePaul Law Review*, Vol. 48 (1998), pp. 1–50.

Petchesky, Rosiland, *Abortion and Woman's Choice: The State, Sexuality, and Reproductive Freedom*, rev. ed. (Boston: Northeastern University Press, 1990).

Phelps, Teresa Goodwin, "The Sound of Silence Breaking: Catholic Women, Abortion, and the Law," *Tennessee Law Review*, Vol. 59 (1992), pp. 547–69.

Pickthall, Marmaduke, *The Meaning of the Glorious Koran* (New York: New American Library, 1977).

Pierard, Richard, "Reagan and the Evangelicals: The Making of a Love Affair," *Christian Century*, Vol. 100 (1983), pp. 1182–84.

———, "Cacophony on Capitol Hill: Evangelical Voices in Politics," in Stephen Johnson and Joseph Tamney, eds., *The Political Role of Religion in the United States* (Boulder, Colo.: Westview, 1986), pp. 71–96.

Pilpel, Harriet, "Hyde and Go Seek: A Response to Representative Hyde," *New York Law School Review*, Vol. 27 (1982), pp. 1101–23.

Pippert, Wesley, "Sen. Mark O. Hatfield," in *Faith at The Top* (Elgin, Ill.: Cook, 1973).

Planned Parenthood, "Who Has Abortion?" [cited July 2, 1999], available from http://plannedparenthood.org/abotion/abortquestions.html@Who has abortion?; INTERNET.

Pojman, Louis, and Francis Beckwith, *The Abortion Controversy: A Reader* (Boston: Jones and Bartlett, 1994).

Poovey, Mary, "The Abortion Question and the Death of Man," in Judith Butler and Joan Scott, eds., *Feminists Theorize the Political* (New York: Routledge, 1992), pp. 239–56.

Post, Robert, "Tradition, the Self, and Substantive Due Process: A Comment on Michael Sandel," *California Law Review*, Vol. 77 (1989), pp. 553–60.

Postema, Gerald, "Moral Responsibility in Professional Ethics," *New York University Law Review*, Vol. 55 (1990), pp. 63–99.

Ranke-Heinemann, Uta, *Eunuchs for the Kingdom of Heaven: Women, Sexuality, and the Catholic Church* (New York: Doubleday, 1990).

Ratzinger, Joseph, ed., *On the Pastoral Care of Homosexual Persons* (Boston: Daughters of St. Paul, 1986).

Rawls, John, *A Theory of Justice* (Cambridge: Belknap, 1971).

———, "Kantian Constructivism in Moral Theory: The Dewey Lectures 1980," *Journal of Philosophy*, Vol. 77 (1980), pp. 517–72.

———, "Justice as Fairness: Political Not Metaphysical," *Philosophy and Public Affairs*, Vol. 14 (1985), pp. 223–51.

———, "The Ideas of an Overlapping Consensus," *Oxford Journal of Legal Studies*, Vol. 7 (1987), pp. 1–27.

———, "The Priority of Right and Ideas of the Good," *Philosophy and Public Affairs*, Vol.17 (1988), pp. 251–76.

———, "The Domain of the Political and Overlapping Consensus," *New York University Law Review*, Vol. 64 (1989), pp. 233–55.

———, *Political Liberalism* (New York, Columbia University Press, 1996 [pbk.] and 1993).

———, "The Idea of Public Reason Revisited," *University of Chicago Law Review*, Vol. 64 (1997), pp. 765–99.

Reagan, Ronald, *Constitutional Amendment* (Washington, D.C.: U. S. Government Printing Office, 1982).

———, "Politics and Morality Are Inseparable," *Notre Dame Journal of Law, Ethics, and Public Policy*, Vol. 1 (1984), pp. 7–11.

———, *Abortion and the Conscience of the Nation* (Nashville: Nelson, 1984), excerpted in *Catholic Lawyer*, Vol. 30 (1986), pp. 99–106.

———, *Proposed Legislation—President's Pro-Life Act of 1988* (Washington, D.C.: U.S. Government Printing Office, 1988).

Regens, James, and Brad Lockerbie, "Making Choices about Choice: House Support for Abortion Funding," *Social Science Research*, Vol. 22 (1993), pp. 24–32.

Rhode, Deborah, "The 'No-Problem' Problem: Feminist Challenges and Cultural Change," *Yale Law Journal*, Vol. 100 (1991), pp. 1731–93.

Richards, David A. J. *Toleration and the Constitution* (New York: Oxford University Press, 1986).

———, "Liberalism, Public Morality, and Constitutional Law: Prolegomenon to a Theory of the Constitutional Right to Privacy," *Law & Contemporary Problems*, Vol. 51 (1988), pp. 123–50.

———, *Foundations of American Constitutionalism* (New York: Oxford University Press, 1989).

Rosenblum, Nancy L., "Introduction," in Nancy Rosenblum, ed., *Liberalism and the Moral Life* (Cambridge: Harvard University Press, 1989), pp. 1–18.

Rotunda, Ronald, and Nowak, John, *Treatise on Constitutional Law: Substance and Procedure* (St. Paul, Minn.: West, 1999).

Rubin, Eva, *Abortion, Politics, and the Courts: Roe v. Wade and Its Aftermath* (Westport, Conn.: Greenwood, 1982).

Rubinfeld, Jed, "On the Legal Status of the Proposition that 'Life Begins at Conception,'" *Stanford Law Review*, Vol. 43 (1991), pp. 599–635.

Ruddick, Sara, *Maternal Thinking: Toward a Politics of Peace* (Boston: Beacon, 1989).

Ruether, Rosemary, *Sexism and God-Talk: Toward a Feminist Theology* (Boston: Beacon, 1983).

Rupp, George, "Commitment in a Pluralistic World," in Leroy Rouner, ed., *Religious Pluralism* (Notre Dame, Ind.: University of Notre Dame Press, 1984), pp. 214–26.

Sandel, Michael, *Liberalism and the Limits of Justice* (Cambridge: Cambridge University Press, 1982).

———, "Morality and the Liberal Ideal," *New Republic* (May 7, 1984a), pp. 15–17.

———, "The Procedural Republic and the Unencumbered Self," *Political Theory*, Vol. 12, no. 1 (1984b), pp. 81–96.

———, "Democrats and Community," *New Republic* (Feb. 22, 1988), pp. 20–23.

———, "Essay in Law: Religious Liberty—Freedom of Conscience or Freedom of Choice?," *1989 Utah Law Review*, No. 3 (1989a), pp. 597–615.

———, "Moral Argument and Liberal Toleration: Abortion and Homosexuality," *California Law Review*, Vol. 77 (1989b), pp. 521–38.

———, "Freedom of Conscience or Freedom of Choice?," in James Davison Hunter and Os Guiness, eds., *Articles of Faith, Articles of Peace: The Religious Liberty Clauses and the American Public Philosophy* (Washington, D.C.: Brookings Institution, 1992), pp. 75–92.

Santurri, Edmund, "Religion, the Constitution, and Rawlsian Justice: A Critical Analysis of David A. J. Richards on the Religion Clauses," *Journal of Law and Religion*, Vol. 9 (1992), pp. 325–46.

Schauer, Frederick, "May Officials Think Religiously?," *William and Mary Law Review Annual*, Vol. 27 (1986), pp. 1075–84.

Schnell, Frauke, "The Foundations of Abortion Attitudes: The Role of Values and Value Conflict," in Malcolm Goggin, ed., *Understanding the New Politics of Abortion* (Newbury Park, Calif.: Sage, 1993), pp. 23–43.

Schopen, Gregory, "Archaeology and Protestant Presuppositions in the Study of Indian Buddhism," *History of Religions*, Vol. 31 (1991), pp. 1–23.

Segers, Mary "The Bishops, Birth Control, and Abortion Policy: 1950–1985," in Mary Segers, ed., *Church Polity and American Politics: Issues in Contemporary Catholicism* (New York: Garland, 1990a), pp. 215–32.

———, ed., *Church Polity and American Politics: Issues in Contemporary Catholicism* (New York: Garland, 1990b).

———, "Moral Consistency and Public Policy: Cuomo and Califano on Abortion," in Mary Segers, ed., *Church Polity and American Politics: Issues in Contemporary Catholicism* (New York: Garland, 1990c), pp. 157–74.

———, "Abortion Politics Post-Webster: The New Jersey Bishops," in Timothy Byrnes and Mary Segers, eds., *The Catholic Church and the Politics of Abortion: A View from the States* (Boulder, Colo.: Westview, 1992), pp. 27–47.

Seigfried, Charlene Haddock, *Pragmatism and Feminism: Reweaving the Social Fabric* (Chicago: University of Chicago Press, 1996).

Sherry, Suzanna, "Women's Virtue," essay on Michael Perry's *Morality, Politics and Law*, *Tulane Law Review*, Vol. 63 (1989), pp. 1591–1672.

Siegel, Riva, "Reasoning from the Body: A Historical Perspective on Abortion Regulation and Questions of Equal Protection," *Stanford Law Review*, Vol. 44 (1992), pp. 261–381.

Silberman, Charles, *A Certain People: American Jews and Their Lives Today* (New York: Summit, 1985).

Sinipoli, Richard, *The Foundations of American Citizenship: Liberalism, the Constitution, and Civic Virtue* (New York: Oxford University Press, 1992).

Smith, Jane, "The Experience of Muslim Women: Considerations of Power and Authority," in Yvonne Yazbeck Haddad and Ellison Findley, eds., *The Islamic Impact* (Syracuse, N.Y.: Syracuse University Press, 1984), pp. 89–112.

Smith, Paul, *Discerning the Subject* (Minneapolis: University of Minnesota Press, 1988).

Smith, Ruth, "Feminism and the Moral Subject," in Barbara Andolsen, Christine Gudorf, and Mary Pellauer, eds., *Women's Consciousness, Women's Conscience* (San Francisco: Harper & Row, 1985), pp. 235–50.

Smith, Steven D., "Separation and the 'Secular': Reconstructing the Disestablishment Decision," *University of Texas Law Review*, Vol. 67 (1986), pp. 955–1031.

———, "The Rise and Fall of Religious Freedom in Constitutional Discourse," *University of Pennsylvania Law Review*, Vol. 140 (1991), pp. 149–240.

Smolin, David, "Abortion Legislation after *Webster v. Reproductive Services*: Model Statutes and Commentaries," *Cumberland Law Review*, Vol. 20 (1989), pp. 71–163.

———, "Regulating Religious and Cultural Conflict in a Postmodern America: A Response to Professor Perry," review of *Love and Power* by Michael Perry, *Iowa Law Review*, Vol. 76 (1991), pp. 1067–104.

Solum, Lawrence, "Faith and Justice," *DePaul Law Review*, Vol. 39 (1990), pp. 1083–153.

———, "Constructing an Ideal of Public Reason," *San Diego Law Review*, Vol. 30 (1993), pp. 729–62.

Sorauf, Frank, *The Wall of Separation: The Constitutional Politics of Church and State* (Princeton, N.J.: Princeton University Press, 1976).

Sullivan, Andrew, "Dead End: Cuomo's Abortion Contortion," *New Republic*, Vol. 204, No. 18 (1991), pp. 16–18.

Sullivan, Kathleen, "Religion and Liberal Democracy," *University of Chicago Law Review*, Vol. 59 (1992), pp. 195–224.

Tamney, Joseph, "Religion and the Abortion Issue," in Stephen Johnson and Joseph Tamney, eds., *The Political Role of Religion in the United States* (Boulder, Colo.: Westview, 1986), pp. 159–80.

Tamney, Joseph, Stephen Johnson, and Ronald Burton, "The Abortion Controversy: Conflicting Beliefs and Values in American Society and within Religious Subgroups," in Ted Jelen and Marthe Chandler, eds., *Abortion Politics in the United States and Canada: Studies in Public Opinion* (Westport, Conn.: Praeger, 1994), pp. 41–56.

Tatalovich, Raymond, and David Schier, "The Persistence of Ideological Cleavage in Voting on Abortion Legislation in the House of Representatives, 1973–1988," in Malcolm Goggin, ed., *Understanding the New Politics of Abortion* (Newbury Park, Calif.: Sage, 1993), pp. 109–22.

Taylor, Charles, "Cross-Purposes: The Liberal-Communitarian Debate," in N. Rosenblum, ed., *Liberalism and the Moral Life* (Cambridge: Harvard University Press, 1989a).

———, *Sources of the Self: The Making of Modern Identity* (Cambridge: Harvard University Press, 1989b).

———, *Multiculturalism and "The Politics of Recognition"* (Princeton, N.J.: Princeton University Press, 1992a), pp. 159–82.

———, "Religion in a Free Society," in James Davison Hunter and Os Guiness, eds., *Articles of Faith, Articles of Peace: The Religious Liberty Clauses and the American Public Philosophy* (Washington, D.C.: Brookings, 1992b), pp. 93–113.

Teitel, Rudi, "A Critique of Religion as Politics in the Public Sphere," *Cornell Law Review*, Vol. 78 (1993), pp. 747–821.

Thomson, Judith Jarvis, "A Defense of Abortion," *Philosophy and Public Affairs*, Vol. 1 (1971), pp. 47–66.

Thumma, Scott, "Negotiating a Religious Identity: The Case of the Gay Evangelical," *Sociological Analysis*, Vol. 52 (1991), pp. 333–47.

Tipton, Steven, "Religion and the Moral Rhetoric of Presidential Politics," *Christian Century*, Vol. 101 (1984), pp. 1010–14.

Tribe, Laurence, *American Constitutional Law*, 2nd ed. (Mineola, N.Y.: Foundation, 1988).

———, *Abortion: The Clash of Absolutes* (Cambridge: Harvard University Press, 1990).

Tushnet, Mark, *Red, White, and Blue: A Critical Analysis of Constitutional Law* (Cambridge: Harvard University Press, 1988).

———, "Flourishing and the Problem of Evil," *Tulane Law Review*, Vol. 63 (1989), pp. 1631–50.

———, "The Limits of Involvement of Religion in the Body Politic," in James Wood, ed., *The Role of Religion in the Making of Public Policy* (Waco, Tex.: Baylor University Press, 1991), pp. 191–220.

Umansky, Ellen, "Feminism and the Reevaluation of Women's Roles within American Jewish Life," in Yvonne Yasbeck Haddad and Ellison Banks-Findley, eds., *Women, Religion, and Social Change* (Albany: State University of New York Press, 1985), pp. 477–96.

U.S. Catholic Conference, "Abortion," in J. Gordon Melton, ed., *The Churches Speak On: Abortion* (Detroit, Mich.: Gale Research, 1989), pp. 6–8.

U.S. Senate, Committee on Labor and Human Resources, 102nd Congress, 2nd Session, S. 25, *Hearings on Freedom of Choice Act of 1991* (Washington, D.C.: U.S. Government Printing Office, 1992).

Wald, Kenneth, "Assessing the Religious Factor in Electoral Behavior," in Charles Dunn, ed., *Religion in American Politics* (Washington, D.C.: Congressional Quarterly Press, 1989), pp. 105–22.

———, *Religion and Politics in the United States* (Washington, D.C.: Congressional Quarterly Press, 1992).

Walzer, Michael, "The Communitarian Critique of Liberalism," *Political Theory*, Vol. 18 (1990), pp. 6–23.

Wasserstrom, Richard, "Lawyers as Professionals: Some Moral Issues," *Human Rights*, Vol. 5 (1975), pp. 1–24.

———, "Roles and Morality," in David Luban, ed., *The Good Lawyer: Lawyers' Roles and Lawyers' Ethics* (Totowa, N.J.: Rowman & Allanheld, 1984), pp. 25–37.

Weber, Paul, "Strict Neutrality: The Next Step in First Amendment Development," in Charles Dunn, ed., *Religion in American Politics* (Washington, D.C.: Congressional Quarterly Press, 1989), pp. 25–36.

Weedon, Chris, *Feminist Practice and Poststructuralist Theory* (Oxford: Blackwell, 1987).

Weigand, Kathryn, "The Secularization of the Law and Sex Discrimination," *Mercer Law Review*, Vol. 31 (1980), pp. 581–94.

Weithman, Paul, "The Separation of Church and State: Some Questions for Professor Audi," *Philosophy and Public Affairs*, Vol. 20 (1991), pp. 52–76.

———, "Taking Rites Seriously," *Pacific Philosophical Quarterly*, Vol. 75 (1994), pp. 272–94.

———, "Introduction: Religion and the Liberalism of Reasoned Respect," in Paul Weithman, ed., *Religion and Contemporary Liberalism* (South Bend, Ind.: University of Notre Dame Press, 1997), pp. 1–38.

Wenz, Peter, *Abortion Rights as Religious Freedom* (Philadelphia: Temple University Press, 1992).

Williams, Joan, "Abortion, Incommensurability, and Jurisprudence," review of *Morality, Politics, and Law* by Michael J. Perry, *Tulane Law Review*, Vol. 63 (1989), pp. 1651–72.

Williams, Susan, "Feminism's Search for the Feminine: Essentialism, Utopianism, and Community," *Cornell Law Review*, Vol. 75 (1990), pp. 700–9.

Williams, Susan, and David Williams, "Note, Reinterpreting the Religion Clauses: Constitutional Construction and Conceptions of the Self," *Harvard Law Review*, Vol. 97, No. 6 (1984), pp. 1468–86.

Williamsburg Charter Foundation, *Survey on Religion and American Public Life* (Washington, D.C.: Williamsburg Charter Foundation, 1988).

Wisconsin Bishops, "Consistent Ethic of Life," *Origins*, Vol. 19, No. 28 (December 14, 1989), pp. 461–65.

Witt, Stephanie, and Gary Montcrief, "Religion and Roll-Call Voting in Idaho," in Malcolm Goggin, ed., *Understanding the New Politics of Abortion* (Newbury Park, Calif.: Sage, 1993), pp. 123–33.

Wood, James Edward, *Religion and Politics* (Waco, Tex.: Baylor University Press, 1983).

———, "Introduction: Religion and Public Policy," in James Wood, ed., *The Role of Religion in the Making of Public Policy* (Waco, Tex.: Baylor University Press, 1991), pp. 1–20.

Woodard, Calvin, "Thoughts on the Interplay Between Morality and Law in Modern Legal Thought," *1984 Notre Dame Law Review* (1984), pp. 784–804.

Woodward, Kenneth, "The Rites of Americans," *Newsweek* (November 29, 1993), pp. 80–82.

Wright, Alexandra, "Judaism," in Jean Holm, ed., *Women in Religion* (London: Pinter, 1994), pp. 113–40.

Wuthnow, Robert, *Christianity in the Twenty-First Century: Reflections on the Challenges Ahead* (New York: Oxford University Press, 1993).

Young, Iris Marion, "Impartiality and the Civic Public: Some Implications of Feminist Critiques of Moral and Political Theory," in Seyla Benhabib and Drucilla Cornell, eds., *Feminism as Critique* (Minneapolis: University of Minnesota Press, 1987), pp. 56–76.

———, "The Ideal of Community and the Politics of Difference," in Linda Nicholson, ed., *Feminism/Postmodernism* (New York: Routledge, 1989), pp. 300–323.

———, *Justice and the Politics of Difference* (Princeton, N.J.: Princeton University Press, 1990).

Zimmerman, Dianne, "To Walk a Crooked Path: Separating Law and Religion in the Secular State," *William and Mary Law Review Annual*, Vol. 27 (1986), pp. 1095–1108.

Index